THE NEW ART OF CENTRAL BANKING

Also by M. L. Burstein

MONEY
THE COST OF TRUCKING: Econometric Analysis (*with others*)
ECONOMIC THEORY: Equilibrium and Change
*RESOURCE ALLOCATION AND ECONOMIC POLICY (*editor with Michael Allingham*)
*NEW DIRECTIONS IN ECONOMIC POLICY
*MODERN MONETARY THEORY
*STUDIES IN BANKING THEORY, FINANCIAL HISTORY AND VERTICAL CONTROL
*OPEN-ECONOMY MONETARY ECONOMICS

**Also published by Macmillan*

The New Art of Central Banking

M. L. Burstein
Professor of Economics
York University, Canada

M
MACMILLAN

First published 1991

Published by
MACMILLAN ACADEMIC AND PROFESSIONAL LTD
Houndmills, Basingstoke, Hampshire RG21 2XS
and London
Companies and representatives
throughout the world

Printed in Hong Kong

British Library Cataloguing in Publication Data
Burstein, M. L. (Meyer Louis), *1926–*
The new art of central banking.
1. Central banking
I. Title
332.1′1
ISBN 0–333–52571–X

For
Eugene Mitchell

*It was among the ruins of the
Capitol that I first conceived
the idea of a work . . . which, however
inadequate to my own wishes, I
finally deliver to the curiosity
and candour of the public.*

Edward Gibbon, *The Decline
and Fall of the Roman
Empire*

Contents

List of Illustrations and Tables

Illustrations

Tables

Preface

This is the book of an American abroad. But the theme of innocents abroad or of American *naïveté* and European worldliness, *à la* Henry James, is quite reversed: Americans are sophisticated about federalism and their romance with it was shattered by a bloody civil war. Mine is a cautionary political-economic tale told at the dawn of 1992. The success of American federalism mainly owes, I think, to two factors. One is unique: the character and persona of General Washington. The other is the American Constitution, a machine that runs by itself. Bismarck almost got it right: God looks after fools, drunkards and the United States of America. It is true that America owes nothing to the wisdom of its Congresses or the perspicacity of most of its Presidents. That is its strength: its Constitution protects its people from the unimpeded impetus of its elected 'leaders', who are condemned by the Constitution to jostle against each other. Do Europeans know that?

The bulk of the book concerns the theory of monetary control. It consolidates and expands bridgeheads carved out by my series of books (1986, 1988 and 1989a) breaking out onto a tundra on which financial institutions and substances cannot be distinctly discerned; one after another innovation in theory and praxis has obliterated once-salient monetary landmarks. Nor is it possible to pick up a regular pulse from the flux of inchoate events evolving on the economic tundra. Not surprisingly, then, the new art of central banking culminates in masterly inactivity.

The principles that survive the book's critique are classical or new-classical. I plodded on, and on, seeking what passes for truth in science; and *this* is what I found. The economic argument is not politically motivated. Nor is it peculiar to private-ownership economies: I recommend it for *perestroika* anywhere. But there is a point in political economy to be made. I should think that the book's principal results are quite ineluctable for the natural action of a private-ownership economy; while a socialist system must *select* modalities conforming to the logic controlling the theory. Professor Hayek has deeply probed this point; I leave the reader to her own devices.

* * *

I have never known what a 'monetary economy' is, importantly because there has never been a barter economy; nor am I intrigued by phantasies about barterers emerging from the primaeval slime. And, on reflection, I think the expression tendentiously inept. For the purposes of this book it suffices to say that radical innovation, going so far as to eject money from the economy, is quite consistent with what is called a monetary economy. The upshot is less anodyne for central bankers who must be dramatically affected by disappearance of money-stuff.

* * *

André Malraux called General de Gaulle a man of the day before yesterday and the day after tomorrow. This image readily transmutes into an essential property of classical art, or of science. To be successful, economic theory must *persist* in time and space. The fact that Galiani, Adam Smith, Thornton, Wheatley and Ricardo so inform the theory of monetary innovation bodes well for economics. Indeed the most brilliantly successful official action reported in the book is the open market purchase by the emperor Tiberius in AD 33.

The Right Honourable Nigel Lawson resigned in November 1989, after this book had been made ready for the printer.

M. L. BURSTEIN

Acknowledgements

I owe much to many people at Banca d'Italia and to that splendid institution, which I visited between September and November 1988; also to Banca Commerciale Italiana of Milan and Aalborg University, Denmark.

I especially benefited from the informed, perceptive crticism of Ambrosio Rinaldi and Giuseppe Tullio. And I hope the book adequately reflects my admiration for Franco Modigliani and his work.

This gratefully acknowledges my indebtedness to T. M. Farmiloe, Keith Povey, and Barbara Dochety.

And I am indebted to Kitty Sokoll in a number of important ways.

The author and publishers acknowledge with thanks permission from the following to reproduce copyright material: *Financial Times*, for Figures 3.9–3.11 (22 June 1989); Banca Commerciale Italiana, for Figures 5.1–5.3, 7.1–7.3, from *Monetary Trends* (February and July 1988) and for Table 5.3, from *Monetary Trends* (July 1988); Federal Reserve *Bulletin*, for Tables 7.1–7.4 (December 1988); P. S. King, for the quotations from D. H. Robertson, *Banking Policy and the Price Level* (1926); and Hogarth Press, for the quotations from M. Finley, *The Ancient Economy* (1985).

Citations from my own work are often in the form (198–) rather than Burstein (198–).

Part I
Foundations of the New Art of Central Banking

1 Introduction

The new art of central banking pivots on a reformed (tabular) monetary standard, 'securitization' beyond the banking principle and other innovations in praxis, including debt-discharge (clearing) mechanisms. Its field of action is constricted by virtual convertibility; the transform of a central bank must operate in real space, the only space left; the 'monetary' authority must operate with real assets. What is more, intermediaries surviving beyond the banking principle (see Burstein, 1988) must back their liabilities with real assets; and public debt will also become virtually convertible into real assets – see Chapters 2 and 5 below.

The theory is woven from several strands developed disjointedly over some years before being integrated in 1988–9.

1.1 THE STRANDS OF ANALYSIS

The *tabular standard* exercises influence in two channels. In the first it reveals that much economic theory hinges on choice of measure – the inflation perplex is an example; and stability properties of difference equations typically depend on arbitrarily selected time dimensions (in economic applications). In the second channel, money-stuff loses its aura of immutability and is sucked into the mass of variably-priced substances.

When the analytic content of the theory of tabular standards is assembled, and then applied to the European currency debate, striking results are obtained. Desirable properties of monetary unity require neither Authority nor deliberate coordination. And virtual convertibility of government debt is imposed by the theory's innovated ECU standard: governments become committed to make virtually real payments. The set of constraints imposed by the theory's liberal régime is like the pre-1914 one; and works more stringently than constraints implicit in the Delors proposal. At national level prospects for *dirigisme* are dismal; pan-European authority proposals, when properly understood, are a retreat by anti-liberals to a final redoubt.

Interest on money leads to certainty that the *LM* curve is vertical. But then it cannot be located. So it must be discarded. (There is no

LM curve in nature; I refer to a conceptualization of ISLM theory – and implicitly invoke the work of Immanuel Kant.)

Competitively determined interest on money makes intermediaries' spreads pivotally important. And it greatly simplifies properties of effects of liquidity-preference vibration: pressure is absorbed by transient changes in spreads; and the laws of motion of effects of monetary policy action are surprisingly intricate.

It is not adequately understood that vibration of liquidity preference is substantially accommodated by covariant fluctuation in the scale of financial intermediation. Intermediaries simply exchange their paper for others' paper; their profits flow from their spreads. Misperception of this point is central for flawed monetary theories of trade cycles and may infect the work of Wicksell, as it surely does that of the Wicksellians (see Part II, especially Chapter 9).

So we come upon another strand, *Wicksell's cumulative process* – which I explored in Burstein (1988). Wicksell's theory, properly understood, concerns money supply and prices relative to a quantity theory hypothesis. And it suffers from a lacuna that should be filled in: Wicksell supplies no motivation to hold the paper generated by the cumulative process. I try to repair this fault in (1988) and in Chapters 3 and 9 below.

Wicksell's cumulative process unfolds against an autonomously evolving own rate of return on physical capital. Wicksell's is *not* a *monetary theory of the real rate of interest*. But Wicksellian economics, especially when given a Keynesian twist, is intensely committed to monetary theories of real rates of interest, as are the City and Wall Street.

It is explained in Chapter 3 that monetary theories of real rates of interest (attacked from a number of directions in this book) have exerted influence along two distinct lines of development. Keynes centres on monetary aggregates in the *General Theory* – save for the Appendix to Chapter 14, which is not integrated into the core argument. (But Keynes may be the creator of the Wicksellian line of development, in his *Treatise*.) Keynes readily acknowledges the mercantilist origin of the idea that the equilibrium real rate of interest is a decreasing function of the nominal quantity of money.

In Wicksell's model, the monetary authority (MA) announces it will deal in paper at a decreed 'paper yield on paper' without limit. Say that this administered rate lies below that consistent with the equilibrium of a competitive banking industry. (The bizarre script is influenced by effects of usury laws and other artificial constraints analysed by Ricardo, 1817.)

The financial press takes a Wicksellian (but not Wicksell's) tack. It reports that the MA takes decisions, day by day, on a spectrum of *real* rates of interest; and that the Phillips curve explains inflation effects – the MA's ploy supplies real stimulus to the economy, perhaps causing it to overheat, so that inflation spurts (the topic is pursued in Chapter 3, section 3.4).

Wicksell's theory is not Wicksellian. In Wicksell's theory the real rate of return on physical capital is autonomous for monetary analysis. When modified to accommodate portfolio equilibrium, his theory runs along the following lines.

Since competitive interest is paid on bank accounts in Wicksell's system, if the real running yield on bank paper is to fall, portfolio equilibrium requires its shadow convenience yield to increase accordingly. And *this* determines the real quantity of claims on banks in equilibrium. So long as the MA insists on real yields of bank loans below the own rate of return on capital, it pays to borrow from banks and redeposit the proceeds (to take round trips): the controlling arbitrage condition assures that the *total* marginal return on bank balances equals that on physical capital – in principle, the process can evolve in a hermetically-sealed monetary circuit. The rate at which bank paper depreciates against goods depends on how rapidly its stock expands: the largesse of the banks would typically be constrained by quantitative controls on bank credit – the script is bottomed on *dirigiste* intervention. In a purely competitive banking industry, rates at which banks deal key on Thornton's mercantile rate of profit; bank spreads transiently vibrate sympathetically with fluctuations in liquidity preference; the vibration's frequency depends on the open-ness of the economy, partially determining the elasticity of supply of liquidity.

Interpolation

Such dealing is partitioned from evaluation of credit risks and marrying suppliers and absorbers of real resources, i.e. from merchant banking. *Circa* 1790, Thomas Jefferson proposed a comparable partition for American finance. Jefferson (and President Andrew Jackson) opposed *issue*, not financial intermediation.

The last strand, *innovations leading to liquidity saturation*, culminates the theory. Liquidity premia are to disappear. And they ought to disappear, since liquidity can now be created costlessly. See *Beyond the Banking Principle* (1988, inspired by securitization prospects; and see Chapter 4 below). In a moneyless monetary economy, the liquidity properties of a very wide spectrum of assets are undifferentiated.

The spontaneous evolution of monetary modalities leads to the own rate of return on physical capital ruling the roost. Samuelson (1947/1983) anticipates this result. Wallace (1983) builds on Samuelson's deep conjecture. And Ricardo (1817) set the table.

The argument is sent into a classical domain of economic thought: an economy saturated with liquidity, as Pareto optimality demands, behaves like the hypothetical non-monetary economy of general equilibrium theory. In particular, the Keynesian theory of interest evaporates: monetary assets cease to be unique; vacua do not rule roosts. So there is no sensible way to contemplate plans being made to divert flows from the income–expenditure stream towards paper assets: paper assets will be wanted only as evidence of claims to real ones.

1.2 CAPSULATION OF CHAPTERS 2–5

Chapters 2–5 are to be capsulated so that their contents are keyed to the strands of analysis.

1.2.1 Chapter 2: The Theory of Monetary Standards Applied to Pan-European Money and Monetary Control

Study of the pure theory of monetary standards leads to sharp conclusions about the ECU, the EMS and pan-European monetary authority proposals: *viz.* the ECU concept should be promoted, after being reformulated; and the pan-European monetary authority idea should be jettisoned; while the purposes of the EMS are better served without its serpent.

The idea of tabular monetary standards contains the seed of these conclusions, but my way has been roundabout. For years, I went backwards from *symmetallism*, studying properties of notional metallic systems, instead of forward into the domain of its ultimate extension, a full tabular standard. True, retrogression continues: this book goes back to the *electrum stater* of Cyzicus in ancient Asia Minor.

Another seminal idea is Einaudi's *imaginary money* introduced to me by the late Professor Earl J. Hamilton. I was able to take this idea no further than an application to eighteenth century British North America, together with the Aureus and Caesara concoctions of (1989a). But Galiani's luminous (1750) analysis, limned by Einaudi (1937), leads to reformulation of the rôle of the ECU in 1992 and beyond. Chapter 2 displays technical features of the analysis. The upshot for political economy is less salient. An ECU *metric* establishes a liberal order with a common money of account *and* free selection of debt-discharge vehicles: agents pay indifferently in DM, KR, FF, lire, sterling, etc. Control is dysfunctional.

An ECU standard *sans* a pan-European authority has other novel features; and if innovation spans tabular properties, the art of central banking is dramatically transformed indeed: *installation* of a tabular standard resolves the inflation perplex.

Banks will find that a cheap way to keep a balanced book is to operate all over Europe. Then exchange risks intrinsic to an ECU accounting unit will mostly wash out. But a French bank cannot effectively evaluate the creditworthiness of Bavarian merchants: pan-European mergers are virtually mandated, further sapping national credit controls.

So long as European economies are on an ECU standard, national authorities will only destabilize their money supply processes if they try to collect inflation taxes. (True, the inflation tax has lost favour in Europe recently.) Indeed controlling joint supply/joint demand logic implies that ECU-dominated prices will be strongly influenced by the policy of the least-expansionary monetary authority; and political-economic reasoning suggests that a pan-European authority is apt to be more inflationist than an independent Bundesbank.

'*IS*' relationships of conventional national economic models will not persist. ECU *accounting* makes investors more indifferent towards where they place their funds.

All of this is brought about by an innovation in reckoning, – i.e., by an accounting device. It is explained in Chapter 4 that little is possible until one assimilates the profound truth stated by Hawtrey (1947): the idea of money depends on that of debt: the material substance, money, is a contrivance of a particular way of discharging debt, necessarily denominated in money of account, ontologically equivalent to the hectare or some other pure measure. Upon assimilating this truth, dramatic progress can be made both conceptually and in praxis.

The *mechanics* of the proposed ECU system are intriguing. The set of admissible ECU prices of constituent currencies lies on a hyper-plane. Transactions costs aside, an ECU *basket currency*, assembled *ad hoc* by traders, would be cost effective. If transactions costs are put into play, an actual ECU currency – or, more likely, currencies, some private – reckons to *evolve*. Indeed, as DM, KR, lire, etc. are seen more and more as vestigial remains of a past age, local currencies will fade away and the ECU will be transformed into a true tabular measure.

Five features of central banking in the ECU régime are studied: (1) The free-lira (free-franc, etc.) concept. (2) Possibilities of dys-synchronization of credit and real savings flows, touching on the credit-cycle literature explored in Chapter 9. (3) Open-market operations. (4) Properties of monetary aggregate-targeted policy. (5) Inflationary bias? (No!)

The lire stock is allocated between *bound* and *free* lire; bound lire are locked into (notional) baskets of ECU reserves. Free lire are held for a number of reasons, some speculative. And analogies to bridging finance and modalities of fiscal stabilization are near to hand. From time to time, the Italian authorities will sell lire at a discount (against other ECU components), planning to buy back lire when the Italian economy regains buoyancy.

Dys-synchronization of credit and real savings flows is, as the book seeks to show again and again, something of a red herring. Intermediaries do not generate real lendable resources; they trade their paper for others' paper, living on a spread. Dilation and contraction of intermediary balance sheets (say around a trend-line) is a quasi-monetary, not a credit, phenomenon. That said, the virtual convertibility properties of an ECU standard, as it sets in, severely cramp credit-cycle possibilities, evanescent as they may be.

Prospects for open-market operations may be discussed at two levels of generality. At the lower level of Chapter 2, it is pointed out that, since the Banca d'Italia cannot print both lire and ECU, it will have to move between lire and real assets, in conjunction with the IRI. At a higher level of generality, contemplating a fully securitized economy, saturated with liquidity and so beyond the banking principle, demand for the liquidity properties of paper evaporates; and open-market operations must be conducted with real assets. Some 35 years ago, Phillip Cagan conjectured about conducting open-market operations with Old Masters; his conjecture will have its day.

The analysis lies outside the attractive field of monetary aggregate theory; and it goes farther out into space as Part I continues. This much is clear. If any low-inflating monetary authority grips its portion of the reserve base, a laissez-faire ECU régime solves the monetarists' problem.

Features (4) and (5) are linked by a weak monetarism. The anti-inflationary bias of the innovated system is not due to cooperation: the most virtuous authority tends to be preponderantly influential. It is explained in Chapter 2 that 'one man/one vote' is potentially destructive in non-homogeneous societies and, so far as inflation is concerned, ambiguous in homogeneous ones (see the 'Concluding Political-Economic Observations' Chapter 2, p. 41.)

Surveying the ground covered by Chapter 2 from a great height, it is clear that Galiani (1750), modulated by Einaudi (1936/1952, 1937), is the progenitor of its most radical, and most important, ideas. It is *not* intrinsic to an efficient monetary system that debt-discharge media be fixed in price – as becomes especially clear in Chapter 4 where, in the limit, anything is a debt-discharge medium. Once Galiani's proposition is digested, the idea of the tabular standard is easy to grasp; and the inflation perplex looks downright silly.

1.2.2 Chapter 3: The *Modus Operandi* of Bank Rate Reconsidered

The first job is to jettison the *LM* curve. A number of the book's central concepts converge to smash up *LM*: interest on money, securitization and other forces taking us beyond the banking principle and so saturating the economy with liquidity, innovated payments networks, etc. In the upshot one can at most conclude that *LM* is vertical, but one cannot know where it is.

The next job is to reflect deeply on *modes of monetary policy*. Monetary aggregate modes link up with the theory of moving equilibria. But the link-up is uncomfortable for unsophisticated readers of the *General Theory*. Following Irving Fisher, we must conclude that a shift to secularly faster money growth entails *higher*, not lower, nominal interest rates; and that real rates are autonomous for the régime of secular money-growth.

Bank rate is passive, or adaptive, in a monetary aggregate mode of policy. And this point has led to serious confusion. Especially before Friedman called attention to the matter in 1968, Fisher's careful distinction of real from nominal interest rates was quite neglected: it may still be widely taught that it is immaterial whether the MA takes a decision on *the* (real?) interest rate or the nominal supply of money.

What is worse, the reduced-form relation is to be $\partial \bar{r}/\partial M < 0$. This doctrine is tenable, if at all, only for effects of changes in base money growth at impact. We have just seen that it is untenable for dynamized descriptions.

Keynes (1930/1971) thought the active voice of Bank rate policy more important than the passive one just limned. For Keynes, the most important strand of Bank rate analysis was a putative direct effect on the cost of capital.

The theory of active Bank rate policy cannot properly be extracted from models of spontaneous economic action. It is properly a set of problems in *control theory*. It concerns acts of *will*. In a highly energized form, which we call *purgative* Bank rate, the government virtually makes war on the economy. Active Bank rate policy is obviously compatible with disequilibrium ideas – but properties of general equilibrium cannot be measured; the concept of departure from general equilibrium cannot be scientific.

These preliminaries being accomplished, the massive work of Chapter 3 is distributed among several economic boxes as follows.

Properties of monetary aggregate modes of policy, in which Bank rate is adaptive, in largely uninnovated economies, are assessed. 'Interest on money' entails results that may surprise the reader; and there is a lot of overshooting, so she will be entertained too.

Active Bank rate policy exploits inertia so that the natural relationship between yields of real and financial assets is distorted. And the economics of deployment of active Bank rate policy, especially in its purgative form, are intriguing, as 'The Economic Consequences of Mr Lawson' (section 3.4) is meant to show. (A control-theoretical reconstruction of Poole's (1970) problem is also supplied.)

Remark

Departure of real yields obtained from holding paper assets from own rates of return on real assets should be sharply distinguished from departure of the own yield of paper from its real yield: see Pierce (1980).

* * *

The work described so far is substantially reconstructive: the machinery of quite conventional monetary theory is lubricated, some parts are replaced, and others realigned, in order to analyse events in largely uninnovated economies. Section 3.3 of Chapter 3 looks ahead, inspired by Samuelson (1947/1983) via Wallace (1983). It is explained that a certain insight of Samuelson is the ark of the tabernacle of the book, the platform for a new art of central banking. If there is no reason for a spread between the yield of any two assets, interest rates are determined strictly 'classically'; the MA's printing press is taken out of play. What passes for open-market operations will be transactions in real assets. Once Samuelson's conjecture is made operational, a number of points made in Part I that might otherwise seem tangential to the main argument, or ill-assorted, are seen to be wholly germane: Part I's density dramatically increases. In particular, securitization (going beyond the banking principle), flexible interest on all financial assets, innovated clearing, etc. work to eliminate liquidity premia and indeed to make *many* assets indistinguishable on the plane of monetary analysis.

* * *

Economics is an applied subject: good economic theory concerns economies that are at least potentially observable. There is a symbiosis in good economics (Keynes's is an example) between the sometimes lurid stories told in the press and beautiful analytic leaps and *vice versa*. So we move from overarching generalizations, flowing from Samuelson's conjecture, to a highly-charged example of purgative Bank rate entitled 'The Economic Consequences of Mr Lawson'. The reader will know how it came out. The narrative of section 3.4 is meant only to carry a tune in economic theory – although the upshot might usefully influence political economy in future.

As a rather wretched episode in economic governance, *circa* 1988–9, staggered on, a purgative policy intended to cool off the British economy (stumbling onto Phillips Curve reasoning) became conflated with defence of the pound, amid tumultuous confusion about what the pound was being defended against, since the Government had been committed to the idea that markets are as wise as they are ineluctable.

Our purposes are better served by the rationale of the original, internal, objective (still the EMS facet of the onset of the troubles is developed). Perhaps the most interesting theoretical material falls under the rubric, 'How things might go wrong under purgative Bank rate' (p. 68). For a number of reasons, deceptively like *cost push*, historically high real Bank rate may lead to a substantial increase in bank lending (see the 'finance' analysis of Chapter 9) and to price hikes by desperate businessmen. Since active Bank rate policy is dual to passive supply of base money, a ratcheting sequence may find Bank rate chasing prices – so that real Bank rate is lower than it seems to be. And if the foreign exchange markets understand 'how things might go wrong', the spot pound will fall as the forward pound is sold short.

* * *

Remark

I cannot supply the analysis of tax effects that ought to supplement the study. See Martin Feldstein's work closing up comparable studies of the American economy.

* * *

It is explained in Chapter 9 that active deployment of Bank rate as an *internal* economic regulator is largely alien to nineteenth-century British thought – although there are uneasy analogies to Bagehot's prescription for combating external drains. The origins of the contemporary (active Bank rate) doctrine lie in a number of misperceptions: monetary theories of real rates of interest; the idea that the MA can regulate streams of real lendable resources, central to Wicksellian economics and to most monetary theories of real economic fluctuation; and, finally, the notion that open economies can be 'regulated' as if they were closed. Purgative contractions of money growth, in monetary aggregate-targeted régimes, often reflect mistaken beliefs by MAs that they are contracting the flow of loanable funds when they are in fact distorting, if not rupturing, the fabric of the matrix of claims so that excess supply of non-liquid assets accompanies excess demand for liquid ones.

It is explained in Chapter 3 that MAF rate is transiently sensitive to the sort of script just written – a point of obsessive interest in 1979 after the Federal Reserve *announced* it would aim at monetary aggregate targets. But elasticity of supply of intermediation (to be sharply distinguished from the supply of loanable funds) is high enough to assure that interest rate bulges promptly recede.

Friedman (1968) explains that monetary policy, including bond price-support programmes, cannot reduce the real cost of borrowing real resources. And Keynes (1930/1971) points out the absurdity of believing that the banking system determines the supply of real loanable funds – although his credit-cycle theory features forced saving (or induced lacking; see Chapter 9).

Volatility of interest rates due to monetary aggregate targeting reflects volatility of liquidity preference *cum* inelasticity of substitution among financial assets.

1.2.3 Chapter 4: Innovated Payments Systems

All of the major pieces of the theory are developed by the end of Chapter 3; they can be deployed in Chapter 4 with little explanatory comment. Chapter 4 is a condensed review of the theory of Part I as well as an exposé of innovated payment systems.

The pieces are put into play in the following sequence. The commandingly important principle, that the idea of money depends on that of debt, admirably stated by Hawtrey (1947), promptly uncovers a crucial corollary: money of account alone suffices for creation of a viable debt-discharge system.

One envisages an innovated clearing system in which continuous electronic monitoring of agents' accounts replaces accounting for transactions one at a time in direct descent of the ancient modality in which coins cross palms. In the upshot, one asset is like another from a monetary standpoint: if everything is money, nothing is money; money goes off the board. This is to say that the economy is saturated with liquidity. A relativity principle is established: there is an essential lack of privilege in innovated monetary nature. And Pareto optimality is served as well: liquidity – which, after all, can be created without burning up real resources – is produced to the point of saturation. And this sucks us into the powerful field of Samuelson's proposition, dextrously deployed by Wallace (1983): very simply, the own rate of return of physical (human and non-human) capital must rule the roost in the innovated monetary, but moneyless, economy.

Perhaps less transparently, the innovated régime entails convertibility. A commitment to pay Aureus-denominated debt requires transfer of real goods and services. It transcends indexation which determines quantities of *paper* to be transferred.

Interpolation
I am more concerned here to put the full panoply of my armoury into play than to sort out necessary from sufficient conditions for the substantive characteristics of an innovated economy. Thus securitization alone takes us fairly far past the 'money principle' as well as the banking principle (see 1988).

* * *

Implications for banking go far beyond elimination of banks' wretched chequery business. Since bank paper is to be worthless unless it represents physical property, and since financial intermediation becomes otiose, banking and industrial activities will be conglomerated – if banking is not reduced to mere evaluation of credit risks and packaging of 'micro' obligations, along the lines of nineteenth-century discount markets, reshaped by more recent securitization techniques.

Central bankers must scurry for cover; they must coalesce with fiscal authorities and Crown corporations to participate, modestly, in a new art of central banking.

The new art of central banking is not altogether uncongenial towards the *General Theory*. Thus the value of Tobin's q may spontaneously fluctuate outside desired boundaries. Open-market operations in real assets may be attempted, subject to an economic version of resonance. But terms must be precisely defined; the controlling economic syntax is complex.

If the private sector imputes the public sector's balance sheet to its own account, open-market operations go off the board along lines developed by Wallace (1981, 1983) and Sargent and Smith (1987). If such imputations are not made, the argument gains transparency if q is transmogrified into the ratio of the Aureus prices of capital and consumption goods, *à la* Hayek and Mises. An authority, seeking to drive down the price of capital in this sense, must supply additional capital assets (cf sales by Crown corporations) while absorbing consumer goods (dual to the public's incremental abstinence, funding its fresh investments). Or the Authority may make virtual consumer loans to the public who will be longer on capital assets and will virtually owe consumer goods in the new portfolio equilibrium.

The flimsy monetary component of Keynesian economics crumbles. In the innovated economy, the veil of money is stripped off altogether so that continuity is maintained with the great classical writers. *This* means that a polished up version of Say's law rules the innovated economy: in the innovated economy, induction of substitution of planned purchase of new for purchase of old assets is generically equivalent to inducing substitution of oranges for apples through relative price changes. Dramatic innovations go far to wipe out two centuries of monetary-theoretical development, so that the 'real world' is modelled by strictly real schemae that may be confused with barter. Indeed, endemic confusion of moneyless exchange with the celebrated double coincidence required for barter exchange has obstructed development of high macro theory.

1.2.4 Chapter 5: A Monetary Analysis of Public Debt

(The following remarks are selective: section 5.1 of Chapter 5 supplies a quite careful summary of its contents.)

Money and public debt are more closely linked than most realize: treasury currency is but a non-interest-yielding perpetuity, saleable because of its convenience yield, but not categorically distinct from public debt in general. (Alexander Hamilton's *Report on the Public Credit* takes the argument further, anticipating that the new republic's debt would do direct monetary work – a conjecture that was more fruitful for monetary theory than for praxis.)

Tobin (1974), while pointing out that money cannot be neutral if supplies of other nominal values are determined autonomously, poses a cogent question capsulating this line of inquiry (Clower and I worked along similar lines: 1960/1988).

> [is] a 'rain' of Treasury bills – promises to pay currency in three months or less – of no consequence for the price level while a 'rain' of currency inflates prices proportionately?
>
> Tobin (1974, p. 87)

Especially in a financially primitive economy, government paper, if it is a widely held liquid asset, is a potentially important monetary contrivance. And the analysis takes a 'Ricardo–Barro' twist: fulfilment of 'defensive estate motivation' generates demand for government stock 1:1 with its creation, while promoting an illusion of thrift – in a closed analysis in which the government is sure to redeem its (tacitly inconvertible) obligations. Parallel themes emerge. One is monetary; the other fiscal.

The fiscal theme is developed quite fully in Chapter 5. For one thing, short of liquidity saturation, monetary and fiscal components of the analysis cannot be strictly segregated; short of the limit, a monetary/fiscal theory is required.

The stark relativity principle of the theory of the innovated economy, requiring that no asset be monetarily privileged, banishes the monetary theme, while reformulating the metric.

Banishment of public debt from the monetary realm entails a dramatic political-economic consequence: public debt must then be virtually convertible to survive. And since convertibility pivots on *taxable capacity*, public debt is apt to lose favour in the innovated future. The day before yesterday foretells the day after tomorrow:

the gilt-edged quality of public debt is a product of the Government's printing press; when governments owe what they cannot print up, their credit tends to be problematical well short of basket cases like Argentina (Chapter 10 shows that public debt was disfavoured anciently). Finally, and more mundanely, inflation taxation is barred in an innovated economy; it will have gone beyond indexation too.

Chapter 5 and its coda (linked to Chapter 2) impinge on *European Monetary Institutions Post 1992* in the following way. The immense, and burgeoning, Italian public debt will become convertible into ECU, if not Aurei, before very long. In a higly open economy under a virtually convertible régime (such as the laissez-faire ECU standard of Chapter 2), *I* residents, however strictly they conform to Ricardo–Barro behaviour, can accomplish their purposes by buying *F* instead of *I* debt; and will continuously evaluate the quality of *I* debt. The classical properties of the unfolding monetary order are vividly robust. The upshot for public finance is emphatic: public authorities will lose much of their freedom of action. So personal liberty can be enhanced: liberty is an absence of duty, not an entitlement. It remains to be seen whether this gift of spontaneous economic evolution, laboriously articulated by innovated economic theory, will be accepted.

2 The Theory of Monetary Standards Applied to Pan-European Money and Monetary Control

2.1 THE THEORY OF MONETARY STANDARDS

2.1.1 Preliminary Ideas

I reported on symmetallism in 1963, influenced by Marshall and Friedman (1951a/1953); and began to understand its ultimate extension, a full tabular standard, in 1986 – expanding this bridgehead in Burstein (1988 and 1989a). But I had no good idea of the theory's praxis until I visited Banca d'Italia. It turns out that the theoretical foundations of a common European currency, and the corollary possibility of a European monetary authority, can be fashioned from these materials.

At the chapter's centre is analysis of an expanded, deepened ECU schema that may achieve the proper objectives of a puissant authority while perhaps dispensing with central banking altogether. And there are a number of other instances in which innovated theory points to innovated practice eliding Authority.

The *raison d'être* of central banking is significantly undermined by ineluctable transformations of praxis, based on new technologies and reformed perceptions of transactions modalities. The upshot is not ideologically-inspired deregulation: spontaneous evolution may leave nothing to regulate!

The analysis about to unfold leads to a sharp political-economic result: it is undesirable to create a pan-European monetary authority. European trade is better freed by elimination of much Authority than by creation of a vast new one. In particular, it would be better to dismantle much national monetary control than to transfer control to a super-authority.

The reader is asked to suspend (dis)belief and to exercise a certain tolerance: the robustness of the theory, making its implications so implacable, does not hinge on any political conviction.

(a) *Milton Friedman (1951a/1953)*

> In principle the ultimate extension of the idea of symmetallism is to include in the standard every commodity and service produced in the economy roughly in proportion to the amounts produced . . . Since the price of this . . . basket would be the price index, stability of the price index would be immediately and perfectly attained.
>
> Friedman (1951a/1953, pp. 213–14)

Interpolation

Note 2 to Chapter 10 concerns the *electrum stater* of Cyzicus in ancient Asia Minor. Electrum is a gold–silver alloy. Symmetallism has a long history! (see Finley, 1985, p. 167; his sources are supplied in note 35).

(b) *Luigi Einaudi (1937)*

(Also see Einaudi (1936/1952, pp. 229–61). I discuss his important work in (1986, 1988 and 1989a).)

> Debtors, customers and employers who are in debt so many dollars [the dollar is merely an instrument for accounting and pricing, p. 259] will pay indifferently in gold, platinum or silver coins or notes, according to the ruling market rate. There is nothing in the system which could expel any of the coins from circulation.
>
> Einaudi (1937, pp. 261–2)

> At first men would be bewildered; but by-and-by they will grow accustomed to seeing daily fluctuations in the dollar prices of silver florins and platinum guineas . . . As already said, almost two hundred years ago by Galiani [Ferdinando Galiani, *Della Moneta* (1750); he was 21 in 1750] coins will gradually come to be seen as subject to price fluctuations like wheat or oil or securities. If the system can be managed successfully, men will find it obvious that a given salary or wage or rent fixed in dollars has a variable buying power in silver or gold . . . but a stable buying power in an assortment of goods.
>
> Einaudi (1937, p. 264)

Pausing to consolidate ideas, under a tabular standard, fragments of many goods and services, perhaps including currencies, comprise the basis for an imaginary accounting unit we shall call the Aureus. Its proper history is supplied by the *Oxford Classical Dictionary* (see 'Coinage, Roman'). And the *tabular standard* was suggested by Wheatley in 1807 and has been interestingly discussed by Hawtrey, Viner and Friedman as well as by Keynes (1930/1971, pp. 351–4, pagination being governed by the 1971 reissue).

Assume that claims against banks are denominated in Aurei and discharged in lire. The lira has an Aureus price: one lira fetches ₳x; a debt of ₳1m is discharged by a lira tender whose mass equals the lire equivalent to ₳1m on the settlement date.

The preliminary ideas are put into play in sections 1.2 and 1.3. An ECU standard is a much diluted version of a true tabular standard – but a dramatic result pops out at once. If agents of Economy E pay indifferently in DM, SF, FF, lire, sterling, USD, yen, etc. prospects for control of money supplies and credit flows are indeed bleak.

2.1.2 Properties of the Innovated System

The unit of account is the Aureus; the standard of value is a composite commodity.

(a) *Preferred Habitation of Paper Issue*

Under an Aureus standard, there is no compelling reason to prefer local issue – again see Einaudi (1937). And this remark has striking implications for the future of European finance. In Italy, for example, *circa* 2000, many currencies will circulate side by side, all valued in an Aureus-like measure: credit emissions from many sources will leave residues mapping into holdings eligible to discharge debt. Nor need the lira survive such currency competition; nor need any national currency.

(b) *Insights from Study of Eighteenth-century British North America*

The history of paper issue in eighteenth-century British North America, interestingly discussed by Adam Smith (1776), suggests that competition between currencies will lead to the following trick being taken. Surely in Italy in the Reform's early days, taxes will be assessed in lire in order to give *currency* to lira paper. Or, if Italian tax obligations are not metricised in lire (they may be stated in Aurei) only lira paper might be tenable (by fiat) for discharge of Italian tax obligations. So there would evolve a secondary circulation with a measurable velocity as the government recirculates its paper – as it absorbs real goods (see B. Smith, 1988: his bibliography is definitive; also see 'Colonial Currency and Contemporary Monetary Theory' (Chapter 7 of 1988).

2.1.3 Analysis of the Innovated System

In economics, but not in physics, choice of numéraire – something that looks deceptively like a mere convention – affects systemic dynamic behaviour. And it has long been (imperfectly) recognized that this is true: see especially Keynes (1936, Chapter 17). King's (1936/1972) discussion of effects of gold discoveries on London interest rates is illuminating.

> Meanwhile, the first gold arrivals from both California and Australia were beginning to have their effect on money rates. Bank rate was reduced to the unprecedented level of 2 per cent in April 1852 . . . Once again, an unnatural depression of interest rates brought in its train a host of new speculative ventures.
>
> King (1936/1972, p. 171)

> A blithe confidence made this fresh speculation particularly dangerous.
>
> King (1936/1972, p. 172)

Remark

Chapter 3 shows that Marshall's slant on speculation is similar to King's. Marshall focused on 'Bank rate and money supply', stressing effects of speculative borrowing on money supply, not on output.

Assess this episode under the stipulation that Britain is off gold, and may be on a tabular standard. Then there would be little difference between increases in gold and shoe supply. Then the price of gold, in say an Aureus measure, would fall, perhaps substantially; impact on relative prices and interest rates would properly be studied through a conventionally microeconomic lens. The thrust of 'imaginary money' is starkly plain.

Results, viewed through a gold-standard lens, are very different. Prices of goods in general must rise for equilibrium to be restored. And prices may be sticky; the process may be slow-dragging. Corollary implications of persisting excess supply of gold include the following.

1. Interest rates may be sharply depressed, since financial markets tend to operate fluidly. Securities prices will tend to increase for at least two reasons: (i) Agents plan to switch from gold to securities more or less permanently. (ii) Agents, seeking to diversify now gold-heavy portfolios, will promptly try to increase liquid security positions – planning to run these down quite slowly, acquiring illiquid assets with the proceeds. An 'illiquid' asset can be promptly purchased, or sold, only at a penalty – in thin markets.
2. Alternatively, holders of gold may be prepared to retain undesired positions for some time. Indeed, if this were not true, prices might not be sticky! This is the pith of the ancient 'temporary-abode-of-purchasing-power' idea.

Alas, the argument is circular. But the old-fashioned counterpart argument, relying on low storage costs of money, is not. The trouble is that gold has *high* storage costs. As for *circularity*, price stickiness makes it safer to hold a standard of value, as Keynes said in Chapter 17 of the *General Theory*; but we are dealing with an *effect* of price stickiness without discovering its *cause*.

(a) *A Rational Expectations Variant of the Analysis Exhibiting Overshooting*

If expectations are formed rationally, programmes will be shaped up, subsequent to an unexpected influx of gold, relative to restoration of near-neutrality by date τ. Interest rates and prices implicit in forward quotations at date 0 for date $(\tau - h)$ must obey arbitrage formulae barring profitable speculation. Generally speaking, interest rates must overshoot. Short rate must plunge on the initially surprising, but quickly digested, information. Subsequently, short rate must rise on the interval $(0+h) \twoheadrightarrow \tau$, reflecting both the evolution of prices and necessary rectification of the *real* rate of interest. Thus, at the end of the traverse, the interest rate at date $\tau - \varepsilon$ for maturity at date τ, ${}_{\tau-\varepsilon}r_{\tau}$, is arbitrarily close to $\bar{r}$ as $\varepsilon \rightarrow 0$.

Interpolation

Why *near* neutrality? So long as gold has non-monetary uses, strict neutrality is barred. This result is interestingly extended, in connection with the Gibson Paradox, by Barsky and Summers (1988).

Recovery speeds of interest rates depend on profitability of modulation of time profiles of programmes; if modulation costs are slight, the process may be rapid. If prices are highly inertial, and so slow to rise, interest rates will be depressed all the longer, with little real effect. And, when money flexibly yields interest, much of the burden of adjustment will be borne by the interest yield of money (Caranza and Fazio, 1983, make a related point about the Italian economy in their 'Methods of Monetary Control in Italy', pp. 66–92).

2.2 PROPERTIES OF AN ECU STANDARD *SANS* A PAN-EUROPEAN MONETARY AUTHORITY

2.2.1 Monetary Mechanics

(a) *Preliminary Comments*

The pure theory of 'the ECU' nests in that of symmetallism. It is well known that bimetallism is flawed: mint and market prices of gold and silver do not stay aligned. The metal that is undervalued at the mint will go out of monetary circulation, save for dual pricing: if gold is undervalued at the mint, prices may be quoted as '$\$1_{Ag}$ or $\$0.95_{Au}$'; but transactions costs of dual pricing may be substantial. Alfred Marshall suggested a *symmetallic* unit so that a debt of one pound is discharged by a compound tender of a_1 grains of gold *and* a_2 grains of silver; the vector representation of the standard of value being (a_1, a_2) or, in an extended instance (a_i). So admissible prices of gold and silver belong to the line

$$a_1p_1 + a_2p_2 = 1 \tag{2.1}$$

or, in extended instances, to the hyperplane

$$\Sigma a_ip_i = 1 \tag{2.2}$$

Both metals are kept in monetary circulation; but their prices are free to vary, under constraint.

The mechanics of a revised ECU régime are near to hand, once the nature of the revision is grasped: prices of the component parts of the ECU are to *float*.

(b) *The Construction's Policy Implications*

1. ECU-denominated prices of goods and services in the revised system will be guided by the policy of the least expansionary national monetary authority. Think of production of chess sets by unintegrated manufacturers, each producing but one component. And ignore non-chess uses of rooks, bishops, pawns, etc. Supply is determined by the 'least inflationary' producer. What if there are significant non-chess uses of chess material? Thus Kings and Queens may have ornamental utility. Then freedom of action is retained by producers wanting to expand their outputs more rapidly. The theory of joint demand and supply provides the controlling logic.
2. Prudential reserving factors promote pan-Europe bank mergers. The representative bank will operate on a pan-European scale – undermining national attempts to control credit directly.
3. National authorities are unable to extract inflation taxes: national obligations, linked to a substantially external monetary unit, become indexed *de facto*. If political authorities seek to elude this constraint, without 'going off ECU', money supply may become unstable.
4. Macro-modelling is harshly affected. ECU accounting makes investors more indifferent about *where* they place their resources. If Italians lose heart as investors in physical capital (if their animal spirits subside), they may be replaced by Germans, investing in Italy, perhaps via intermediaries who collect Italian savings – or Italians may make portfolio investments in Belgium, Holland, etc. (with concomitant positive trade balance effects if the placements are not offset by alien investment in Italy). All of this occurs without supernational authority and without deliberate policy coordination. 'All of this' follows from a mere change in modality – i.e., adoption of an ECU metric.

'*IS*' relationships of conventional national economic models cannot persist; and '*LM*' is swept off the board.

(c) *Joint Demand in Symmetallism*

The accounting unit, the dollar, is defined so that a tender of a_1 grains of gold *and* a_2 grains of silver discharges a one-dollar debt:

$$V(a_1, a_2) = 1; \text{ or } V(a_i) = 1$$

Arbitrage strictly enforces equations (2.1) and (2.2).

Now take account of non-monetary, as well as of monetary, demand for gold and silver, after reviewing the following glossary.

Glossary

a_1, a_2	=	the gold and silver contents of the dollar
p_1, p_2	=	the dollar prices of gold and silver
p	=	the general price level of 'commodities'
$\hat{x}_1, \hat{x}_2$	=	end-period stocks of gold and silver
x_{11}, x_{21}	=	demands for monetary gold and silver
x_{12}, x_{22}	=	demands for non-monetary gold and silver

The system is depicted in an obvious, but misleading, way by equations (2.3) – (2.5).

$$x_{11}(p_1, p_2, p) + x_{12}(\cdot) = \hat{x}_1 \tag{2.3}$$

$$x_{21}(\cdot) \qquad + x_{22}(\cdot) = \hat{x}_2 \tag{2.4}$$

$$a_1p_1 + a_2p_2 = 1 \tag{2.5}$$

Why is the system misleading? Because monetary demands for gold and silver are *not* independent. Dependency nests in the definition of the monetary unit: cf the notation (a_1, a_2). Gold and silver cannot be substituted for each other for monetary purposes. Indeed they are perfect complements, subject to this. An agent can make forward deals so that he may, for example, have a virtual negative position in gold, although he has substantial (symmetallic) monetary holdings. So demand for monetary gold, x_{11}, can be written

$$x_{11} = (a_1/a_2)x_{21} \tag{2.3a}$$

The complete system is obtained by repeating equations (2.4) and (2.5) and replacing equation (2.3) with equation (2.6).

$$(a_1/a_2)x_{21}(\cdot) + x_{12}(\cdot) = \hat{x}_1 \tag{2.6}$$

Remark

End-period stocks, $\hat{x}_1$ and $\hat{x}_2$, are parametric – as they are not in the more difficult analysis of a related problem I made in (1989a, Chapter 8).

* * *

The system's comparative statics may be illustrated informally. Say that the stock of gold ($\hat{x}_1$) increases, *ceteris paribus*. Equilibrium requires that the total demand for gold increase correspondingly. And the following is a plausible change in the equilibrium price system. The price of gold falls; the prices of silver and 'goods' rise. (equation (2.5) requires that $d\bar{p}_1 = -(a_1/a_2)d\bar{p}_2$.) The quantity of gold absorbed by industrial and decorative uses will increase, as will the supply of monetary gold. The stock of monetary silver increases correspondingly; and that of non-monetary silver falls *pari passu*, suggesting that the price of silver rises relatively more than that of goods in general.

(d) *Related ECU Mechanics*

The ECU unit is defined as (a_i) – reflecting a deviation from the ECU schema *en vigeur*: weights are now endogenous in ways not discussed here.

$$\sum a_i p_i = 1 \tag{2.7}$$

Admissible ECU prices of the constituent currencies lie on a hyperplane, but a two-space illustration conveys the economics quite well. See equations (2.8) and (2.9), along with Figure 2.1.

$$a_1 p_1 + a_2 p_2 = 1 \tag{2.8}$$

$$p_1 + (a_2/a_1)p_2 = 1/a_1 \tag{2.9}$$

Graphically, the situation can be depicted as in Figure 2.1.

The *diet problem* of linear programming illuminates the schema's *arbitrage* properties. One is indifferent, always subject to arbitrage, between holding the constituent parts of an ECU and a claim definitively worth one ECU. Or, along lines interestingly studied by

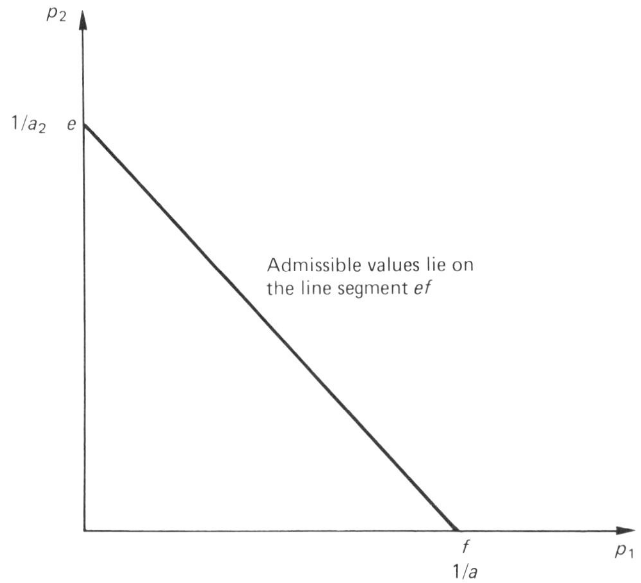

Figure 2.1 Admissible prices of gold and silver

Wallace (1983), save for official restrictions and transactions costs, one is indifferent between holding ka_1 grains of gold and ka_2 grains of silver versus k unit value coins. Transactions costs aside, one can cover an exposure of k ECUs by buying k ECUs forward *or* the vector (ka_i) of constituent 'currencies'. Furthermore, the ECU may merely be a *basket currency*, assembled *ad hoc* by traders.

As for *transactions costs*, an ECU metric (cf an 'imaginary' ECU currency) under laissez-faire would evolve towards 'creation' of an actual ECU currency, a vehicle capable of discharging debt – always distinguishing ECU property (cf incorporeal heraditaments) from the abstract measure, ECU, clumsily carrying the same title.

(e) *Concluding Remarks, Modulating Towards Section 2.1.1 (f)*

Assume that national vehicle currencies enjoy monopolies under an ECU standard. On the surface, little has changed: thus in Italy debts are discharged by lire tenders as before. But, beneath the surface, much has changed. For one thing, operations formerly entailing 'mere' local currency risk now entail ECU risk that can be laid off by options dealings or internalized by merger. And consider this corollary implication. As an ECU standard covers more ground, demands for local currencies, other than as parts of ECU ordered packages, fall; demand for domestic monetary balances for all but direct vehicular (debt-discharge) purposes will fall. And external demand for Italian, German, French, etc. currencies will increase: the harmonized process may lead to a wash.

An ECU currency (private ECU) could be generated by the private sector. But governments will seek to preserve seigneurage profits; and since international swap lines have long been in place, MAs are well placed to succeed in open competition. Still national monetary authorities must surrender much of their mystique: they cannot print up non-local currency components of their ECU-denominated obligations.

(Implications for *public debt* are profound: see section 2.2.4 and Chapter 5.)

(f) *Reserve Principles*

(See section 2.2.2.)

The logic controlling some rather implausible cases unties a number of technical knots.

Consider a bank whose deposits are guaranteed in ECU, in an economy in which local currency remains the vehicle currency; and whose loans are strictly denominated in the local currency. (Prudential reserves should be ECU-based.) And specialize the problem to Italy. Italian banks are short ECU′ – the prime denotes deletion of the lira component of the ECU. Italian banks may acquire put options from insurers who balance their books, to desired degrees, by investing their capital in ECU-based packages of securities. *And* pan-European banks are substantially self-insured – while official entities are apt to operate naked: they have access to swap facilities.

Turning to the *insurance* operation just put into play, there are automatic set-offs making insurance more plausible and conducing towards spontaneous creation of pan-European banking entities. Thus consider a problem in two-space in which $a_1 = a_2 = 0.5$.

$$0.5p_1 + 0.5p_2 = 1 \tag{2.10}$$

If the local currencies are pounds and dollars, Economy 1 is short dollars and Economy 2, pounds. A bank spanning both economies (as a pan-European bank spans Europe) may find its risks washed out; and indeed can quite easily wash out its risks.

In a counterpart gold-standard problem, the financial institutions of both economies are short the *same thing*, gold. If one successfully covers its risks, there is less gold available for the other to cover *its* exposure (non-monetary gold is ignored for simplicity's sake, see Chapter 10). In our ECU régime, both economies are exposed to the risk of having to supply assets they cannot print, but one can print the stuff the other needs.

(g) *Currency Competition and Reserve Principles*

(A. Rinaldi of the Banca d'Italia has saved me from error in this connection.)

If the DM were the slowest growing component of the ECU package, and persistently appreciates, it is attractive as a substitute for ECU-equivalent reserves, subject to interest arbitrage factors: rational expectations appear to require expected appreciation to be matched by correspondingly lower running yields. But in life expectations are blurry; expectations vary across persons and are weakly, diffusedly, held. Some may take uncovered long DM positions, defying forecasts implicit in the interest parity; but their expectations will be too weakly diffuse for massive positions to be taken.

Remarks

1. If one holds only DM reserves against ECU obligations, one is shorting the other ECU components.
2. The fact that obedience to interest parity enforces relatively low yields on certain DM money market instruments does not entail a correspondingly low cost of capital in Germany. The cost of capital is an own rate, determined in imperfectly arbitraged global markets.

Call the global cost of capital r^*. Then the basic German interest rate becomes $r^* + \pi_{DM}$ and the basic Italian interest rate $r^* + \pi_{DM} + \xi$ – where π_{DM} is the German inflation rate and ξ the excess of the Italian over the German inflation rate.

2.2.2 Banking

In a limiting case, the vehicular currency is privately-generated ECU. And the régime is one of *convertibility*: ECU paper is redeemed by packages of government issue in local currencies. The non-banking public may hold 'warehouse receipts' for 'ECU packages' – i.e., appropriate sets of supporting paper. Or they may hold constituent elements, but not necessarily in 'proper' proportions; they may *speculate*. All ECU-guaranteed debt is foreign debt to a significant degree.

In a limiting case, demand for 'local currency' is merely for a reserve asset. And reserves are freely 'manufactured' within the European community. Other members' expansion paths impose constraints. Is *concerted* inflation elided? I suggest it is.

Bank reserves should consist of assets readily convertible into ECU components. So liaison with individual central banks is less useful – save for their access to swap privileges. And monetary bases of member economies are endogenous, as under a gold standard.

In section 2.2.2 bank lending is ECU-denominated. And efficiency is promoted by pan-European procedures – e.g., by integrated clearing of ECU-denominated transactions. Pan-European banking is encouraged; Europe-wide clearing is as natural in Europe as US-wide clearing in America.

As a laissez-faire ECU régime matures, the ECU will become predominant as a vehicle currency. Spontaneous evolution will be engendered by the simple expedient of freeing people to *choose* ECU modalities.

(a) *Tying up a Number of Loose Ends*

1. *Intra-European Financial Disequilibrium (?).* Shifts of reserves from Italian to French residents become no more important than those from Romans to Paduans. And banks are no more French than Italian – but integration is spontaneous.

   As for shifts of reserves from say Italian to say French residents, see positions taken by Sir Terrance Burns and the Chancellor (at the end of November 1988) that the 1988–9 British trade deficit was quite anodyne, since it was sparked by private agents who are sure to be subject to market discipline: the deficit-generating process drains liquidity in ways leading to homeostatic correction.
2. *Indexation* becomes a snare. Say that Italian authorities seek to promote demand for their securities by guaranteeing their ECU value against depreciation of the lira. Then the rate of growth of the stock of Italian liquid assets becomes a monotonically increasing function of the growth rate of the Italian monetary base,

assumed to determine the lira's rate of depreciation against ECU. Excess supply of Italian debt, corresponding to excess demand for foreign securities, generates correspondingly higher rates of growth of nominal supply of such debt. The canonical dynamics are

$$\dot{x} = f(x);\ f'(x) = (+)$$

2.2.3 Central Banking

Discussion is organized around five topics: (1) The free-lira (free-franc, etc.) concept; and properties of markets in free lire, etc. (2) Implications of the schema for possibilities of dys-synchronization of credit and real savings flows, referring to the credit-cycle literature touched on in Chapter 9. (3) Open-market operations. (4) Monetary aggregate-targeted policy in the new régime; (5) Does the new régime have an inflationary bias? (No!).

(a) *The Free-lira Concept; Properties of Markets in Free Lire, etc.*

Recall free electrons from physics or free molecules from old-fashioned chemistry. The lira stock can be similarly allocated between *bound* and *free* lire. Banca d'Italia (BI) may want to absorb free lire; or the government may want to increase the supply of free lire as part of a programme supplying stimulus. Free lire are held by dealers (including giant multinational banks and speculators – but speculation is universal; rational agents contemplate price-profile likelihoods). Dealers in free lire hope to profit from 'turns': processes generating free lire will unwind so that there will be excess demand for bound lire, supplied from overhanging stocks of free lire. *Bridging finance* analogies lie near to hand. Stabilizing speculation would virtually supply bridging finance under floating rates.

Lire become bound in the following ways.

1. As part of 'packages' backing ECU-issue, strictly imitating the (a_i) coefficients.
2. As part of the reserves backing ECU issue that do *not* strictly imitate (a_i) – reserves that might be out of phase for speculative reasons.
3. In stocks, including transactions balances, supporting local currency dealings (here lire). In the early days of evolution of an ECU standard, such stocks will be very substantial.

The following *corollary discussion* will be deepened later.

1. A monetary authority can make its 'currency' more scarce by selling real assets for it. Then its currency's ECU price will increase.
2. There is room for differential rates of monetary growth within Europe with corresponding changes in ECU-defined foreign indebtedness. Think of monetization of a deficit caused by a recession localized to Italy. Free lire are bought in by the market; and will become bound when the Italian budget goes into surplus during a subsequent period of economic buoyancy in Italy. During the recession, there is at least a tacit commitment to cut back Italian monetary base growth later. Credibility will erode, or shatter, if the commitment is dishonoured.
3. In Canada, limitations of nation-wide fiscal policy are acute: regional trade cycles are dys-synchronous. Europe's case is doubtless the same: 'local' fluctuations are often out of phase for reasons unrelated to monetary/fiscal policy divergences. We seek a structure supple enough to accommodate differential macro-policies.

   Changing the situs, the Bank of France, reacting to a local recession, may monetize public sector borrowing requirements in French francs, creating free French francs. The French francs are bought in at a discount for ECU′, (for ECU minus its French franc component) – increasing French liquidity and relaxing the French Government's budget constraint. The free French francs are stocked. When the French economy recovers, so that the public sector borrowing requirement falls, free French francs become bound. The process is operated by profit-seeking private agents. Stocks of free 'currencies' rotate according to trade-cycle phases.
4. So long as prices are quoted in ECU, speculation in component currencies seems unlikely to play back to terms of trade. Effects of speculation then seem largely confined to the free currencies markets, noting that prices in the currency markets will be quoted in ECU.

   Speculators in the 'free currency' markets will be vulnerable to bear squeezes by MAs: if they begin to accumulate DM, creating a shortage of bound DM, the German monetary authority may flood the market with DM paper, bloodying up the speculators.

   Eligible stocks are vast; they include public debt stocks, but cf *infra*. And, as the ECU price of the DM rises, it is increasingly attractive to sell DM-denominated holdings to agents seeking to accumulate ECU reserves . . . By definition the ECU price of (a_i) is unity; reserve-accumulating agents can obtain non-DM components for less when the ECU price of the DM increases.

5. At the genesis of the reformed régime, ECU values of the various monetary bases must be aligned. (Initial ECU prices of member currencies will reflect the initial state of play; and may be misaligned relative to equilibrium vectors.) If there is an initial shortage of DM relative to the appropriate ECU supply, the Germans can make a special issue – out of the equivalent to British *tap stock* – of DM securities.

   If underlying stocks of potential ECU reserves are vast, relative to ECU reserve requirements, no intervention would be called for in any plausible circumstances. And if the relevant monetary basal aggregate is ill defined, price behaviour in an ECU measure will be correspondingly hard to track, let alone control.

   In the reformed régime's early days, demand for local currencies for transactions balances purposes will be very substantial indeed; the bulk of bound currency stocks will be explained by local currency transactions balances motivation. But, finally, local currencies will look like vestigial remains and the European Currency idea will be fulfilled in a liberal order. Finally, local currencies will cease to be debt-settlement vehicles (*pace* the tacit stipulation controlling the corollary discussion).

(b) *Dys-synchronization, etc.*

Centring on modalities controlling 'creation' of credit by banks, and on debt-discharge modalities, the discussion sharpens up analysis of the appropriate monetary aggregates, preparing the way for section (d) below.

Banks, seeking to make additional ECU-denominated loans, in effect trade their paper for private sector open-market paper. Or merchant banks, playing a pure intermediary rôle, arrange for clients to transform chequeable ECU positions into holdings of paper issued by deficit spending units.

So, on a pan-European scale, there is ample opportunity for dys-synchronization between the volume of intermediation and real savings flows. But the constituent sub-systems are much more heavily constrained than they are now: national monetary authorities cannot 'print' the reserves that must back monetary expansion.

(c) *Open-market Operations in the New Régime*

Open-market operations must be remodelled: the BI will not be able to move freely between ECU and lire. It cannot print *both*. It will have to move between lire and real assets, in conjunction with the IRI; monetary authorities and Crown Corporations will collaborate in executing monetary policy. Consider sales of plant and equipment or shares for lire. Such sales mop up free lire; and reverse operations increase the supply of free lire.

Demand for local currencies can be influenced quite overtly. If the French Government were to insist that French francs be tendered for taxes, and other obligations to it, demand for French francs would be stimulated, just as recission of such regulations would reduce (schedule) demand for French francs. Demand for paper money has long been manipulated in this way: fascinating examples can be extracted from the annals of eighteenth-century British North America (see B. Smith, 1988).

Remark

Of course, 'local' MAs can trade their currencies for ECU, and *vice versa*, like other agents can. But MAs will no longer be privileged: they are constrained as they were under the classic gold standard.

(d) *Monetary Aggregates in the New Régime*

So far a diluted monetary aggregate concept has been deployed: public debt issue has been included. And a *principle of reflux* operates. When demand for ECUs increases, appropriate sets of near-dated bonds, etc. are 'warehoused', and 'ECU certificates' are issued. When such demand recedes, there is a reflux: the certificates are redeemed for underlying stock. Measured velocities of plausible monetary aggregates are thus apt to be volatile. Are basal aggregates controllable? If *any* low-inflating monetary authority tightly grips its portion of the reserve base, the monetarists' problems seem to be solved. (The query is not pivotal under a tabular standard; adoption of a tabular standard blots out inflation.)

(e) *Inflationary Bias(?)*

The joint production/joint demand properties of 'our' ECU schema make across-the-board cooperation unnecessary: it suffices for *one* authority to be virtuous. Nor is that all. Going back to 'our' markets in 'free' currencies, if an economy is a net debtor externally, slower monetary growth yields seigneurage profit to it *comme* 'issuer' of reserves, subject to a complex interest-arbitrage qualification (I owe much to A. Rinaldi on this point).

Finally, choice between uncontrolled ECU systems and ones based on powerful pan-European authority is like that between market-based and heirarchical industrial structures (the labels are Oliver Williamson's). In the uncontrolled ECU system, overt agreement is unnecessary: not even tacit concertization is required. Indeed one shudders on contemplating the bargaining intrinsic to pan-European authority, necessarily attuned to politics. Once so powerful a MA were established, politicians, skilled professional power-seekers, would swarm towards the new honey pot. Monetary laxity often permeates solutions of resulting games. In our schema, the lowest inflator predominates (and all the more in a dynamic assignment procedure for weight-determination). High-inflators are likely to come out on top in pan-European politics. Nor should economists neglect the theory and praxis of 'one-man/one-vote', a potentially destructive idea in non-homogeneous societies and ambiguous in homogeneous ones.

2.2.4 Public Finance

(See Chapter 5.)

ECU-denominated debt of say the Italian Government has the principal properties of external debt: the government is committed to tender foreign exchange to holders of its paper. And corollary analysis contributes *another* reason why public debt should not be deemed net social wealth: one's holdings are valuable only to the extent that the government can obtain devisen it cannot create.

So long as the lira, for example, is a vehicular currency, lira bonds, *comme* liquid assets supporting lira-denominated positions, will command a market. To this extent member governments retain powers of fiscal action. Recall how the Italian Government may sell lira bonds for ECU supplied by dealers anticipating profitable resale when the lira's ECU price rises, once the Italian economy regains buoyancy so that the Italian government reverses its fiscal gears.

Prospects for fiscal action will, however, dissipate as European economies become more fully integrated after 1992. Relevant multipliers may approach *zero*; GNP and GDP will become wholly disjoint. Think of prospects for the Commune of Rome (SPQR) to exercise Keynesian fiscal policy! And 'local' currencies will wither away. In early days, the ECU and (e.g.) lira standards will operate side by side – and, indeed, the lira may predominate at first. But the ECU will come to the fore fairly swiftly, prevailing by say 2000.

2.2.5 Macro-modelling

ECU accounting reckons to make investors more indifferent towards the patria in which they entrust their resources – leading to an amorphous 'real economic space'. If the French lose heart as investors in physical capital, German may replace French entrepreneurship in France, an upshot entailing larger French placements with German intermediaries and increased lending to and investment in German entrepreneurship by German intermediaries. The matrix of claims will jiggle about under the pressure of fresh transitions and new arteries of financial circulation may be carved out, but net effects on national trade and capital accounts could well be *nil*. (See Svensson (1988) for a penetrating related analysis.)

Implications for stability, and for freer choice of milieux in which to act are attractive; just as those for national model builders are chilling. Investment plans of Italian entrepreneurs, even in Italy, lose importance in a proper model; and the reaction functions, and action-determinants of agents *partout* become highly important, and indiscernible to traditional macro-models, if discernible at all.

2.3 DISCUSSION OF THREE 'BANCA D'ITALIA' PAPERS INTERSECTING THIS STUDY

(I merely refer to work generated and/or discussed in the Bank. The papers do not bind Banca d'Italia(!); and authors may have left the Bank.)

2.3.1 Tullio and Contesso (1987)

The authors show that, so long as the ECU is not a standard of value, it cannot be an optimal hedge for the most part. And they make a point (based on work by Dr H.-J. Dudler) especially interesting here:

> The low risk/high return characteristics of the private ECU have been a cause of its development, thanks to transactions costs. With

> zero transactions costs, investors and borrowers could diversify their risk by forming their own baskets of currencies and the private ECU would never have developed.
>
> Tullio and Contesso (1987, p. 2)

(See Chapter 10 of (1989a) for a related line of development – in which I emphasize potentials of options transactions.)

This point appears again at p. 15, in a context displaying the central difference between my approach and others: I emphasize ECU metrics (measures, standards of value), playing down embodiment of the ECU idea in say an official currency; I should wish to rely on spontaneous processes rather than juridical reform – along an azimuth described in section 2.1 above.

> In a world without transactions costs, private agents wanting to diversify their risks would form their own baskets and the ECU would lose its diversification function.
>
> Tullio and Contesso (1987, p. 15)

What is truly decisive is installation of an ECU *metric*: an imaginary ECU may serve perfectly well (see Chapter 4). What is important is not ECU property, but rather an ECU idea that can be implemented by an imaginary ECU. (True, in time, 'real' ECUs, perhaps private ones, may predominate.) Under an ECU standard, ECU-denominated contracts would tend to be optimal feasible risk-allocation devices.

Tullio and Contesso conclude that a common European accounting unit must be accompanied by coordinated member economy monetary/fiscal policies. But, if a European *metric* is properly selected, necessary coordination is slight, if not nil.

Liberal and *dirigiste* outlooks become sharply distinguished. The distinction is like that between a chess authority who merely defines the game's rules the way von Neumann and Morgenstern define their games and one who does this *and* lays down say the first twenty moves for each contest.

2.3.2 Russo and Tullio (1988)

The following passage conveys the flavour of the Russo and Tullio analysis.

> Four rules [are] discussed that could lead, under a broadly unchanged institutional setting, to an improvement in the function of the EMS system . . . They are not intended to be proposals for reform but only working hypotheses.
>
> (1) a common EMS-wide money supply target, à la McKinnon fixed ex ante.
> (2) a rule which consists in setting the growth rate of the domestic component of the monetary base in each country on the basis of the inflation target and of potential output growth (coupled with no sterilization).
> (3) [a nominal demand] income target . . .
> (4) a rule to target monetary policy (and fiscal policy?) at a commonly agreed inflation rate . . .
>
> The need for concentrating on a final target (i.e. inflation) and adopting policy response to the nature and origin of the shock [must control implementation of and choice between rules] in the present institutional context.
>
> Russo and Tullio (1988, pp. 36–7)

I reckon the four rules to be politically infeasible: thus pro-inflationary politicians are apt to overwhelm technocrats in setting target values. So the following points are the more intriguing.

1. Why not simply install an ECU *standard*? (Some revision of monetary charters, including legal tender acts, may be required – but preliminary investigation suggests required revision is quite slight.) This would engender a spontaneous evolution going far to integrate a *de facto* European monetary system. Creation of rights and corresponding duties is not entailed; the reform confers powers to make offers that indeed change the legal map (nexus) but which have substantive effect only if *voluntarily* accepted. The upshot, shaped in part by Hohfeld's juridical theory, obeys Hayekian tenets of liberal ordering.
2. More flexibility than is possible under the four rules seems required. Thus the political-economic personalities of member economies must be accommodated for reform to work. Consider Italian public finance and, in particular, Italian public debt (for the most part held internally). *How* could Italian public debt become ECU-convertible overnight? But, if exchange rates were fixed and

financial dealing wholly denationalized, it would be virtually convertible. If, more realistically, Italian debt is to continue to be lira-denominated and convertible only into basal lire stock, *the lira must float*. (Galli and Masera (1988) take a somewhat different slant.)

3. The German political-economic personality is identified with low monetary growth and so, all in all, with low inflation. (See Modigliani, 1986, pp. 42ff, for a qualified dissent, at least in the Italian context, from this remark's underlying premiss.) The German ethos is more likely to prevail under laissez-faire than under collective *dirigisme* where the German delegate's vote counts for little. (Nor, in September 1989, is it clear how *Germany* will be defined in 1993 or say 2000. And will the Board of the European MA include Poles and Hungarians, if not Russians and Romanians?)
4. One need only recall the symmetallic properties of the ECU idea to see that an ECU standard is consistent with floating rates among the ECU's constituent parts – and to see that the ECU can feasibly be *imaginary*.

Further Commentary on Russo and Tullio (1988)

Russo and Tullio remark that 'in an n-country world, there are only n–1 exchange rates' (p. 34). This need not be true. Thus Patinkin (1956/1965) points out that the following is a valid normalization rule.

$$\sum p_i = 1 \tag{2.11}$$

And the set of such rules is indefinitely large (our ECU proposals nest in a normalization like that of equation (2.11)).

Finally, Russo and Tullio say that

> A properly functioning fixed or adjustable exchange rate system needs a rule governing inflation. The gold standard had such a rule, albeit an imperfect one. Bretton Woods and the EMS do not. To the extent that in the latter two systems the nth country (the 'leader') has also provided an acceptable inflation anchor, the system has operated satisfactorily, but asymmetrically.
>
> Russo and Tullio (1988, p. 36)

This line of development probably commands very wide consensus and is flawed in at least two ways, one on the plane of general economic reasoning, the other on that of political-economic praxis.

Establishment of a tabular standard wipes out the inflation perplex at a stroke. And an ECU standard goes far, *per se* to establish 'an acceptable inflation anchor'.

As a practical matter, German leadership on 'inflation' is promoted by spontaneous evolution; for one thing, it then can be exercised without consultation. Nor need virtuous authorities then coordinate their plans with sinful ones.

Finally, the Bundesbank is now exceptionally independent of political authority. Would a Brussels behemoth grant special patents to the putatively virtuous Bundesbank? Indeed translated Bundesbank officers, sitting on a European board, would be outvoted by a consortium of Greek, Italian, Spanish, Turkish and Hungarian politicians.

2.3.3 Masera (1987)

> It needs to be recognized, however, that *complete* integration of national financial markets entails exchange rates remaining fixed. Otherwise financial assets held in different currencies will not be perfectly substitutable, an indispensable condition for full integration. Financial integration itself calls for monetary convergence. In principle, sovereignty in monetary matters . . . is not compatible with the objective of creating a *single* European financial market.
>
> Masera (1987, p. 5)

This is strong stuff. Indeed, since financial integration on Masera's terms looks infeasible, impatient readers may simply drop the matter – further encouraged to do so by Herr Pöhl's remarks in Autumn 1988. So this study's schematization, based on 'mere' commitment to freedom of transactors' choice of measure (leaving them free to choose an ECU measure), is the more interesting. A *spontaneous* alternative to strict monetary convergence looks more feasible as well as more liberal.

(a) *Public Debt*

Italians cannot accept Masera's conclusions, and implicit proposals, unless the immense overhang of Italian public debt is wiped out (see

Chapter 5). And this point shows how important is the political dimension of European economic reform. Comparable American public debt disharmony, *circa* 1783–91, was resolved by a famous compromise under which the capital was located in a fetid lowland in exchange for support of Hamilton's closely-reasoned Assumption plan. Resolution required an act of immense political will at the apex of American politics (cf Washington, Hamilton, Jefferson and Madison) in the aftermath of a monumental revolution that still exerted great emotional force. The American example does *not* encourage European emulation.

(b) *Brussels Hegemony*

Masera supports a powerful pan-European fiscal authority as well as a monetary one. And the fiscal authority is to be amply endowed with powers to enforce a stern *dirigisme*.

> It is necessary to limit and prevent rigidities – or even perverse movements with respect to productivity – in wage rates in the countries forming the area. The minimization of the costs associated with overcoming balance-of-payments problems cannot be achieved exclusively by exploiting the mobility of factors of production, but must also be able to rely on fiscal measures that are coordinated at *[European]* level and, when necessary, on recourse to corrective instruments such as incomes policy.
>
> Masera (1987, p. 6)

Europe is to be governed by a heavily-armed nanny. Nations are to be instructed by Brussels to enact wage–price controls or to expand public spending. National parliaments had just as well be prorogued. If these are truly the necessary conditions for European economic integration, the concept will be quashed, unless the voters are gulled. But such conditions are *not* necessary for economic integration and indeed would impede pan-European economic efficiency. A liberal ordering, nested in an ECU metric (or standard), can do Dr Masera's job for him.

Concluding Political-economic Observations

Dr Masera elevates a neo-Keynesian world view to the status of received truth: 'Thou shalt not be beguiled by the new classical macro-economics and other heresies'. An immense political upheaval is to be motivated by implicit propositions of a not-very-successful science. European polity is bound to crumble if necessarily half-baked concoctions are embedded in a constitution that will be profoundly revised as other concoctions come to the fore. (I oppose 'balanced budget' amendments to the American Constitution on the same ground.) And there is a more opaque ground for dissent as well.

Models are not intrinsically true or false. The ideas of the Phillips curve and monetarism, expressed as sets of propositions avoiding self-contradiction, can be neither true nor false. Science's essentially instrumental constructions are retained or jettisoned because of their utility or practical futility. Nor indeed need such constructions be *wholly* adopted or rejected, as the oft-repeated instance of Newtonian mechanics shows. So it is fundamentally improper to write hypotheses into constitutions; just as the *operations* of governments, and of *all* agents, *must* pivot on provisionally maintained hypotheses.

The British Constitution embodies 'my' view. It is not surprising that the methodology of the transition to a different Europe is more hotly contested in Britain than anywhere else.

3 The Modus Operandi of Bank Rate Reconsidered

3.1 THE ANALYTICAL FRAMEWORK

3.1.1 Preliminary Comments

The purport of *interest on money* seems ill-understood. (But see Modigliani, 1986, Modigliani and Papademos, 1980 and Chapter 3 of (1986), including its references to Tobin.)

What are the implications for central bank policy of flexibly interest yielding money in a competitive system? Changes in yields of monetary assets relative to those of other financial assets are then barred – although transient changes of yields of financial assets relative to those of *real* assets *are* permissible; thus Pierce (1980) nicely distinguishes Fisherine real rates of interest from own yields of physical assets.

So substitution effects within the financial sector are barred. The upshot is sometimes confused with that of a vertical *LM* curve – in a Keynesian context faithfully reproduced by 'ISLM' to this extent. Indeed it is said that nominal money supply drives real interest rates. What really happens is that *LM* is indeed known to be vertical, but its location becomes undetermined – a point amplified in an innovated economy saturated with liquidity: see Chapters 4 and 5 below and (1988). Of course, if *LM* cannot be located, it ought to be abandoned.

(a) *Modes of Monetary Policy*

Monetary aggregate modes of monetary policy can link up with the theory of moving equilibria – i.e., differential equations in the canonical form

$$\dot{x} = f(x); \quad 0 = f(\bar{x}) \tag{3.1}$$

where x may be a vector of deviations from a vector-valued equilibrium growth path. But Bank rate policy can be properly assessed only as a problem in optimal control, quite divorced from 'equilibrium' except in the seemingly perverse way in which in a moving equilibrium higher (lower) Bank rate maps into higher (lower) inflation.

The theory of active Bank rate policy is exceptionally difficult and remains perplexing. Why? It cannot be extracted from models of spontaneous economic action. The well-known contrast of active with passive exchange rate management is helpful. Active Bank rate policy manipulates Bank rate (which communicates directly with a set of money market rates) the way an Authority may manipulate exchange rates in order to impose terms of trade inconsistent with general equilibrium. A passive Authority merely adapts exchange rates to autonomously evolving equilibrium terms of trade. The behaviour of the 'active' authority is wilful; it cannot be modelled by counterparts to physical models of gas behaviour.

Active Bank rate policy reckons to control the economy's motion rather than merely respond to it. And the proper paradigm for modelling active Bank rate policy has long been near to hand: cf dynamic programming, the (Pontryagin) maximum principle or the theory of optimal control.

Interpolation

Bank rate can be passive when the MA is otherwise active. Thus if the secular rate of monetary expansion is altered by the MA, Bank rate is made higher in order to validate resulting higher secular inflation.

* * *

In Section 3.4, 'The Economic Consequences of Mr Lawson', the revised theory is applied to an interesting 1988–9 episode. The British Chancellor deployed active Bank rate policy to try to cut back British inflation, said by some to be due to earlier substitution of the sterling/DM rate for money growth as a prime policy target: control of the monetary base may have been lost. The theory suggests that the Chancellor's policy is flawed. For one thing it pivots on the 'Phillips curve' premiss that the path of price inflation depends on the level of aggregate demand rather than on 'money'. And Mr Lawson's policy entails closed-loop control, contrasting with the open-loop properties of, say, Friedman's rule. In a régime of Bank rate targeting, inflation is easily fuelled on a feedback channel.

Section 3.5 reconstructs Poole's problem so that it nests in an optimal control framework eschewing monetary theories of real action.

3.1.2 A Preliminary Exercise: Properties of a Prototype Change in the Monetary Régime

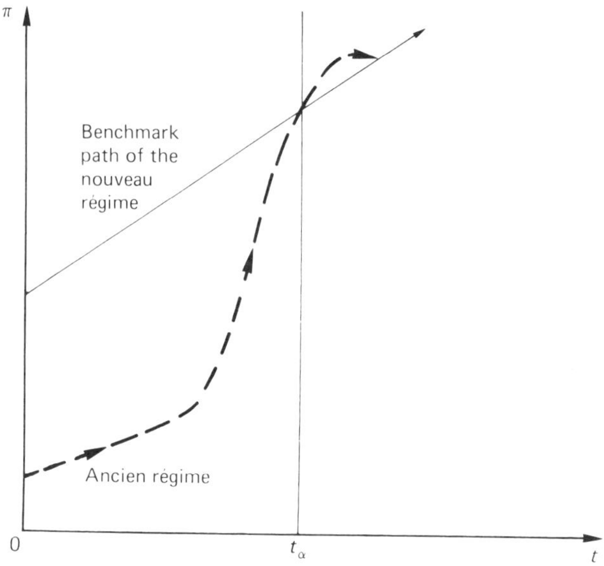

Figure 3.1 A change in the monetary régime confronting price inertia

Notes for Figure 3.1

1. See Friedman (1969) for a keen analysis of a related problem. Prices must accelerate on some interval so that the process regains its equilibrium track. The propulsive force is supplied by a build-up of liquidity.
2. The inflation rate overshoots. The 'overshoot' dries up excess liquidity existing at date t_α.
3. Figure 3.1 pertains to a monetary aggregate policy mode.

Figure 3.1. displays characteristic features of aftermaths of changes in money growth régimes. For one thing, the inflation rate must overshoot, as the notes explain. We seek a theory consistent with 'interest on money' that accounts for these characteristics.

At impact, a switch to faster money growth pushes down the market yield of monetary authority funds (MAF). The fall in MAF rate induces lower deposit rate, leading to lower financial asset yields in general. Some stimulus may also be supplied to share markets. But share markets are supposed to be very forward looking. And plans to move towards consumer durables and inventories, and to foreshorten investment – expenditure streams (cf Hicksian diminuendo), take time to be formulated and executed. Even transient 'real' stimulus is problematical.

One piece of the puzzle is still to be put into place. An increase in financial intermediary liabilities, absorbing faster growth of MAF, must be *willed* by the financial intermediaries; their increased demand for reserves must be voluntary, as must be complementary expansion of demand, as well as of supply, of intermediary liabilities. (Of course, intermediaries must *want* to increase their assets, as well as their liabilities.) The theory must supply *motivation*.

If elasticities of substitution among financial substances are high, the volume of intermediation can massively increase without spreads appreciably narrowing. If elasticities of substitution are low, spreads must narrow substantially to induce the public to hold more assets indirectly.[1] Finally, note that expansion and contraction in the volume of financial mediation is quite consistent with autonomously evolving real action.

3.2 MONETARY MECHANISMS

3.2.1 Monetary Aggregate Targeting

A decision is made on the expansion rate of MA debt (asset) holdings – acquired with its funds (MAF). The decision nails down the equilibrium path of *nominal* interest rates; secular *real* interest rates evolve invariantly against purely nominal magnitudes.

Securities transactions implementing decisions on monetary aggregate targets are quite small on a scale measuring total activity in say the thick, deep markets for American public debt. Nor should open-market operations making decisions on MAF rate effective (i.e., open-market operations incidental to active Bank rate policy) be confused with ones implementing achievement of monetary aggregate targets. The latter engender no more than transient, incidental, sometimes random, effects on interest rates. The former are keyed on nominal interest rates; they *must* affect nominal yields under the operational control of the MA.

Now consider markets made in MAF funds. Some banks characteristically obtain part of their resources this way; just as others characteristically lend out MAF. (Agents do not necessarily play one rôle or the other: see Gowland, 1984, pp. 57–8.)

Agents must be indifferent at margins between obtaining resources by selling notes, long bonds, equity or attracting deposits, etc. – *or* borrowing MAF. The simplistic equation (3.2) suggests the upshot.

$$r - r' = 0.9r - \hat{r} \tag{3.2}$$

$$r' - \hat{r} = 0.1r \tag{3.2a}$$

Glossary

r = the open-market lending rate on primary (not financial intermediary) flotation
r' = the MAF rate
$\hat{r}$ = the deposit rate

A reserve requirement is imposed so that only 90 per cent of resources obtained by attracting deposits can be lent out. Reserves are lodged with the MA, who does not pay interest.

The formulae would ideally be adjusted for at least one class of risk: embarrassing urgency is more likely to be experienced by an intermediary dependent on MAF for a substantial portion of its resources than by one who characteristically lends MAF and has a large capital base. And the formulae do not specify the cost-based determinants of spreads.

Finally, MAF rate and deposit rate are positively covariant. And when 'covariance' is linked to a stipulation that the financial intermediary system is competitive, the properties of 'transmission' are determined, as Modigliani and Papademos (1980) and Modigliani (1986) show.

Remarks

(a) Banks do not typically obtain incremental funds by attracting depositors; rather they sell paper the way Ajax Ltd does.

Inframarginally, banks may realize large economic rents. Thus the huge deposit base of the Bank of America once made its lucrative business fairly immune to costs of funds.

(b) As for *seigneurage*, if more MAF are pumped into the system, less government debt need be sold to the public. (The MA receives tap stock.)

3.2.2 A Fragment of Bank Rate Theory

The MA's lending rate describes the terms on which it is prepared to exchange MAF now for MAF later. Is the MA's rate, Bank rate, *effective*? If Bank rate is ineffectively low, fortunate borrowers can relend proceeds of loans from the MA at open-market rates – as Ricardo explains in a famous (1817/1951) passage. If Bank rate is ineffectively high, the market will not borrow from the Bank. The American Federal Reserve Board did not grasp the controlling logic for some years after beginning operations in 1914: see section 3.2.3, which relies on Keynes (1930/1971) – as well as the comprehensive explanation by Friedman and Schwartz (1963) of the origins, implementation and flawed operation of the Federal Reserve System; and Dykes and Whitehouse (1989).

The MA makes targeted rates *effective* by offering MAF for securities or securities for MAF. Portfolio equilibrium requires that the shadow yield of MAF corresponds properly with the market rate for MAF funds, r': see equations (3.2) and (3.2a) and their gloss.[2]

3.2.3 Keynes on Bank Rate

We arrange Keynes's materials around two themes: (1) the relationship between Bank rate and money growth, the proper subject of Wicksell's *cumulative process*; (2) deployment of Bank rate to influence real costs of capital. Keynes comes back to the second theme in the Appendix to Chapter 14 of the *General Theory*, as I explained in (1988).

Keynes contrasts Continental and American with British praxis. And the critical characteristic of the British system of his day (and I should think ours) is that advances by the central bank to the 'member' banks should normally be *nil*: 'resources' are normally to be supplied to banks through open-market operations, if at all – and not at the discount window (however indirectly – e.g., through the agency of the discount houses). Under the British system the MA controls its total liabilities, as it does not in the prototype Continental and American systems Keynes discusses.

(a) *Keynes on the Continental System*

(This material illuminates the context of Wicksell's analysis. Also see Leijonhufvud, 1981.)

> Since the member banks were not tied by reserve ratios and were not prevented from freely discounting . . . the control exercised over them by the central bank was very imperfect . . . This weakness was balanced by the fact that, if member banks as a whole were inclined to increase their lending, they would get back as deposits a much smaller proportion of the amount lent, because a much larger proportion of the new loans would be taken out in the shape of bank notes . . . [So] an expansion of [business] borrowing would quickly show itself in an expansion of the central bank's portfolio of bills and a nearly corresponding expansion of its note issue. Thus it was to these symptoms that the attention of the controlling authorities was primarily directed.
>
> Keynes (1930/1971, II, pp. 208–9)

It becomes clear in Chapter 9 that expansions of central bank note issue responding to increased demand for cash (in the schedule sense of demand) importantly differ from expanded note issue incidental to increased bank lending, responding to say an increase in the marginal efficiency of capital or to concerted reductions in banks' lending rates *à la* Wicksell. In the latter instance, there is excess supply of bank issue at impact; and there may, or may not, be *forced saving*.

(b) *Keynes on the American Federal Reserve System*

> When the Federal Reserve System was planned . . . it was not understood how vitally important to the control of the central bank was the London technique which secured that the 'advances' of the central bank to the member banks should be normally nil . . . The full latitude allowed to the member banks to rediscount . . . and the maintenance of buying rates at which the Federal Reserve banks will discount bills for their member banks or will buy bankers' acceptances commonly bear a relation to market rates which makes it habitually profitable for some bills at any rate to be brought to the reserve banks.
>
> Keynes (1930/1971, II, pp. 210–11)

The Federal Reserve was conceived in real bills-doctrine sin (cf also the Principle of Reflux or the Commercial Loan Theory of Banking). Bank rate was habitually significantly below market rate.

> The first phase, before the above flaw in the system had been discovered was clearly seen in the great inflation of 1920 . . . [The Board] had not yet realized the enormous latent possibilities of inflation resulting from its failure to imitate [penal British Bank rate] . . . No one seemed to notice that the main check on which the Bank of England relies was missing from the machine. The Federal Reserve System's holdings of discounted bills [rose 30 per cent from an 'enormous' base from January to October 1920]. . . Then, with the great deflation, by August 1922 the figure had fallen 85 per cent.
>
> Keynes (1930/1971, II, pp. 213–14)

By 1925, the flaw in the system's *modus operandi* was discovered; and corrective steps were taken. But Original Sin was ineluctable. The Federal Reserve contracted its credit during the Great Depression, responding in part to perceived reductions in the 'needs of trade'.

There is wider consensus that the operational procedures of the Federal Reserve impeded money supply control (even when 'money' was easier to identify) than on 'why does this flaw matter?'. Some, perhaps taking a lead from Marshall (cf *infra*), have emphasized effects on price behaviour. (American experience *circa* 1920–2 supports Marshall's 'speculation' hypothesis: wholesale commodity prices were very volatile.) Others, taking a lead from 'Austrian' theory, look towards distortions in the structure of production, enforced by 'forced saving' and causing investment to exceed saving in the *Treatise*'s convoluted sense of these terms. (But the latter hypothesis does not explain why the public increase their cash holdings during an industrial boom when claims against banks look relatively unattractive.)

(c) *Keynesian Insight into the Arbitrage Formulation of Equations (3.2) and (3.2a)*

Section IV of Chapter 32 (*Treatise*), 'Will member banks borrow from the central bank at a rate above the market?' pp. 218–24 is primarily concerned with the relation of a bank's coefficient of expansion (much larger for a monopoly bank than for a member of a competitive system) to the penalty (on borrowing from the Bank) imposed by penal Bank rate.

> So long as market rates are below the official rate, it will always appear to a bank, which is desirous of increasing its reserve balances, that it will pay it better to steal away the reserve balances of other member banks than to borrow itself from the Reserve bank. Why . . . should a member bank rediscount if it can increase its reserve resources more cheaply by withdrawing funds from the call market or by selling an acceptance or an investment? . . . If each member bank is doing this, no one is, on balance, any the better off.
>
> Keynes (1930/1971, II, p. 223)

We have transposed this passage into terms tenable for analysis of the Federal Funds market. And the transposition alters Keynes's characterization of the situation: a bank can lend out all the funds it borrows by issuing paper it need not reserve against; but it can lend out only a fraction of reserve-eligible deposits it takes. The deposit rate must be correspondingly lower in equilibrium; and the convenience yield, at the margin, of such deposits must be correspondingly higher.

(d) *Open-market Policy Further Analysed (Keynes, 1930/1971, II, pp. 224ff)*

The following passage sharply distinguishes the logic of active from that of adaptive (passive) Bank rate policy.

> Now in the last resort it is certainly the case that Bank rate policy and open-market policy cannot be carried on, except within limits, along different lines. The importance of the difference between the two methods is not, however, affected by this. For it arises out of the fact that the *kinds* of effect produced by the two methods are materially different. Changes in Bank rate may, amongst other things, affect the volume of central bank advances; but they do much else besides, and their influence on central bank advances is an uncertain, incidental result of a much wider complex of consequences which a change in Bank rate sets up, [*Voilà*! Keynes is a Wicksellian out of tune with the economics of Knut Wicksell.] Open-market operations, on the other hand, produce a direct effect on the reserves of the member banks and hence on the volume of deposits and of credit generally, by their immediate consequences and apart from their indirect reactions. Moreover,

changes in Bank rate primarily affect the short rate of interest; whereas open-market operations – so far as they relate to the central bank's holdings of long-dated securities – influence the long rate of interest [*sic?*].

Keynes (1930/1971, II, p. 225)

(e) *Critique of the last (Keynesian) Passage*

Keynes correctly points out that deliberate expansion or contraction of MA assets may be offset by countervailing *recourse* to the MA – countervailing recourse blocked by the British system. Nor does the revised American system block such recourse, as Meigs (1962) shows in an important study. But, if the coefficient of countervailing recourse is predictably less than unity, there survives only a distinction without a difference for the efficiency of 'classic' monetary aggregate targeting – although the MA's ability to impose crunching squeezes *is* then impaired.

Indeed open-market operations directly affect bank reserves. But Modigliani (1986) shows that banks' reserve positions must accommodate to non-bank portfolio equilibrium: a bank can always buy reserves from or sell them to the market. Thus so long as bank reserves are excessive, deposit rate falls; and the system cannot regain equilibrium until deposit rate and MAF rate are realigned with primary yields, relative to a cost-based spread. Section 3.3.2 shows that this task is discharged by changes in the general price level – or, in a dynamic analysis, by changes in the inflation rate.

Finally, it is implausible that changes in MA holdings of long-dated securities, on the scale of open-market operations, should much affect long rates: the order of magnitude of the relevant stock dwarfs that of MA operations (see Chapter 7). What is more, when Modigliani–Miller-like adaptations are put into play (cf countervailing private sector issue), the idea that operations in long-dated stocks can control long rate becomes preposterous.[3]

3.3 TOWARDS A REVISED THEORY OF BANK RATE

3.3.1 Resolution of the Classical and Neo-classical Chords

It is said that 'interest on money' leads to a vertical *LM* curve; the concomitant implication being that real economic action is determined by the quantity of money! It is even said that this horrid proposition is monetarist. No! Monetarism boils down to a theory of nominal income: the allocation between real and nominal effects of monetary action is 'open' along a Hicksian traverse, which may be very short for expected monetary changes; secular real action is invariant against secular monetary growth.

ISLM becomes incoherent when money flexibly yields interest – but the *CC/LL* construction, based on work by Metzler and Patinkin, supplies a more suitable framework. (See Patinkin, 1956/1965; and I vividly recall Professor Metzler's lectures *circa* 1955.) Figure 3.2 describes the upshot. The flat *CC* curve depicts a natural rate of interest while properly eschewing real balance effects. The vertical *LL* curve does *not* require that the elasticity of demand for money be zero; it simply reflects the stipulation that the spread earned by the financial intermediary sector is rigidly determined by competition. So the only equilibrium values affected by changes in money growth are inflation rates, mirrored by changes in nominal interest rates.

The immediate sequel shows how the *CC/LL* paradigm sharpens up contrast between monetary aggregate and Bank rate orientation. Monetary aggregate-targeted policy conforms to equilibrium models (see Figure 3.2). But active Bank rate policy does not: it is intrinsically interventionist.

3.3.2 Some Exercises in Praxis

(a) *Open-market Sales are to Reduce Base Money Growth: Interest Rate Dynamics*

Open-market sales by the MA are to reduce base money growth. Excess demand for MAF drives up the MAF rate in secondary markets and, in turn, the covariant deposit rate. The quantity of money demanded increases: money now yields more relative to non-monetary assets. And money growth is slowing.

The strict covariance of yields on money and non-monetary financial assets, imposed by the competitive spread stipulation, drives the process. Financial sector rates in general and the yield on money chase each other in an expanding spiral so far as we have gone. See Figure 3.3, describing a closed-loop dynamic that cannot resolve itself until slower inflation curtails money-demand – via a negative expansion effect; competitive interest on money quashes substitution effects.

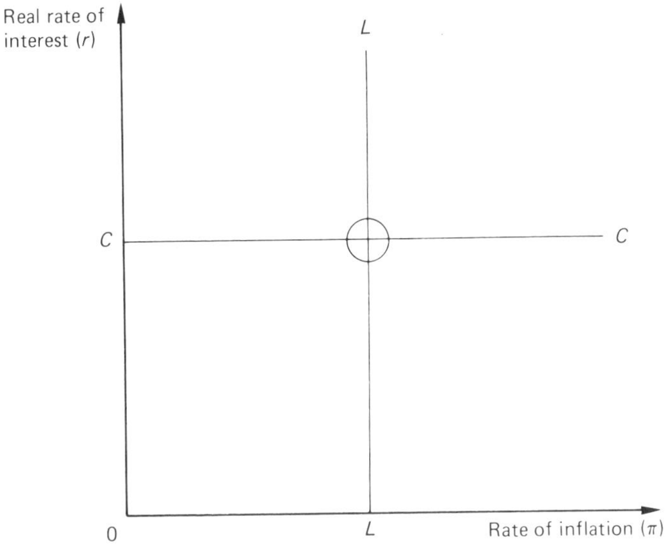

Figure 3.2 The *CC/LL* construction *à la* Metzler and Patinkin

Notes for Figure 3.2

1. The inflation rate is substituted for the Metzler–Patinkin price level. A tacit initial condition assures that the money supply is initially 'right'.
2. The locus of points comprising *LL* is consistent with money market equilibrium; and the locus of points comprising *CC* is consistent with commodity market equilibrium. But it is misleading to call this a *full employment* construction. Rather, aggregate output is essentially autonomous for the monetary analysis.

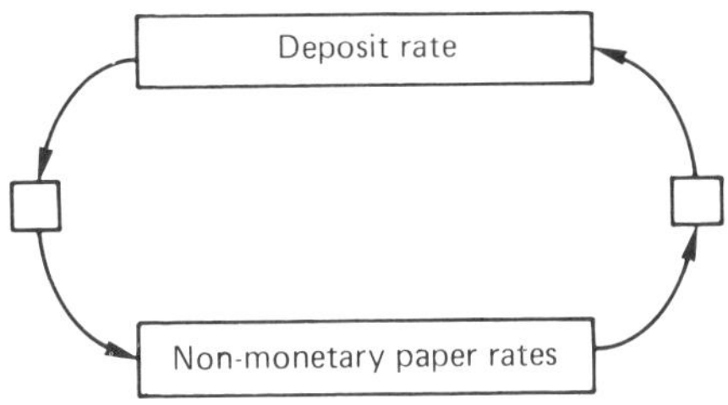

Figure 3.3 Deposit rate and non-monetary yields chase each other until disequilibrium is resolved by a lower inflation rate subsequent to slower money growth

Effects on primary security yields are ill-defined and surely incidental to the exercise. And Bank rate merely tracks the evolution of money market rates in order to stay effective – so that monetary aggregate targets are hit.

Now relax the stipulation that the banking system is strictly competitive. What if deposit rate falls *relative to* other rates, in the wake of contracted MAF growth? Monetary demand contracts correspondingly so that disequilibrating pressures are absorbed and the financial markets are temporarily equilibrated. What is more, the puzzle can now be solved without *any* market rate, other than deposit rate, changing. In the upshot, deposit rate falls(!) because of monetary contraction. And price inertia becomes easier to understand: a relatively lower deposit rate induces agents to reduce the monetary composition of their portfolios so that monetary velocity increases; and *vice versa* for monetary expansion.

Relaxation of the stipulation of strict competition in banking markets puts the distinction of adaptive from active Bank rate policy into high relief: in principle, monetary-targeting exercises can be conducted without affecting real yields of any substance but money.

(b) *Bank Rate is Increased in a Régime of Active Bank Rate Policy*

The MA is prepared at all times to deal in MAF at a rate it decrees . . . Bank rate is put up. The policy mode is not amenable to equilibrium analysis: in equilibrium, a permanent increase in Bank rate is validated by a corresponding increase in secular inflation. The proper problem concerns optimal control: see section 3.4. Thus prices *may* decelerate; and the system *may* be eased onto a new track (or put into a new orbit) at the episode's conclusion.

(c) *Bank Rate is Cut in a Régime of Active Bank Rate Policy*

The analysis is taken quite pure: relative rates are invariant in the theory's competitive financial sector.

Since primary own rates evolve autonomously (see Thornton's 'mercantile rate of profit') relative to money market yields, bank lending is encouraged – so that money supply, a residue of intermediary asset purchases, accelerates. Two comments are called for.

1. In an equilibrium mode of analysis, pertinent for monetary aggregate targeting, lower nominal bank rate maps into slower money growth and slower inflation.
2. The 'mercantile rate of profit' may evolve strictly autonomously; and a cut in Bank rate *still* fuels faster money growth. It becomes attractive to take *round trips*, to redeposit borrowed funds. What is more, this paradigm seems to conform to Wicksell's.

* * *

Lord Kaldor's notion that causality runs from the inflation rate (determined by non-monetary forces) to money growth is speciously plausible in an active mode of Bank rate policy; see section 3.4 below. Demand for nominal cash balances, when money yields interest competitively, is an unambiguously increasing function of the inflation rate: substitution effects are quashed.[4] But, *pace* Lord Kaldor, the engine propelling the process *is* monetary: the process is circular only if allowed to evolve in a closed circuit.

(d) *Open-market Purchases by the MA Under Monetary Aggregate Targeting; Primary Capital Markets do not Evolve Autonomously*

MAF are offered for 'bonds'. MAF rate, in the secondary market for MAF, falls, inducing higher bond prices. Arbitrage pushes down deposit rates. *And* Tobin's q increases transiently: yields of primary assets fall sympathetically.

Enter the *supply-side liquidity trap*. In strictly competitive financial markets, bank spreads cannot narrow; at the initial general price level, demand for chequeable accounts may not increase; at first, monetary aggregates may not change. But a yawning gap, between depressed money market rates and the own rate of return on physical capital, may provoke agitated motion; attempts to move into real assets, including consumer durables, may accelerate prices. The transmission process starts *before* money growth changes. Price acceleration induces increased demand for money. Money supply growth trails inflation – although the lag may be short.

Finally, nominal yields increase in line with targeted increases in MAF growth;[5] real equilibrium paths are regained.

The alternative policy modes *are* disjoint. In a monetary

aggregate-targeting episode, excess supply of (demand for) MAF incidentally affects interest rates across an imprecisely located spectrum of asset yields. In (active) Bank rate episodes, there is neither excess demand for nor supply of MAF: the MA's offer curve is perfectly elastic. Not only are the modes' dynamics disparate: the theory of a régime of active Bank rate lies outside the domain of equilibrium analysis.

Coda to Section 3.3.2: Flexible Competitive Interest on Money Leads to a Vertical LM Curve that cannot be Located

Label a subset of financial assets *money*. Competition establishes a strictly cost-based gap between yields of monetary and non-monetary financial assets so that monetary equilibrium is consistent with *any* real interest rate index. (see Patinkin, 1961/1972, for a corollary analysis).

Two *uncertainty principles* emerge.

1. If the gap between yields of monetary and non-monetary financial assets is 'logarithmically invariant', the quantity of money is indeterminant over a wide range: the mix of intermediary liabilities supported by the reserve base becomes determined by demand. Wallace expands this point; see section 3.3.3. And a surprising ancient counterpart is explained in Chapter 10.
2. If the gap between yields of monetary and non-monetary financial assets is invariant on a log scale, nothing about the level (intercept) of the interest rate index – in real space – can properly be extracted from monetary theory.

Figure 3.4 describes the principal implication of these uncertainty principles, evoking the name of Heisenberg.

(The two-sigma confidence region for the location of *LM* is *very* wide.)

It is explained in Chapter 4 that the conflation of innovated clearing systems with such devices as securitization and 'interest on money' leads to very high elasticities of substitution between financial assets: no subset is then clearly distinguishable as *money propre*; preferences among financial holdings become very weak indeed; demand for money looks 'unstable'

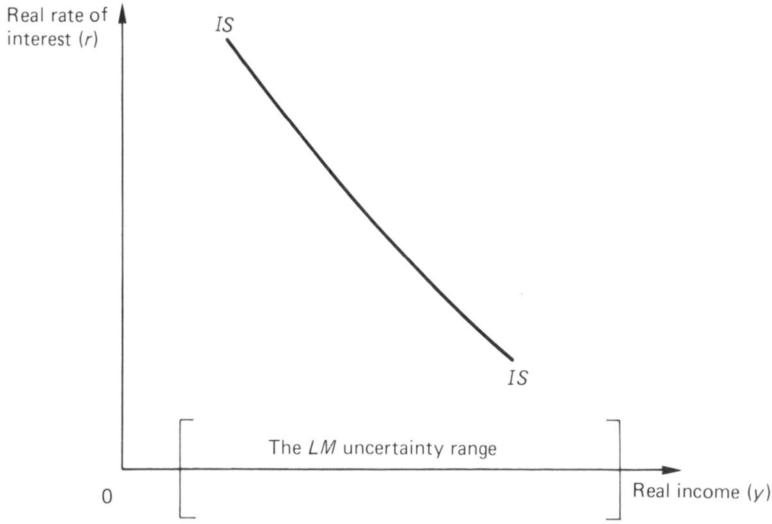

Figure 3.4 *LM* is vertical but we do not know where it is!

The Heisenberg Uncertainty Principle

> This is the way Heisenberg stated the uncertainty principle originally: if you make the measurement on any object, and you can determine the x-component of its momentum with an uncertainty Δp, you cannot, at the same time, know its x-position more accurately than $\Delta x = h/\Delta p$, where h is a definite fixed number given by nature. It is called Planck's constant . . . This is a special case of the uncertainty principle . . . The more general statement is that one cannot design equipment . . . to determine which of two alternatives is taken without . . . destroying the pattern of interference.
>
> Feynman *et al.* (1965, 3, pp. 1–11)

3.3.3 Wallace's (1981, 1983) Contributions

The monetary and fiscal authorities of a hypothetically perfectly liberal economy cannot extract seigneurage profit through *legal restrictions* (see Wallace, 1983). And if the 'mechanical' functions of the authorities' paper are equally well performed by private issue, switches between component parts of the public sector's balance sheet are anodyne, so long as the public sector's *aggregate* deficit or surplus is preserved (see Modigliani and Miller, 1958 and Wallace, 1981). Refunding operations supply an example. If the public sector's debt were shortened, private agents would lengthen their issue on net, washing out the public sector operation.

(a) *Wallace's (1983) Schematization*

Treasury bills supply 100 per cent reserve backing for the currency operations of private enterprises. Private currency is a perfect substitute for Treasury currency. In the upshot, Treasury bills are perfect substitutes for Treasury currency, so that the latter must yield interest to survive. Wallace writes,

> [Consider] an open market purchase of Treasury bills. This results in the private sector holding fewer bills and more Federal Reserve notes. Under laissez faire, the equilibrium adjustment is a contraction in the scale of operations of private note-issuing intermediaries, a contraction that exactly offsets the open market purchases. If it is costly in terms of resources to carry out this private intermediation, then the contraction frees some resources . . . With technological symmetry between the private sector and the government, these are precisely the resources the government needs in order to provide and maintain the larger outstanding stock of government currency . . . The open market purchase does no more than change the location from the private sector to the government of a given quantity of economic activity . . . Nothing else is affected . . . A similar argument applies to open market sales.
>
> Wallace (1983, pp. 4–5)

Wallace also claims that 'the result that central bank intermediation does not matter laissez-faire also holds for central-bank exchanges of Federal Reserve notes for other assets – risky mortgages, risky commercial loans or common stock. It is a straightforward extension . . . of the Modigliani–Miller theorem (p. 5, note 5; also see Stiglitz, 1969, and Wallace, 1981). But Wallace's generalization of his model – in which currency notes are warehouse receipts for Treasury bills of larger denominations – may not hold up. Thus insert a singular element into the economy. Granted a sophist may say *this* imposes a legal restriction. Then open-market operations are not anodyne: MAF is a unique asset, a reduced financial substance not reproducible by the private sector; symmetry is lost (Example (d), p. 55, deepens this conclusion).

(b) *Samuelson's (1947/1983) Profound Conjecture*

Samuelson (1947/1983), cited by Wallace (1983), makes a conjecture that, when somewhat amplified, suits our purposes even better than Wallace's. Once the implicit liquidity premium of Samuelson's securities boils off, so that real assets discharge historic monetary functions, the own rate of return on real assets must rule the interest rate roost; and monetary authorities are taken out of play even more decisively than in Wallace's schematization.

> It is true that in a world involving no transaction friction and no uncertainty, there would be no reason for a spread between the yield of any two assets, and hence there would be no difference in the yield on money and on securities. Hicks concludes, therefore, that securities will not yield interest. It is equally possible and more illuminating to suppose that under these conditions money-yield adjusts itself to the yield of securities. In fact, in such a world securities themselves would circulate as money and be acceptable in transactions; demand bank deposits would bear interest . . . And if money could not make the adjustment, as in the case of the metal counters Aristotle tells us are barren, it would pass out of use, wither away and die, become a free good.
>
> Samuelson (1947/1983, p. 123)

(In Wallace's model, 'uncertainty seems not to be relevant because the hypothetical note issuing intermediary . . . is perfectly hedged' (Wallace, 1983, p. 4).)

Samuelson's profound insight becomes the ark of the tabernacle for this book. Almost all of its principal propositions turn out either to issue from or lead into Samuelson's passage. It is the platform for the new art of central banking.

3.3.4 Crystallization of the Theory

(Section 3.3.4 tacitly modifies Poole's model; see Section 3.5.)

The simplest, and most revealing, examples nest in a régime of fiat paper money.

Say that base money is fixed in supply and that there is a 'federal funds' market in meteoric (liquidity) stones. (We can elide specific modelling of banks.) There is a deceptively precise arbitrage condition, linking the own rate of return on physical capital with the liquidity services (convenience yield) of money. And yields are calculated at margins.

Remark

The services of money, as an institution, in facilitating debt-discharge are imbedded in the implicit model.

* * *

(a) *An Arbitrage Condition*

$$r' + \lambda = \ell \tag{3.3}$$

The own rate of return on physical capital (r') plus its rate of appreciation against money, in a metric in which money is numéraire, equals the total yield of money.

The arbitrage condition *is* deceptively precise. Physical capital is not malleable; it is not feasible to slice off slivers of physical capital, planning to invest the proceeds in money, say. Lumpiness and indivisibility controls. So money market yields may plausibly exceed '$r' + \lambda$' quite substantially for some time without provoking massive reaction. True, primary yields will react to *some* extent. Thus 'q' will fall if a squeeze pushes up 'ℓ'. But in forward-looking markets this reaction reckons to be slight: share prices discount very long-lived streams: present values may be little affected by dramatic blips in money market yields. True, the channel of communication of money market action to the 'real economy' is not altogether blocked: Bank rate effects run in this turbid channel.

(b) *Quasi-Federal Funds Markets*

The shadow price of liquidity can be read from yields in markets made for meteoric (liquidity) stones. And since this material comprises truly instant funds, its yield reckons to lie below that for loans of money, leading to *another arbitrage condition*.

$$\xi + \Gamma = \ell \tag{3.4}$$

where ξ is the 'federal funds' rate and Γ the premium adhering to 'federal funds'. Fluctuations in liquidity preference are reflected by the quasi-rent ξ

(c) *Intervention: the Rôle of the MA*

The intrinsic vibration of the real sector has been tacitly stipulated to be quite small; and that of the monetary sector quite large – so that monetary aggregate-targeting maps into substantial fluctuation in money market yields, imparting an ill-specified, but putatively small, forcing term onto the real economy. Enter a monetary authority (MA) who might seek to reduce the vibration of the funds rate by transforming the meteroric stones into a control variable in a régime of money market rates targeting.

There is a rub. The arbitrage condition of equation (3.3) implies that 'real economy' events force vibration of ℓ and ξ that may be observationally indistinguishable from effects of liquidity preference vibration. Indeed, if most of the 'radiation' emanates from the real economy (see *IS* vibration in Poole's paradigm) the MA will act pro-cyclically – granting that the feeble, erratic linkage between the money and real assets markets will cause most of the process's energy to be dissipated by frictional heat.

(d) *Review of Some Potentials of MA Action*

Bank Rate $< r'$ The literature moves along two azimuths. One is based on *forced saving*: see Chapter 9, in which the paradigm is rejected. The second azimuth is Marshallian and may indeed be that of Knut Wicksell, leading to a distinction of Wicksellian economics from the economics of Wicksell. Along the second azimuth, the discrepancy of Bank rate from say Thornton's mercantile rate of profit maps into increased, or depressed, money growth. But the second azimuth requires caution: *motivation* to *hold* burgeoning money supplies must be provided (see Burstein, 1988). Aided by Ricardo's deep (1817/1951) analysis, we see that the process is anodyne for the real economy. Nor, *sans* money illusion (of the MA) is it cumulative: it simply maps into an equilibrium rate of inflation.

Bank Rate > r′ This is the game being played in Britain in August 1989; see section 3.4. And it seems bizarre for a government to make war on the economy.

Several comments on this case follow – to be embellished by section 3.4.

1. Real Bank rate well above the intrinsic own rate of return on capital is transiently sustainable with surprisingly little depressing effect: entrepreneurs understandably prefer to operate at losses, or at less than Ricardo's required rate of return, for some time – instead of surrendering their enterprises, folding their cards, ceding present values of long-running earnings streams conditioned on firms being intensely active *sans cesse*.
2. The *taxable capacity* of governments lets them offer towering yields on their securities over longish intervals.
3. Purgative Bank rate does encourage borrowers to try to liquidate positions, or not to acquire new ones – so long as going concern values are not undermined. This explains the transient sensitivity of real estate and housing prices to monetary policy. But the sensitivity of *aggregate* consumer expenditure to asset prices should not be exaggerated. Thus it is absurd that a *society* should be able to make itself wealthier by bidding more (of what?) for each other's assets! More precisely, one must beware of 'metrical illusion'. Say that housing prices increase – think of spectacular recent rises in the south of England or Toronto. Aggregate wealth, measured in house price units (cf Keynes's *wage unit*), *falls*. And note that the opportunity cost of house occupation rises correspondingly. Think of a polar case in which a house owner *must* live in Belgravia(!). The implicit cost of holding his position in the City increases with Belgravia property prices so that the present value of this flow precisely offsets the rise in his house price . . . A complete analysis of this fascinating problem is beyond this book's scope.
4. Active Bank rate policy modes entail an elastic supply of base money. Thus section 3.4 shows that purgative Bank rate can trigger a ratchet sequence in which desperate businessmen raise prices in order to preserve margins. If the increases stick, elastic

base money supply ratifies price escalation, so that prices seem to drive money supply.

Coda to Section 3.3.4: Bank Rate and Exchange Rates

Interest rate parity is pivotal. If money market rates rise in London, the forward pound must go to a discount. This is most plausibly accomplished by a rise in spot sterling.

Another facet of the term structure of foreign exchange rates is less transparent. A British borrower of foreign exchange – or one guaranteeing the foreign exchange equivalent of the *sterling* he pays on maturity – can obtain loan terms dominating those available to ordinary sterling borrowers (on a purgative Bank rate interval), subject to transactions costs. *If a borrower is prepared to take an open short position in DM*, he pays Frankfurt interest rates, although the vehicle currency, coming and going, is sterling.

Say that a British resident takes out a virtual DM loan. By effectively buying forward DM (selling sterling forward), she can obtain precisely the terms available on a domestic loan, always subject to a transactions cost calculus. Thus she could take out a DM-denominated loan, simultaneously acquiring the right to put DM for sterling on stated terms over the loan's life – locking in more favourable terms at the cost of the option.[6]

The distance between covered and uncovered borrowers' positions can be narrowed. Thus open short positions in DM can be covered by purchase of BMW cars. Effects of interest rate differentials on trade balances look very intricate, as do responses of multinational traders to interest rate differentials.

ECU lending becomes especially interesting. The law of large numbers imposes a stronger central tendency on the spectrum of possible outcomes of ECU lending than on that of loans in ECU components: an open position in ECU is less risky than one in an ECU component.

Implications for *Aureus lending* are still more striking. If proceeds of Aureus loans are spent on productive goods, an automatic hedge is obtained. So Aureus lending would evolve indifferently to Bank rate policy – assuming that international capital flows are not legally restricted. Aureus lending is equivalent to contracting out of the ambit of state control and is tantamount to a spontaneous contrivance creating truly stable money.

3.3.5 Further Development of the Theory: Reflections on Majnoni and Zautzig (1980)

Majnoni and Zautzig keenly analyse facets of Bank rate theory in the context of operational problems naturally encountered by central banks, here Banca d'Italia.

In Italy, as in many other places, banks must over-reserve: reserve requirements have long been divorced from prudential criteria. So clearing banks cannot offer fully competitive yields independently of convenience yields (shadow yields) enjoyed by 'depositors'. Thus clearing banks, as such, 'issue' lower-yielding deposits eligible to discharge debt – a business that will disappear in the fairly near future.

Interpolation

Yield relationships are heavily constrained both by competitive arbitrage and by regulation. Modigliani (1986) deepens this result in an Italian context.

So regulation and the intrinsic risk of clearing make clearers high absorbers of MAF: clearing houses require immediate settlement; regulation imposes reserve requirements beyond prudential ones.

(a) *Implications for the Theory of Monetary Policy*

Assume that bank deposits comprise an exclusive clearing medium; and that MAF are widely held and actively traded in MAF loan markets.[7]

MAF growth is to increase. At impact, the MAF rate will fall. Even if price inertia deters an increase in inflation, bank deposits will expand: it is highly plausible that the spread between deposit rate and open-market yields should transiently narrow. So, at the outset of the transmission process, the velocity of narrowly-defined aggregates falls more than that of more broadly-defined ones. And demand for transactions balances receives a further fillip when inflation begins to increase: second-round transactions balance growth may lag inflation even in a schematization with broadly monetarist properties.

(b) *The MA and Public Finance*

Majnoni and Zautzig discuss Banca d'Italia's obligation to support public sector financement. It remains substantial even after the 1981 Divorce – much like the Accord(!) between the US Treasury and the Federal Reserve about thirty years earlier.

It is instructive to work through a model in which the MA serves the government as an ordinary bank, as the Bank of England has traditionally done. In the 'first round', money supply increases 1:1 with public spending – as does MAF, since cheques on the MA are deposited in 'member banks'. In later rounds, pressure is transmitted by interest rates.

If MAF yield interest at free market rates, and there are no legal restrictions, MA debt is merely substituted for potential holdings of Treasury debt in the public's portfolios. (The MA takes tap stock.) For the public, the switch is a virtual wash. We have Wallace's (1983) result! Then inflation, and everything else, is invariant against monetization of public debt or public debt sales to the public.

3.4 THE ECONOMIC CONSEQUENCES OF MR LAWSON

The Spring 1988 forecasts of the Chancellor of the British Exchequer, Mr Nigel Lawson, did not pan out. Inflation substantially exceeded forecast levels and the British trade balance proved more negative than was forecast. On 24 May 1989, Bank rate stood at 14 per cent. On 8 May 1990 it stood at 15 per cent.

3.4.1 How it Happened[8]

Defying monetarist tenets, Mr Lawson keyed on the sterling/DM rate, not on money growth (however *money* may be defined). Common sense, often misleading in economics, suggests that a currency shadowing the DM will behave well at home. And orthodox theory, based on purchasing power parity (PPP), holds that British costs cannot long be out of line with German ones if the pound shadows the DM: unsustainable losses of reserves lead to exhaustion of swap lines, etc. eerily evoking Keynes's 'The Economic Consequences of Mr Churchill' (*Essays in Persuasion*).

3.4.2 Implications of Mr Lawson's Putative Policy

Consider the policy's implications when: (1) purchasing power parity is readily violated and works with long, erratic lags – and is a weak economic force; (2) a free sterling/DM rate strongly responds to portfolio management motivation – and, indeed, to speculation. Speculation may engender self-sustaining episodes, or bubbles. It follows that British monetary growth may go out of the control of British authorities and *not* imitate the profile of German monetary growth. Thus, especially in 1987, British purchases of DM, whenever the pound threatened to exceed its target DM value, expanded the British monetary base (Bank of England liabilities correspondingly increased – and sterilization would have pushed up the pound). And since short- to medium-run forces on exchange rates are erratically speculative, British base money growth reckoned to be erratic.

3.4.3 A More Formal Statement of the Theory

Preliminary Remark

The German system is stipulated to operate without feedback – i.e., to be under open-loop control. This stipulation puts into high relief the 'paradoxical' way in which attempts to imitate German performance, imposing closed-loop (feedback) control on the imitator, can lead to the antithesis of the German system.

Glossary

x = excess demand for sterling (excess supply of DM) at the target rate – measured in sterling
y = the index of departure from PPP
A = the index for an autonomous process
$\{m\}$ = the time path of m

The Model

$$\dot{m} = f(x) \tag{3.5}$$

$$\dot{x} = \phi(y, A) \tag{3.6}$$

$$\dot{y} = \psi(\{m\}) \tag{3.7}$$

Equation (3.7) displays the dependence of $\dot{y}$ on past behaviour of money growth. It suffices here to work with virtual distributed lags.

Since $(x, \dot{x})$ evolves independently of the volition of the British MA, the British 'm' process goes out of control – and the stipulation that $\partial\dot{x}/\partial y$ operates weakly and with long, erratic lags promotes this upshot.

(a) *Reaction to the Perplex*

Having got into a spot of trouble – an accelerating general price level accompanying unexpectedly large trade deficits – Mr Lawson sought to get back on track through a purgative Bank rate policy. Monetary aggregate targeting was neglected, partly because definitions of *money* are mere gratuitous concoctions. If all goes well, if a putative transversality condition is obeyed, there will be a soft landing (see Figure 3.5).

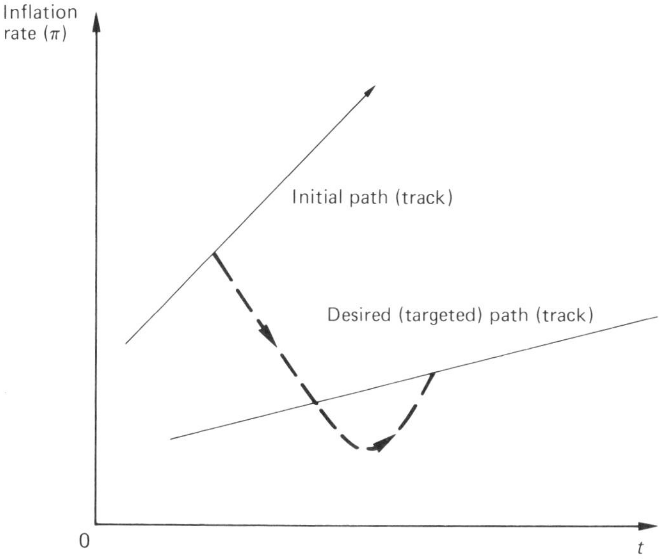

Figure 3.5 A soft landing after some overshooting

Real Bank rate is put up to a level well above Thornton's mercantile rate of profit or Wicksell's natural rate of interest. Prices are to decelerate for a number of tried, and possibly true, reasons. *Videlicet.* Firms will want to reduce their indebtedness: they will try to reduce inventories; investment programmes, including introductions of new product lines, will be deferred or cut back. Asset prices fall as portfolio holders scramble to *try* to reduce net indebtedness. 'Speculative' property holdings are undermined by sharply higher costs of sustaining levered (geared) positions.

Interpolation

But attempts to liquidate stocks may induce a collapse of aggregate demand causing involuntary accumulation so that actual (*ex post*) stocks (inventories) *increase*, leading to *increased* demand for credit. (See Chapter 9.)

There reckons to be some overshooting. Inertia must be overcome. As Figure 3.5. makes clear, prices must accelerate, however briefly, whilst attaining a new equilibrium track; there is an interval on which monetary expansion is more rapid than on its new secular path. Bank rate will transiently fall *below* its new targeted level (i.e., the implicit dynamic programme calls for the MA to put Bank rate below its 'new targeted level'). On this interval, credit taken will expand, as will money supply *comme* residue of credit expansion . . . What will *really* happen?[9]

(Note 9 concerns Alfred Marshall's conception of the modus operandi of Bank rate, glossed, and extended, by Keynes, 1930/1971. Marshall thought of Bank rate as primarily a device for regulating the quantity of money. And for Marshall mediant action was by *speculators*.)

(b) *How Things Might go Wrong Under Purgative Bank Rate*

Figure 3.6 pictures a less benign scenario. At first property prices, and other prices sensitive to credit, crash. But recall at least the connotative penumbra of Henry Thornton's mercantile rate of profit, Demand for loans of money is contingent in part on the real rate of interest corresponding to what might be called the natural rate of profit. Merchants and manufacturers, taking loans at higher nominal rates, relative to an initial equilibrium state, must expect a correspondingly higher inflation rate (rate of depreciation of money against goods), subject to this caveat. A sharp, unexpected increase in key interest rates will not promptly choke off demand for loans: huge going concern values would be dissipated by shutdowns; and one must remain solvent when liquidating one's business. Furthermore, profit deterioration partially increases demand for finance. See the Treatise's charming parable of the Widow's Cruse and the Danaen Jar, as well as Asimakopoulos (1983).

It is not difficult to explain segment (*a*) of Figure 3.6. But segment (*b*) is rather perplexing.

Let us translate the analysis into the language of properly discredited cost-push inflation hypotheses. Supply prices increase so that competitively mandated profit margins are preserved. Higher nominal Bank rate, accompanied by passive monetary aggregate management, becomes compatible with real equilibrium.

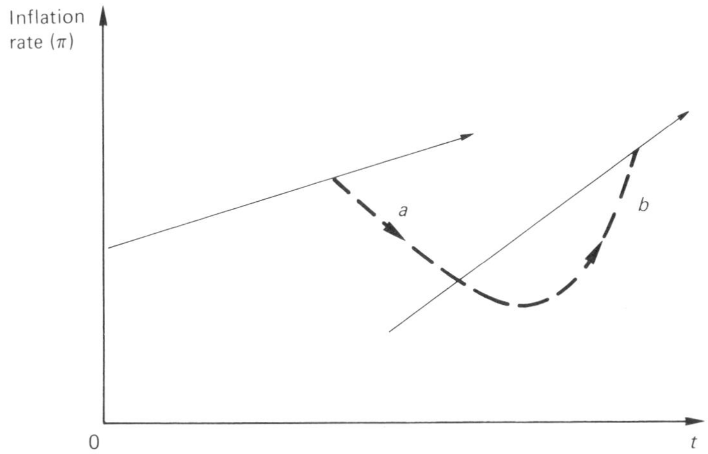

Figure 3.6 Higher Bank rate leads to higher inflation if the *MA* dwells in twilight

Interpolation

I do not say that a principal effect of higher Bank rate is on the cost of doing business. Rather I point out that in moving macro-economic equilibrium the own rate of return on real capital conforms to the rate of interest on loans of spot money to be repaid with money in future – adjusted for expected depreciation, or appreciation, of money against goods.

* * *

If the MA, dwelling in analytical twilight, is disappointed with the upshot of 14 per cent Bank rate (accompanied by elastic supply of MAF), it may raise Bank rate to 16 per cent. At impact, prices may again declerate. But inflation soon becomes embedded at a rate 2 per cent higher than before: Bank rate and the inflation rate chase each other in an expanding spiral. So long as agents are surprised by Bank rate increments, the real economy may deteriorate; stagflation is quite plausible. As agents learn the structure of the process – so that the economy defends itself more successfully against the government's assault on it – a 'mere' inflationary spiral ensues.

Remark

Keynes (1930/1971, I, pp. 174–5), relying in part on a fine passage in Tooke's *History of Prices*, magisterially rebukes literal cost-push explanations of the story just told.

(c) *An Analytical Reduction of the Argument*

Recall the well-known consequence of a rule based on *real* cash balance targeting.

$$\dot{m} = f(\pi) \qquad f' > 0 \tag{3.8}$$

And there is another reason for an expanding spiral of inflation and money growth. To the extent that 'speculators' defend forward sterling, which must go to a discount if the interest parity is to be preserved in the wake of higher Bank rate, capital inflow further augments the monetary base (*sans* sterilization). And indeed there was heavy capital inflow into Britain after the exercise in purgative Bank rate was put into operation in 1988: see Paul Fabra in *Le Monde* 8 November 1988, p. 44). But by mid-1989, as sinister potentials of the purgative policy became more salient, capital outflow pressures developed, encouraging still higher Bank rate. By June 1989, *defence of the pound* joined the *battle against inflation* as a *raison d'être* for official action.

Denoting Bank rate, Z and DZ/Z, z,

$$z = \phi(\pi) \qquad \phi' > 0 \tag{3.9}$$

$$\dot{\pi} = \psi(z) \qquad \psi' > 0 \qquad (!) \tag{3.10}$$

$$\dot{\pi} = \psi(\phi(\pi)) \qquad \partial\dot{\pi}/\partial\pi > 0 \tag{3.11}$$

The impressionistic schema does not explain price deceleration during early stages of aftermaths of unexpected increases in Bank rate. And a complete model must take Lucas's (1976) point: the model's structure must accommodate integration by agents of the set of official policy rules, including programmed corrective responses.

3.5 A RECONSTRUCTION OF WILLIAM POOLE'S PARADIGM

3.5.1 Preliminary Remarks

Why is Poole's (1970) paradigm still so influential? True it ingeniously sharpens up a number of fundamental points. But it is deeply committed to monetary theories of real action. It ignores both 'interest on money' and term structure, so that relative interest rate adaptation is elided. It is an offshoot of simplistic ISLM theory. It makes no provision for 'course correction' in interest rate-targeting. Nor does it distinguish own rates of return on real from those on paper assets. (Still, Poole's construction contributes to a ceaseless process of creative destruction.)

Reconstruction begins at the deepest foundations of the theory. We want to show that, if the frequency and amplitude of the vibration of '*IS*' is lower (higher) than that of '*LM*', interest rate-targeting (monetary aggregate-targeting) need not be preferable.

(The following two paragraphs are from (1986, pp. 70–1).)

> There is a line of communication from the real to the monetary sector complementing that from monetary disturbances to the real sector. Thus a massive *IS* shock, leading to deterioration of private-sector balance sheets, makes lenders reluctant to extend or renew credit to private agents. If such situations can be identified in time, central banks should vigorously expand their assets, defending against internal drains *à la* Bagehot. This seems the proper *raison d'être* for expansion of Federal Reserve assets during the Penn Central and Chrysler crises and the crisis of liquidity feared in 1982–3 [and in the aftermath of the Crash of 19 October 1987]. It seems proper for the central to augment supplies of riskless debt in the aftermath of certain interactive *IS*/*LM* shocks, rather than wait for deflationary effects of 'commodity market' disequilibrium to do the job.
>
> Distilling the analysis's principal conclusion, assume that liquidity-preference parameters do not vibrate intrinsically, that the supply of a well-defined *money* can be firmly controlled and that *IS* vibration is erratically substantial. It does *not* follow that open-loop is preferable to closed-loop control: if the properties of the *IS* shock can be read in time, closed-loop control may be mandated. One reason is that strict adherence to a money-growth rule does not shut off real effects of *IS* vibration – a point explained in Chapter 5.

3.5.2 Reconstruction of the Choice of Target Problem

Say that a secular rate of money-base growth, m^*, feeds into a secular inflation rate, π^*, in the following way – where ϱ symbolizes real output growth.

$$\pi^* = m^* - \varrho^* \tag{3.12}$$

Next we define 'the natural secular *nominal* rate of interest'.

$$r^* = \bar{r}' + \pi^* \tag{3.13}$$

This is a Fisherine concept: the 'natural secular nominal rate of interest' equals the natural real rate of interest ($\bar{r}$) plus the secular rate of inflation (π^*).

(a) *Laws of Motion*

(Lags are eschewed. Nor are expectations modelled.)

The variables of the dynamic system are defined as follows.

$$x = \pi - \pi^* \tag{3.14}$$

$$u = m - m^* \tag{3.15}$$

$$q = r - r^* \tag{3.16}$$

'u' is a control variable; and m is instrumentally decisive. 'u' may be targeted on x directly, or on q.

$$\dot{x} = \dot{x}(x, q, u) \tag{3.17}$$

$$\dot{q} = \dot{q}(x, q, u) \tag{3.18}$$

Evaluating partial derivatives of Equations (3.17) and (3.18),

$\partial\dot{x}/\partial x < 0$,
since liquidity is drying up (3.19)

$\partial\dot{x}/\partial q < 0$,
on conventionally 'Wicksellian' grounds (3.20)

$\partial\dot{q}/\partial x > 0$,
along Fisherine lines (3.21)

$\partial\dot{q}/\partial q < 0$,
since a higher interest rate stimulates
loan supply and discourages loan demand (3.22)

As for a sign analysis of the dynamic system's Jacobian matrix,

$$J = \begin{bmatrix} (-)\,(-) \\ \\ (+)\,(-) \end{bmatrix} \tag{3.23}$$

The trace is negative; and the determinant is positive.

Stability analysis must be approached cautiously. In the system's open-loop variant, stability hinges on the negativity, or not, of the real parts of the eigenvalues of the quadratic characteristic equation (and saddlepoint (in)stability must also be considered). Not that stability suffices for endorsement of open-loop control: a loss function must be defined, and evaluated, relative to consequences of alternative control régimes. *The proper style of analysis of Poole's problem is that of optimal control.*

(b) *Closed-loop Control*

Stability The stability of a closed-loop control mode must be assessed relative to characteristics of the corollary schema of *course correction*. I remarked (in 1986, p. 71) that interest rate *range*-targeting is more effective than *point*-targeting in Poole's model. And interest rate-targeting can be enhanced in other ways – so that it is not true that 'there is no interest rate rule that is associated with a determinate price level' (Sargent, 1979, p. 362)

Modalities In a régime of closed-loop control,

$$\dot{u} = \dot{u}(x, q) \tag{3.24}$$

And equations (3.25) and (3.26) are plausible partial descriptions of closed-loop control.

$$\partial\dot{u}/\partial x < 0 \tag{3.25}$$

$$\partial\dot{u}/\partial u > 0 \tag{3.26}$$

Granted, the régime would be better described by mixed strategies beyond the scope of this sketch.

(c) *Discussion of Inequality (3.25)*

On the face of it, the rule of Inequality (3.25) contributes to 'stability'. This becomes obvious if we stipulate, along 'Phillips curve' lines, that the economy is overheated so that x is positive; or if MAF growth has exceeded its norm for some time, so that, again, x is positive.

The rule of Inequality (3.25) is more problematical in a less simplistic setting. Inflation at a point in time is a resultant of complex lagged effects of the path of MAF growth over some time – to take a monetarist slant. Expectations, always difficult to model, are important. Thus inflation may be about to fall of its own weight when the rule calls for money growth to be checked. Friedman's scepticism about closed-loop control is more plausible as the model becomes denser and more intricate.

(d) *Discussion of Inequality (3.26)*

This policy mode entails mortal danger. What if real interest rates are initially at natural levels? But inflation expectations change. Authorities adhering to Inequality (3.26) may change their planned course, thus feeding – indeed, validating – the new expectations. In general, active manipulation of *nominal* interest rates is apt to distort real ones and, when conflated with speculative motivation in the markets, to make *ex post* real interest rate evolution more erratic. These remarks anticipate the principal theme of Part II: confusion between the real and nominal domains is ineradicable in the Street; and often plagues the Academy.

3.5.3 A Proper Paradigm for Poole's Problem

State variables are x and q. The control is u. A loss function, defined by equation (3.27), is to be minimized, subject to the macrodynamic structure described by Equations (3.28) and (3.29).

$$\min \int \phi(x, q)dt \tag{3.27}$$

subject to

$$\dot{x} = \dot{x}(x, q; u) \tag{3.28}$$

$$\dot{q} = \dot{q}(x, q; u) \tag{3.29}$$

A richer model accommodates control strategies deploying both MAF and Bank rate and introduces uncertainty. In the paradigm, and in Poole's problem, the stochastic properties of an underlying dynamic model must first be established; perforce, there will be errors in the equations and other specification errors. And a properly specified analogue to a variance/covariance matrix may correctly imply that confidence intervals for location of say the nominal rate of interest at date t are very wide. Furthermore, there will surely be substantial errors in the date – of the sorts described by say Metzler's *three lags*. In the upshot, closed-loop control may have prospects like those for control of events on a distant star.

3.6 CHAPTER 3's IMPLICATIONS FOR OPTIMAL MIXES OF FISCAL AND MONETARY POLICY

These are among the implications that can be readily extracted from Chapter 3.

1. The theory precludes any systematic relationship between the secular growth rate of base money and the natural real rate of interest: the theory bars trade-offs between monetary and fiscal policy tenable for equilibrium analysis.
2. Since elasticities of substitution between financial assets are very high in a modern economy, the collective financial intermediary balance sheet expands and contracts covariantly with MAF motion; *but*, since such balance sheet dilation and contraction is so easily accommodated by small changes in spreads, inflationary effects are slow to unfold (see Figure 3.7).

   An extended episode of high base money growth leads to a massive increase in the volume of intermediation before substantial inflationary pressure is generated – a variation of the price inertia theme.

Figure 3.8 reworks Figure 3.7 for a case in which elasticities of substitution between financial assets requiring base money support and other financial assets are low.

Fiscal policy retains the power to exert influence in 'real economic space'. For example, increases in government purchases, or a switch from tax- to deficit-finance of government purchases, plausibly leads to higher real rates of interest and/or rates of capital inflow, along with trade deficits. But the notion that effects of more expansive fiscal policy can be countered by contractive monetary policy, bringing

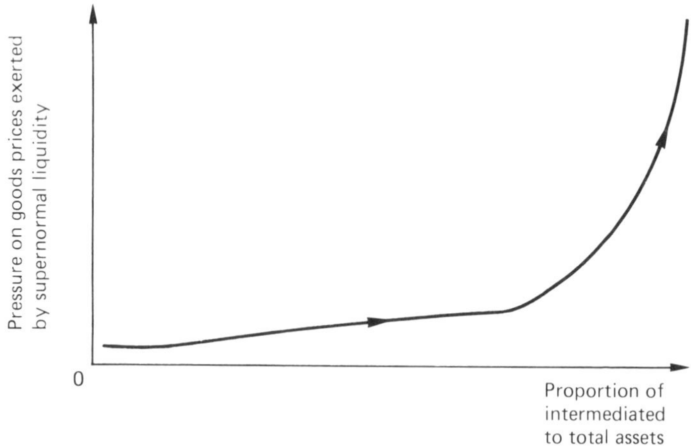

Figure 3.7 Build-up of excessive liquidity pressure when elasticities of substitution are high

Notes for Figure 3.7

1. Over a considerable interval, the pressure level may be nil.
2. Inflationary pressure may develop via a variant of Tobin's '*q*' theory. Own rates of return on 'physical' assets get out of line with yields on 'paper' in the underlying script.

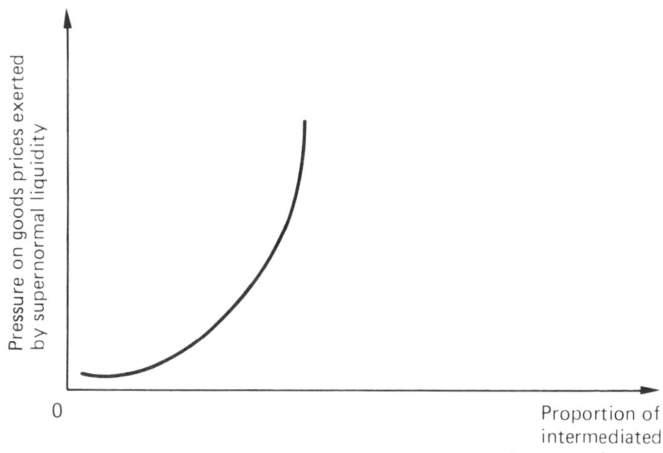

Figure 3.8 The scenario is rewritten when elasticities of substitution are low

about a new temporary equilibrium in ISLM space, seems an improper mélange of real and nominal variables in a macroeconomic pudding.

The theory implies that monetary velocity reckons to fluctuate widely over quite long intervals.

As for the *rôle of monetary policy*, shorter-run monetary-policy action is best analysed in an explicitly dynamic schematization leading to control-theoretic paradigms. In the long run, monetary policy reduces to a decision on the secular growth of base money that is anodyne for the real economy – and to much less under fixed foreign exchange rates.

Notes and References

1. Elasticities of substitution reckon to be very high. Surely non-financial intermediary lenders to companies are prepared to hold financial intermediary paper, *ceteris paribus*. They will readily substitute claims against intermediaries for claims against non-financial companies – so that intermediaries hold non-financial sector paper thus released.

   The equilibrium mass of the financial-intermediary sector is thus left open in the way the output of an industry whose supply curve is perfectly elastic is determined by demand.
2. A bank can reduce its deposit liability by lowering its deposit rate on new money, including rollovers – obviously thus discouraging influx. And there will be natural attrition as accounts are chequed out in the ordinary course of business.
3. The Keynesian conspectus of the foundations of central banking probes into the ontology of banking. See *Treatise* (1930/1971 II, Chapter 31, 'The Problem of Management of Money', pp. 189ff).

> The modern banker performs two distinct sets of services. He supplies a substitute for State money by acting as a clearing house and transferring current payments backwards and forwards between his different customers by means of book entries on the credit and debit sides. But he is also acting as middleman in respect of a particular type of lending, receiving deposits from the public which he employs in purchasing securities, or in making loans to industry and trade mainly to meet demands for working capital.
>
> This duality of function is the clue to many difficulties in the modern theory of money and credit and the source of some serious confusions of thought.
>
> Keynes (1930/1971, II, Chapter 31, p. 191)

(An earlier Chicago School's 100 per cent reserve proposal sought to break up the 'duality of function'.)

Will Keynes's 'modern banker' persist? Chapter 4 describes an innovated clearing system eschewing banks – who do not now cherish this side of their business. And beyond the banking principle there is no need for intermediaries to provide liquidity for a hyper-securitized economy

Keynes on a Motley Gang of Heretics

> There is a common element in the theories of nearly all monetary heretics. Their theories are alike in supposing that in some way the banks can furnish all the real resources which manufacturers and trade reasonably require.
>
> Keynes (1930/1971, II, Chapter 31, p. 194)

> 'The ample stocks of gold in the Federal Reserve System indicate', we commonly read in the financial press, 'that the banks will have no difficulty in financing all reasonable requirements of trade and industry'. Thus, if we are to believe the bankers, the amount of working capital for industry seems to depend in some way upon the amount of gold in the Bank of England or in the Federal Reserve system.
>
> Keynes (1930/1971, II, Chapter 31, p. 196)

Chapter 9 shows that this heresy continues to exercise powerful force and lies behind most monetary theory of trade fluctuations. Alas, the author of these passages went on to project monetary theories of the real rate of interest with monumental panache.

4. Fresh lines of credit or loan authorizations may precede increases in credit *taken*. Attempts to use new credit lines may intensify inflation. Higher inflation spurs increased demand for nominal balances, inducing clients to take down their authorizations. True, MAF accommodation is necessary for feasibility of the sequence.
5. See Gibson's Paradox. The key to its resolution is that, until the First World War, the general price level, not price inflation, was central. Friedman and Schwartz (1982, Chapter 10) discuss the paradox, citing Klein (1975) – and they supply a copious bibliography. Also see Barsky and Summers (1988) and Chapter 8 of (1989a).
6. Sterling cover for a DM loan can be obtained by selling DM forward – or an option to put DM for sterling can be purchased. Banks are as anxious to lock in towering interest rates as clients are to avoid them.

   Careful integration of the theory with that of the interest parity is mandatory.
7. In a hermetically sealed system, excess supply of an asset that is a 'reduced financial substance', so that it is not convertible into anything else, can be cured only if the general price level increases (the 'reduced substance' being numéraire); the nominal quantity of the reduced financial substance is conserved.

   Financial substances typically are *not* conserved; they are highly mutable. Undesired financial substances (long bonds from time to time, for example) are transmuted into desired ones (say short bonds) by refunding operations. However, in the 'real economy', resources must be spent in order to change commodity sets – financial assets can be costlessly transmuted.

Careless financial analysts are repeatedly surprised that financial equilibrium is so speedily regained.

8. Brittan (1989) assesses the episode rather differently, in an interesting commentary. He writes that

> MO on its own has not had a good record in warning of inflationary dangers. It did not rise decisively above its target range . . . until well into 1988 . . .
>
> Advocates of broad and narrow money . . . have tried to make common cause against any use of the exchange rate for policy. But it really does not wash. For the prescriptions of the two camps have often suggested diametrically opposed policies. So demands . . . to 'go back to monetarism' are literally without meaning.
>
> Brittan (1989, p. 19)

Figure 3.9, supplied by Brittan, must trouble monetarists. (Figure 3.10 shows how mortgage interest payments affect the all-items retail price index, RPI.)

> The mistake was not to shadow the DM, but to do so at too low a rate.
>
> Brittan (1989)

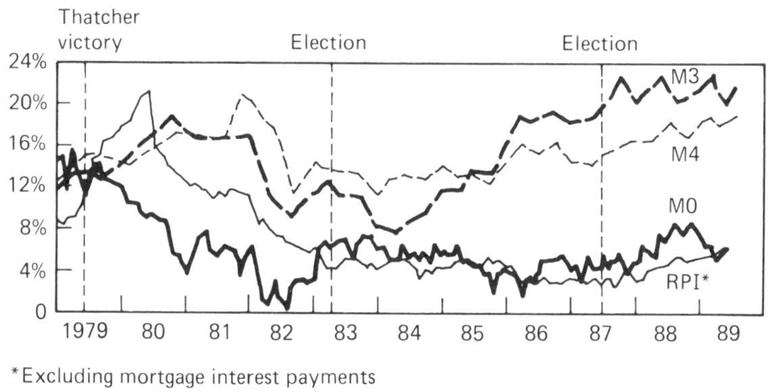

Figure 3.9 Money and inflation, *year on year increase* (Bank of England data)

Source: *Financial Times*, 22 June 1989, p. 19

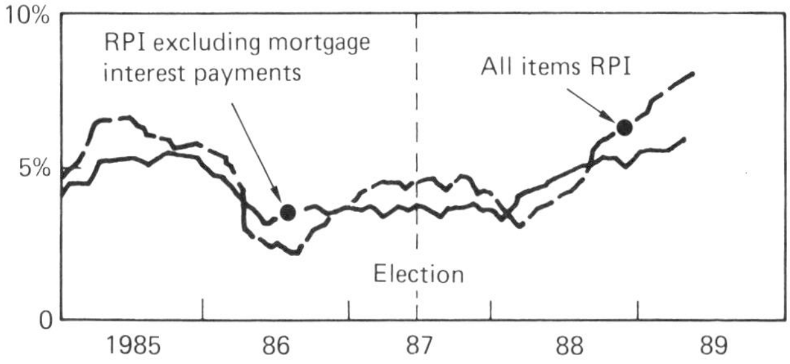

Figure 3.10 RPI inflation, % changes on a year earlier (CSO and *Financial Times* data)

Source: *Financial Times*, 22 June 1989, p. 19

Figure 3.11. amplifies Brittan's supporting analysis.

> In the search for scapegoats, the blame for the current inflation is sometimes put on Nigel Lawson's shadowing of the DM in 1987–8. [Such] borrowing [of pounds to buy DM] is ultimately financed by gilt-edged sales . . . There is indeed very little correlation between the period of maximum intervention to hold down sterling in 1987 and the build-up of broad money growth, which started a great deal earlier.
>
> Brittan (1989)

Brittan points out that the trend of sterling against the DM is downward (see Figure 3.11.). He argues that if Britain had, on Treasury advice, joined the EMS in 1985, when sterling exceeded DM 3.5, net pressure would have been for less expansive British monetary growth – thus tossing a crumb to monetarists and monetary theorists of balances of payments and exchange rates.

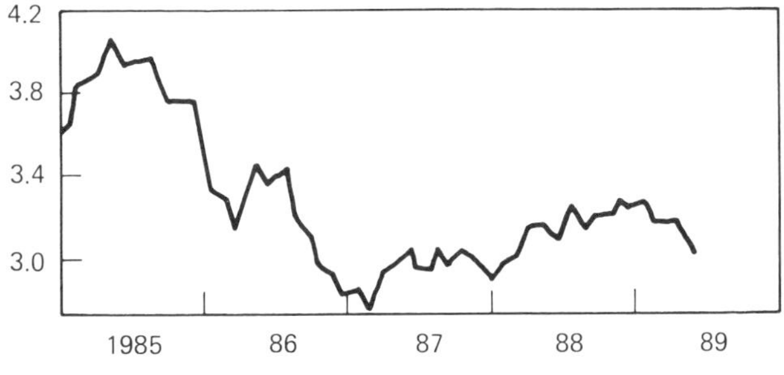

Figure 3.11 Sterling against the DM (DM per £)

Source: *Financial Times*, 22 June 1989, p. 19

* * *

My text is more concerned with the Chancellor's response to the inflationary episode than with its origins. But there is a line of communication from Brittan's analysis to mine. 'Membership of the EMS does not support a currency by magic. Credibility has to be gained' (Brittan, 1989) I write about a shadowing of the DM by a British Government that had made a decision at the highest level, against Treasury advice, *not* to join the EMS. It is reasonable to suppose that credibility was lacking. True, my argument does not undermine the utility of a *credible* British commitment to the EMS. Other arguments must be marshalled to assess that option.

9. (Keynes (1930/1971) on Marshall's conception of the modus operandi of Bank rate.) The text studies deployment of Bank rate to modulate money growth prior to 'reentry'; see the problem limned by Figure 3.5. Marshall solved the problem along similar lines, as Keynes shows.

> The traditional doctrine, which has been developed in the 90 years which have since elapsed, has been woven of three strands of thought, difficult to disentangle, to which different writers attach differing degrees of stress. All of them have been obscurely present from the beginnings of the discussion.
>
> The first of these regards Bank rate merely as a means of regulating the *quantity* of bank money. This is the basis on which the practical method of Bank rate as the characteristic instrument of the Bank of England was developed in the middle of the nineteenth century. Lord Overstone, for example, . . . regarded Bank rate as the correct and efficacious method for reducing the demand on the Bank for discounts, and so for contracting the volume of circulation.
>
> This notion that an upward change in Bank rate is associated with a diminished quantity of bank money . . . was an important part of Marshall's thought in his *Evidence Before the Gold and Silver Commission*,[a] none the less because he believed that it was through speculation or speculative investment that the new money found its way onto the world.[b] . . . Professor Pigou's theory of Bank rate seems to descend almost exclusively from this strand of Marshall's thought. He conceives of Bank rate as acting directly on the quantity of bank credit and so on prices in accordance with the quantity equation.[c]
>
> Mr Hawtrey's scattered remarks in his *Currency and Credit* seem to be on the same lines.[d]
>
> In the same way Professor Cassel explains that the price level is regulated by the Bank rate because the Bank rate regulates the supply of the means of payment.
>
> Keynes (1930/1971, I, pp. 167–9)

a Keynes cites Marshall's *Official Papers* (1926 p. 48) where Marshall writes, 'I do not myself put the rate of discount into the first place; my own way of looking at it was rather to lay stress upon the actual amount of money in the market to be loaned'.

b Marshall wrote that, 'there is more capital in the hands of speculative investors, who come on to the markets for goods as buyers, and so raise prices'.
c See Pigou's *Industrial Fluctuations* (1929, p. 241).
d Keynes cites the third edn, pp. 131–3. Also see Hawtrey's *The Art of Central Banking* (1932)

All the great writers cited may overlook, or insufficiently stress, that increases in bank assets need not reflect fresh credits to the public, but instead, anodyne increases in bank-mediation.

Keynes's *second strand* concerns 'Bank rate policy, not as a means of regulating the price level, but as a means of protecting a country's gold reserves by regulating the rate of foreign lending' (Keynes, 1930/1971, I, p. 169). Bagehot develops this strand in *Lombard Street*. I should attribute great importance to it. See Sayers (1957).

The *third strand* is

> the nearest to what seems to me the essence of the matter . . . [it] conceives of Bank rate as influencing in some way the rate of investment, or at least the rate of some kinds of investment, and, perhaps in the case of Wicksell and Cassel, as influencing the rate of investment relatively to that of saving [*sic*?].
>
> Keynes (1930/1971, I, pp. 170–1)

The principal theme of the *Treatise* is extracted from the 'third strand'. (See Friedman and Schwartz, 1982, Chapter 10, for a related analysis.)

Marshall's Views

Keynes extracts part of Marshall's Memoranda and Evidence Before the Gold and Silver Commission (1887) (pp. 17–195 of Marshall, 1926), and also refers to his Evidence Before the Indian Currency Committee (1899) (pp. 263–326 of Marshall, 1926):

> On the whole I am inclined to think that uppermost in Marshall's mind was the idea that what raises prices is the creation of additional purchasing power, but that in the modern economic world the organization of the credit system is such that the 'speculators' are the people into whose hands new money is most likely to find its way in the first instance, Bank rate playing an obvious part in this causal train. This seems to me to be the doctrine on which I was brought up.
>
> Keynes (1930/1971, I, pp. 172–3)

Keynes quotes from Marshall's Evidence Before the Gold and Silver Commission (1887):

> If there is an extra supply of bullion, bankers and others are able to offer easy terms to people in business, including the bill brokers, and consequently people enter into the market as buyers of things, as starting new businesses . . .
>
> The supply of loans on the one hand and the desire of people to obtain loans on the other, having fixed the rate of discount at anything, 8, 6, 5 or 2 per cent, then the influx of a little extra gold, going as it does into the hands of those who deal in credit, causes the supply to rise relatively to the demand, the rate of discount falls below the equilibrium level, however low that was, and therefore stimulates speculation . . . This is the main issue: when the gold comes into the country it is well known, and people expect that prices will rise . . . The influx of gold into the country by making people believe that prices will rise increases the demand for capital, and raises, therefore, in my opinion, the rate of discount [*sic*?].

Marshall could have referred to Mill's (1848/1940) analysis at this point; and see Cagan (1972) for a penetrating discussion of Mill's theory.

At note 1 (1930/1971/ I, p. 172) Keynes ponders on the extract's last sentence.

> There seems to be more perplexity in Marshall's mind as to whether the new gold raises or lowers the rate of discount. Before the Indian Currency Commission, he [states] 'the new currency . . . in the first instance lowers discount, but it *afterwards* raises prices and therefore tends to increase discount'. But here it is the higher prices which increase discount whereas in the passage quoted above it is the demand for *capital* due to the *expectation* of higher prices which does so.

Conflate Irving Fisher's distinction of real from nominal rates with subsequent rational expectations literature. If Marshall had taken proper heed of Fisher's (perhaps unborn!) analysis, he would have written that the real rate of discount would transiently fall and the nominal rate would rise because of price expectations.

Continuing with Marshall's evidence,

> Having this extra supply, lenders lower still more the rate at which they charge for loans and they keep on lowering it till a point is reached at which the demand will carry off the larger supply. When this has been done there is more capital in the hands of speculative investors who come on the markets for goods as buyers, and so raise prices. [So Marshall declines the forced-saving gambit.] Having been raised [prices] would be sustained because, the methods of business remaining stationary, if a man within an income of £1,000 keeps on the average £12 in his pocket, and if there is more currency in the country so that his share is increased from £12 to £14; then what was bought by £12 would in future be bought by £14.
>
> *Official Papers of Alfred Marshall*, (1926, pp 51–2
> *Gold and Silver Commission*, No. 9686)

But expansion of bank assets need not concern primary credit markets. Holders of primary debt may, in effect, sell it to intermediaries, taking back claims on banks. (Laidler, 1988, notes that Marshall *et al.* emphasize changes in *direct* intermediary lending.) Huge bulges in mediation, or massive disintermediation, are plausible in innovated economies – featuring very high elasticities of substitution among financial assets.

Reflecting on transmission of MA impulses in innovated economies in which the real deposit rate acceptable to the market is rigidly determined by the mercantile rate of profit, excess supply of MAF sends the MAF rate to zero, putting downward pressure on the deposit rate, leading to massive disintermediation. But disintermediation entails plans to switch from claims on intermediaries to consumer durables and producer's goods. The resulting inflation process is apt to be jerky and confused.

4 Innovated Payments Systems

4.1 FOUNDATIONS

Sir Ralph Hawtrey supplies the controlling logic.

> The idea of money is dependent on that of a debt, while that of a debt is not dependent on that of money . . . A sovereign is a coin, put a pound is not. The coinage acts valued a sovereign at a pound . . . A debt of a pound could be discharged with a sovereign . . . The word 'shilling' is ambiguous, meaning equally a twentieth part of a pound and the coin with which a debt of that amount may be paid . . . The money of account must exist before the money.
>
> Hawtrey (1947, pp. 7–8)

Indeed the money of account must precede the money. The *measure* and the property, including money, that is measured are ontologically distinct. What is more, there need be no money at all: money of account alone suffices for a viable debt-discharge system.

Chapter 10 shows that Roman law came close to taking Hawtrey's point: see Nicholas (1962/1969, p. 174). The principal contention of the Proculians, who prevailed, perfectly mirrors the perceptual knot that even modern theorists are often unable to untie: '*If the price is not in money, buyers cannot be distinguished from sellers.*'

Overcoming quite intense resistance, Roman law held that exchange or barter was not sale. But in innovated payments systems buyers *cannot* be distinguished from sellers; there are no distinctive transactional arrows or traffic signals. Innovated payments systems make otiose the ubiquitous money/barter dichotomy, but *not* the principle that double coincidence (of 'wants') is a disastrously inefficient necessary condition for exchange.

4.1.1 An Innovated Clearing System[1]

Envisage an electronic clearing system (or giro) eliding banks, and central banks. Money of account is the Aureus, defined relative to a full tabular standard along lines developed in Chapter 2. An open set of assets comprises the means of payment.

Clients' daily statements from clearing house members, read on video display, reflect the day's events; indeed continuous monitoring is feasible. Sometimes clients are called on to deposit more collateral against debit balances; collateral is created by sales generating giro credit. Or clients may instruct members to purchase more stocks for them, thus working off undesired credit positions equivalent to call loans to members.

Clients' credit positions resemble money – as do their unused drawing rights, comprising reserves of immediately available purchasing power. So does eligible collateral not yet put up. In principle, anything may be collateral; just as in principle any set of claims may be collateralized (beyond the banking principle). If everything is money, nothing is money; money goes off the board.

Analogies to international payments modalities lie near the surface. An agent, up against her debit limit with a house-member, will compel *her* debtors to reduce credit taken from her. Or she will offer higher yields on paper she floats; or sell capital; or cut back outlays on consumption. Governments like the United States Government are more sternly constrained in the innovated global economy; since the economy is saturated with liquidity (because of new techniques in praxis), seigneurage cannot be obtained from paper sales. The starkly innovated system yields results rather like those of the classical gold standard.

The clearing house is not a monetary authority. It neither borrows nor lends: negative balances reflect indebtedness to other members, not to the house, which exercises no more than oversight – it may enforce limits on negative balances, and, in counterparts to Keynes's bancor system, on positive ones too.

Members of the clearing house borrow and lend from each other. Positive clearing house balances (cf clearing house funds) may be assigned to borrowers. But *anything* may be lent: the borrower sells whatever has been lent to him (the loan being designated in Aurei); Aurei proceeds are credited to his account. If *A* lends *B* ₳1m by turning over a car to *B*, *B*'s obligation is *not* to return a car but to direct that Aurei credits summing to ₳1m, plus interest, accrue to *A* on the due date (*B* may sell cattle to *C*). Or a loan can be made by turning over a set of miscellaneous objects to the borrower or directing that sales proceeds be posted to the credit of the borrower's account with a member of the clearing house.

The process, eliding the clumsy contrivance of reducing proceeds to an intermediate substance (money), is frictionless. There is money of account, equivalent to metres or hectares, but no money-stuff. Once it is understood that the Aureus is no more substantial than the kilohertz (kHz), everything is clear; otherwise nothing is clear.

All debt is virtually (but not literally) convertible into commodities; this is intrinsic to the operation of full tabular standards. Would-be monetary authorities cannot acquire assets by issuing paper: the economy is saturated with liquidity; seigneurage cannot be collected. Real assets can be acquired only by selling other real assets or claims to real assets – or promises to transfer credits enabling creditors to purchase stated amounts of well-specified real assets on maturity. (We catch a hint of the way incipient modalities resurrect Say's Law.) In the upshot, the Bank of Italy cannot put pressure on asset markets; it has no real assets to sell. But IRI (the mammoth Italian state holding company) can.

It becomes obvious why the house does not lend or borrow: its insignificant capitalization leaves it with virtually nothing to sell; and a bid to buy is dual to an offer to sell.

4.2 SELECTED PROPERTIES OF THE SCHEMATIZATION

4.2.1 The Metric

All claims are measured in Aurei (₳). An ₳1 claim is discharged by a transfer registering ₳1 on display screens. Aurei-denominated positions are *real* ones. Indeed, since the economy is saturated with liquidity, ancillary properties of paper assets are worthless; assets are valued only as claims to underlying real streams. Commodity convertibility properties are obtained, but the thing into which debt is convertible is imaginary.

The purchasing power of a bundle worth one Aureus is invariant, but no object has an invariant Aureus price. See Einaudi (1937); and recall from Chapter 2 that ECU prices of component currencies are flexible. What is more, properties of an ideal commodity standard (See Friedman, 1951a/1953) are captured without there being a currency.

4.2.2 Liquidity

Sales proceeds of *any* asset generate giro credit, thus discharging indebtedness. Recall Robertson's (1922/1948) chaps lugging ale to sell at a fair. They drink it up in transit. A coin crosses a palm at each swig. In an innovated economy no coin is required. But Robertson's 'agents' could agree ahead of time to drain the vat *per stirpes*. And, since his agents fail to forecast the process's evolution while at the height of their powers, Robertson's parable violates rational expectations. Less vivid developments of this point show that a monetary economy, as it has long been called, naturally evolves from the conflation of uncertainty about the future and heavy costs of acquiring and processing information – and, indeed, of deciding what model to build *and* what models others are building. All the properties of a monetary economy are preserved by the moneyless innovated one: so the idea of *liquidity* is preserved too. (Liquidity concerns full value at short notice; assets are illiquid in thin markets.)

Securitization, going beyond the banking principle, requires drastic transformation of the idea of liquidity. Non-intermediated packages of otherwise illiquid paper may become almost perfectly liquid. *In the limit*, liquidity premia disappear so that the yield of Professor Knight's Crusonia plant rules the roost. Well short of the limit, enough liquidity is generated to annihilate peculiar liquidity properties of small subsets of assets; monetary theory is transformed far short of a limit that is nonetheless important as a polar concept: see Chapter 3's discussion of Samuelson's (1947/1983) conjecture, extended by Wallace (1983).

4.2.3 Public Debt

(See Chapter 5.)

A remote analogy to Samuelson (1958) may be contrived, in Samuelson's model, the population's intrinsic growth rate generates a biological rate of interest in an otherwise barren economy. Here the government's taxable capacity lets it offer more than the yield intrinsic to the economy's organic growth rate. The government may supply high yield paper to pensioners, for example. The paper will immediately go to a premium so that secondary buyers obtain only the economy's intrinsic or organic yield. Nor is the analysis taken into the limit: we elide questions about the *ultimate* sustainability of such policies.

4.2.4 Closure

Since the moneyless system is saturated with liquidity, analysts are tempted to believe, mistakenly, that it is not closed. But closure is tight: obligations are virtually real: there is virtual convertibility. And *collateralization* is important at all levels. Thus the members of the clearing house may hold clients' property in (Wall) Street name, assuring solvency of the clearing house. (Black, 1970, starts from a point rather like this.)

Remark

In Wall Street, a broker often becomes the legal owner of his client's stock. He supplies a 'deposit slip' proving the client's beneficial interest in the shares. And shares are sometimes virtually monetized by a corollary modality: shares held in Street name collateralize bank overdrafts guaranteed by makers' brokers.

4.2.5 Implications for Banking

It follows from sections 4.2.2 and 4.2.4 that, for bank paper to have a market, it must be backed by physical property or claims keyed to yields of such property. So banking and industrial activities will become conglomerated; light is shed on ongoing (September 1989) Italian controversy over merger of industrial and banking companies. (Also see Chapter 2.)

Central bankers must scurry for cover; they will no more be able to print high-powered money than they could under the classical gold standard. Central bankers must coalesce with fiscal authorities (cf taxable capacity) and Crown Corporations (cf régies, IRI *et al.*) – just as banks will be absorbed in industrial/financial complexes.

Reformed authorities (no longer *monetary* ones, since money is no more) are well placed to practise a new art of central banking. Thus an Italian authority encompassing IRI can supply vast new credits by lending shares to borrowers who would either sell them or put them up as collateral in exchange for say giro credit (member houses would assign positive balances on their books). Or the reformed authority might offer tax-anticipation certificates for giro credit which it might then extend to members of the public. In a contractive policy mode, the authority sells real holdings and raises taxes, diverting resulting giro credits to its house member account.

There are equivalents to inflationary bubbles caused by bank credit expansion in the innovated system. The upshot takes an Austrian twist. There are possibilities for distortion of relative prices and unsustainable changes in the period of production (or roundaboutness), subject to the following caveat. Since an extended tabular standard quashes inflation, Automatic or Induced Stinting (in Robertson's 1926/1932) phrase; see Chapter 9) must be generated along quite different lines than are taken in the Wicksellian literature. And the idea of *neutrality* is correspondingly altered: see Patinkin and Steiger (1989).[2]

4.3 EXERCISES IN SOME OF THE TECHNIQUES OF THE NEW ART OF CENTRAL BANKING IN INNOVATED PAYMENTS SYSTEMS

(See 1988, pp. 63–84, especially pp. 79–82.)

First consider some policy targets.

4.3.1 Targets *q*

Tobin (1978) supplies an attractive format based on his *q*, *q* being

> the ratio of market value to replacement cost . . . a summary measure of one important impact of financial markets on purchases of goods and services, in particular of durable goods.
>
> Tobin (1978, p. 422)

The normal value of *q* 'sustains capital replacement and expansion at the natural growth rate of the economy' (Tobin, 1978, p. 422). And, as Keynes (1936, Chapter 12) vividly explains, self-sustaining asset market episodes can thrust up *q* well above, and drive it down far below, its normal value, inducing real disturbances and disequilibrium (whatever *that* means). Intervention may be called for, subject to an economic version of *resonance*, rooted in work of Milton Friedman and extended along lines suggested by R. G. D. Allen in ways I describe in (1986), (1988), (1989a) and, less formally, in Chapter 9 below. Very briefly, attempts at stabilization may be counterproductive because of data lags and errors in data and in models. Keynes describes the upshot in his bismuth/castor-oil cycle (1930/1971).

4.3.2 Targets: Stability of the Purchasing Power of a Unit of Public Debt (here determined by its risk premium and interest rate behaviour)

(See Chapter 5.)

The innovated régime quite transforms the essential characteristics of public debt. In particular, the government's printing press cannot assure service of Aureus-dominated debt. Nor can seigneurage profit be extracted from an economy saturated with liquidity. The line of force Sir Robert Walpole imparted onto political economy dissipates. Indeed public debt may, in future, be downgraded: the sovereign's courts may not supply remedies for its defaults; and taxable capacity may bob like a cork on political seas (there is no danger that the government will refuse to run its printing press when obligated to tender fiat paper). Historically, skittish markets have known that governments may be remiss debtors; it is shown in Chapter 10 that Caesar's paper was badly received indeed. In the innovated régime, categorical distinction of say American from say Brazilian public debt evaporates: if indeed American debt continues to be preferred, the explanation is in the American Government's taxable capacity and/or the stability of American political institutions. But the United States then cannot extract seigneurage revenues from a global economy saturated with liquidity.

In the innovated régime, the purchasing power of a unit of public debt depends only on a risk premium (or on ongoing repudiation) and on real interest rates evolving autonomously relative to monetary policy which, indeed, ceases to exist! And the purchasing power of the basket of (*many*) goods comprising the imaginary Aureus is immutable.

If public debt is backed by real assets, including implicit contracts to supply police services, traffic control, etc. for fees (including local taxes), it may command a premium the way debt of first-class companies does. But so far as public debt finances transfer payments (negative taxes), the upshot is much dicier. (Chapter 5 discusses transfers differently.) The political dynamic impelling such transfers may preclude collection of taxes to service them. The government may have to roll the dice, betting its financial viability on the robustness of the Ricardian-equivalence principle – and then only if it can be assumed that taxes can be collected.

(Chapter 5, a model is built in which the feasibility of debt-financed welfare states pivots on the status of public debt as a virtual money, supplying leverage unavailable to governments in the innovated régime.)

Sovereign lending is less attractive in the upshot: governments will find it more attractive to be project borrowers; as we shall explain, viability of public finance may hinge on the massiveness of stocks of productive assets controlled by the government, so that there is an interesting trade-off between conventional resource use efficiency and the efficiency of fiscal policy.

Interpolation

Until the time of Sir Robert Walpole (the exemplar of Alexander Hamilton) public debt theory and monetary theory were quite disjoint. But the conflation of Walpole's system with fiat paper money led to an intersection of the subjects – which are about to be broken apart again.

* * *

Chapter 5 shows that these points are especially important for Italy and Canada. But the celebrated, misunderstood, American public sector borrowing requirement has a very different rationale. If one departs from Friedman's intriguing rubric, *the deficits that are taxes*, the American PSBR can be ascribed to over-absorption and, in any case, runs parallel to increases in foreign claims on American output, claims accompanied to some extent by concomitant increases in American productive assets and which, if unindexed, can be shrunk by American inflation.

Turn now to *devices* for attaining targets. Instruments include:

1. manipulation of balance sheets of Crown Corporations along lines described by Dacey (1951, 1956): *cf* (dis)funding policy.
2. quasi-fiscal tactics embodying cash-flow effects of modulations of taxation and public-spending flows.
3. innovated open-market operations in which public-sector entities offer to buy and sell various securities and real assets.

4.3.3 Implications of the Theory

Say that government paper is depreciating undesirably against real assets. Real Crown assets can be indirectly offered for government paper; the authority offers simultaneously to buy government paper and sell Crown assets on the giro.

Privatization

Looking ahead to illustrations of open-market operations in real assets, and back to political-economic fragility of tax revenues, we see that the logic of privatization cannot be wholly extracted from a mélange of analysis of micro-economic efficiency effects and points of view on the ethical value of public ownership. In particular, the art of central banking can persist only if the public sector controls large quantities of real assets.

Some will say *good riddance* to the art of central banking but, still, the discourse must be pitched up. And supporters of economic control must acknowledge that enhancement of Control may be subject to an intrinsic trade-off against micro-economic efficiency.

4.3.4 Two Problems Illustrating the Devices

1. *Excess demand for credit balances* Recall that the house does not borrow or lend on its own account, but members may have positive, or negative, balances, summing to zero. And giro funds are traded.

   Assume that agents plan to hold infeasibly large credit positions so that the algebraic sum of planned (indirect) giro positions is positive. The Aureus price of giro credit will increase (the giro funds rate will fall); but small, perhaps miniscule, price changes reckon to equilibrate the market, since any good traded on a thick market is much like giro credit: elasticities of substitution reckon to be very high.

   Government intervention tactics may pivot on a basic credit balance it accumulates with members of the clearing house. An authority leaning against the wind supplies giro credit when it is in excess supply; and buys it when it is in excess demand, perhaps stepping up tax collections as well.

   Should the authority (formerly the MA) lean against the wind? Under a tabular standard, the perfect stability (i.e., the complete absence of volatility) of the general price level is never in doubt. And the economy seems strongly homeostatic, especially since the authority, constrained by the virtual convertibility of its liabilities, cannot easily impart a forced vibration onto the system (which Part II suggests is the predominant monetary characteristic of trade cycles). And *control* may be chimerical: the authority may not be able to accumulate a fund, which must now be *real*, large enough to exert decisive influence.

The last paragraph further extends a characteristic feature of the theory: virtual convertibility, imposed by the Aureus standard, stringently constrains the authority so that political economy reverts to a pre-Walpole condition in which the Crown plays without a printing press. The mirror image of the analysis shows how immense have been the powers accumulated by government under fiat monetary systems, ringing another change on Hayek (1976).

Interpolation

In principle, in uninnovated systems, real liquidity can be generated, however dubiously, by falls in general price levels. (See Tobin, 1978, Chapter 1, which I glossed in 1986, Chapter 9, and Lando, 1989.) This is impossible in innovated systems where paper assets are *per se* worthless. Innovated systems are saturated with liquidity.

2. q-*oriented strategies* The market, feeding on its excited greed, may push q up to towering heights, leading to unsustainable diversion of resources towards durable goods manufacturing; or frantic fear may send the market 'south', bringing capital accumulation to a grinding halt.

   A knowledgable, calm, proficient stabilizing authority may transform the script – selling Crown assets, funding its debt, triggering massive sales of public pension fund assets, instructing Crown corporations to float huge offerings, etc. to block expansive bubbles – or, in the obverse case, diverting the market from stewing in its own juice.

   The authority buys assets when selling pressures may lead to panic; and sells when the market is euphoric – and yet the schematization is 'beyond money'. And there is a parallel to Friedman's (1953b) conjecture on stabilizing speculation in foreign exchange markets: the authority may characteristically buy near bottoms and sell near tops; if it reacts sluggishly, it may buy as the market is turning up and sell as it is turning down. Then the profitability of 'stabilizing' operations is dearly bought: heavy official selling occurs as the market is falling of its own weight; and the authority places large purchase orders as the market is about to soar.

4.4 IMPLICATIONS FOR HIGH MACRO-ECONOMIC THEORY

The ground is prepared by Chapter 3's discussion of seminal work by Samuelson (1947/1983) and Wallace (1983). The roost becomes strictly ruled by the equivalent to Thornton's mercantile rate of profit or Ricardo's 'rate of profits which can be made by the employment of capital, and which is totally independent of the quantity, or the value, of money' (1817/1951).

(Keynes argues in Chapter 17 of the *General Theory* that the convenience yield of cash balances rules the roost; this lurid proposition bottoms his book's theory of interest.)

The dominion of 'real goods' results from 'liquification' analogous to securitization taking the economy beyond the banking principle: the technological innovation of the payments system synergetically vastly increases the liquidity of 'ordinary goods'.

Enter *Say's Law* (see 1989a, Chapter 7). The possibility of intractable planned net diversion of savings from the income–expenditure stream into monetary hoards vanishes. True, agents may plan to divert receipts towards purchases of 'old' assets instead of building up new ones. But then Tobin's '*q*' increases: it becomes more attractive to build *de novo* than to buy assets in the bourse. Induction of substitution of purchase of new for old assets is generically equivalent, in the innovated economy, to inducing substitution of oranges for apples through changes in relative prices.

When liquidity properties are continuously distributed across asset fields, shifts in asset preferences are fully comprehended by the generic case just explained; or there may be switches away from housing, towards cars, affecting average durability of assets as well. 'Moneyness' becomes so diffused that 'excess demand for money, or liquidity' is drained of all operational content; paper assets have utility only so far as they symbolize claims to real assets.

Laidler (1988) points out that the classicals did not seriously explore money except as a debt-discharge vehicle. Were they blind to potential diversion of the income–expenditure stream into hoards? No! The explanation nests in properties of commodity money systems going back to ancient times (see Chapter 10, Barsky and Summers, 1988 and (1989a, Chapter 8)). In the eighteenth and nineteenth centuries, the mercantile rate of profit ruled the interest rate roost. The convenience yield of cash balances easily adapted itself to the autonomously evolving rate of profit because of fluidity of movement between monetary and non-monetary precious metal shocks. The latter much exceeded the former, so that the convenience yield of non-monetary precious metal stocks evolved autonomously relative to demand for money – while adapting itself to the evolution of the mercantile rate of profit. Changes in the propensity to hoard induced sympathetic switches in the distribution of precious metal stocks between monetary and non-monetary uses.

4.4.1 Coda: Further Vindication of the Classics: Inflation and Commodity Money; Bimetallism

(a) *Inflation*

The preponderant importance of non-monetary precious metal stocks meant that an increase in global gold supply led to an increase in the general price level (where gold is numéraire) via the impetus of excess supplies of non-monetary gold. If prices (expressed in gold) were sticky in the wake of expanded gold supply, it was appealing to take gold to the mint – to an extent based on the elasticity of demand for non-monetary gold. Anciently, such demand was highly elastic: gold discoveries, or infusions of spoils of victories, did not work through to substantial declines in gold's purchasing power: the ancient counterpart to modern inflation was depreciation of chronically debased coinage relative to a standard quantum of gold of given fineness. (See Chapter 10.)

(b) *Bimetallism*

Gibbon (1776) reports that silver secularly depreciated against gold in Roman times. The standard bimetallism drill dwells on the difficulties of aligning mint and market ratios; and silver did seem rather persistently over-valued at the Roman mint. More interestingly, the *electrum staters* of Cyzicus, discussed in Chapter 10, note 2, circulated at an invariant price in a *stater* metric, but exhibited properties of Chapter 2's innovated ECU: the *stater* price of silver could fall and that of gold rise, in ways constrained by the generic formula $\Sigma\pi_i = 1$.

4.5 SUMMARY OF CHAPTER FOUR

The materials of Chapter 4 are usefully reassembled and in some cases deployed along new lines of attack.

On the giro, liquidity premia tend towards zero for reasons given by Samuelson (1947/1983) in a different context. Monetary theory dissolves: the veil of money is stripped away, revealing the plain, if not hideous, features of the real economy. Thus assume that a frictionless economy is saturated with liquidity so that *no* asset yields *valuable* liquidity services at the margin. Then only real yields can be defined; then no permutation of the class 'the wheat rate of return on housing' is privileged. (See the *General Theory*, Chapter 17.) A perfectly fluidly operating giro leads to this result, as, for that matter, does securitization *à outrance*.

The paradise of the demonetized giro can be confused with the inferno of barter exchange. Of course, barter exchange is excruciatingly constrained by double coincidence: classical monetary exchange is much more fruitful than barter. But computerized direct debit schemae, eliminating intermediate substances (such as coins crossing palms), do not entail barter. They simply cut out a costly step in the trading process.

The innovated clearing network is operated by data processing specialists who do not give or receive credit: the famous hybrid rôle of the banking system – operation of the clearing network with counters ('deposits') it supplies and which in turn are residues of its lending – is abandoned. Banks of issue are no more. And most bankers will welcome the end of their chequery rôle: it is a low-margin, boring business now that 'interest on money' has destroyed the huge mass of zero-interest, or sub-market-rate, deposits that once backed the clearing system. All pretext for *regulation* of banks is dismissed.

There are plangent implications for the theory of money and finance. Market yields are determined invariantly against whatever remains of monetary phenomena. Concomitant adoption of an *Aureus standard*, explained in Chapter 2, locks in this result. Professor Knight's Crusonia plant becomes a quite plausible generalization of praxis instead of a problematically illuminating phantasy. And the 'Wicksell business' crumbles: only real (often implicit) interest rates remain, and are explained by theories of real economic action. Classical economists believed that economics should turn out this way.

As things stand, transient economic data cannot be fully explained if the action of the financial sector, influenced by central banks, is ignored. This is where Thornton and Wicksell come in and where the theory of banking and monetary control has long nested. Keynesian monetary theory has dwelt on a fringe of the domain carved out by

Thornton, Wicksell, Fisher, Keynes (*Treatise*) and Robertson. At its worst, it projects a purely monetary theory of real yields; midstream Keynesians display the hybrid ISLM construction, nested in a simplistic general equilibrium format and implying far-reaching possibilities for central bank determination of real yields. Dramatic innovations go far to wipe out two centuries of monetary-theoretical development, so that the 'real world' is modelled by innovated schemae that may be confused with barter.

So much that is monetary is stripped away that the new art of central banking operates in real asset markets. Sometimes it may be necessary for the public sector to increase its holdings of productive assets in order to capitalize the new art of central banking. The innovated authority must acquire adequate working capital; a trade-off between micro-efficiency of public sector asset management and efficiency of macro-policy execution is generated – always subject to the caveats of Friedman's formal analysis of stabilization and correlative 'resonance' analogues.

Notes and References

1. *Tobin (1985)* Tobin deals with actual or potential changes in money-stuff (e.g. private currency) and in network properties (including giro transfer), but not with metrics: he does not contemplate systems based on imaginary money. He remarks, in a section entitled 'The Mirage of Private Money',

   > I find it difficult to imagine a system in which there is no governmentally issued store of value in the unit of account. Some discussions of 'private money' in the literature seem to suggest that the government can define the 'dollar' as the unit of account without printing and issuing any dollars. Private agents could issue promises to pay dollars and these would circulate.
   >
   > Tobin (1985, pp. 2–3)

   Private money *is* probably a mirage. Examples of chits issued by Wisconsin narrow-gauge railroads to a few transactors in 1884 are not persuasive. Short of metrical innovation, it is hard to conjure up a feasible praxis exceeding Tobin's boundaries. But deep innovation *is* metrical; and Tobin does scale Mt Nebo, if he fails to see the promised theory.

> Private money makes more sense for commodity money. The government can define a dollar in terms of gold or silver, or plywood or wheat, or some combination of goods.
>
> Tobin (1985, p. 3)

Take one more step. A virtual commodity standard emerges if the unit of account is defined like our Aureus and debt-discharge praxis is innovated; *and* no entity, public or private, issues a circulating medium (although seigneurage may be extracted from issue of a medium discharging small-valued transactions off giro).

Finally, this book's principal results do *not* depend on innovated clearing systems: a 'securitized' economy is saturated with liquidity so that the 'mercantile rate of profit' rules the interest rate roost.

2. *Patinkin and Steiger (1989)* probe the origins of the idea of *monetary neutrality* and the *veil of money* with scholarly *panache*.

Neutrality and the Quantity Theory

I pass over the question whether it is a 'basic quantity-theory proposition that it is only the absolute price level of an economy, and not relative prices and the rate of interest, and hence real outputs, that is affected by changes in the quantity of money' as Patinkin and Steiger claim. In the only sense that Friedman, for one, accepts this interpretation, the theory becomes trivial, if not meaningless: no experiment can test for asymptotic convergence of a process driven by biological agents: the quantity theory is then a proposition in theology. Nor can neutrality be central for the transient intervals Friedman is interested in. See the exchanges between Friedman and Patinkin in Gordon (ed.) (1974).

* * *

Patinkin and Steiger greatly clarify *monetary neutrality* in the Wicksellian domain. Wicksell is concerned with the absolute price level: the natural rate of interest is neutral with respect to commodity prices to that extent. And Wicksell stipulates that the real rate of return to capital evolves autonomously relative to the cumulative process – accordingly an *absolute price* process. So Hayek's stricture on Wicksell, reported by Patinkin and Steiger, for adopting so limited a neutrality idea seems misplaced: Wicksell's neutrality idea is proper to his theory.

Patinkin and Steiger interestingly discuss more extensive notions of monetary neutrality, referring to Johan Koopmans:

> In our terminology, money is neutral if, and only if, the properties of a monetary economy correspond to the ideal type of a pure exchange economy, according to the laws of equilibrium theory.
>
> Koopmans (1933, p. 228, emphases deleted)

Patinkin and Steiger conclude that 'Koopmans meant an exchange economy without money, i.e. a barter economy'. Our innovated system yields precisely the results attributed to barter economies that are so important here: changes in 'real' data must be functions of 'real' forces and nothing else. Of course, the correspondence is merely notional: barter economies are imaginary constructions.

A Footnote to the Theory of the Cumulative Process

Otto Steiger informs me that in 1916 David Davidson called attention to Henry Thornton's priority in deriving a cumulative process; and that Wicksell acknowledged this in the German edition of his *Lectures* vol. II, p. xii, note 1, in 1922. In 1988, I gave priority to Hawtrey (1938) and Hayek (1939) for staking Thornton's claim. Fortunately, Otto Steiger has not read the rest of my book.

5 A Monetary Analysis of Public Debt

5.1 INTRODUCTION

Sections 5.1 and 5.2 pivot on the criterion for the optimum quantity of public debt, generalizing that for the optimum quantity of money – see Friedman (1969). The study is at the juncture of monetary and fiscal theory.

Since debt can be costlessly created (see tap stock), its marginal convenience yield ought to be nil, so that its yield in equilibrium is that of 'physical' capital.

Section 5.3 shows that, in a closed economy, public debt, viewed through a 'Ricardo–Barro' prism, has a bizarre property: upon its marginal convenience yield evaporating, so that its running yield is that of physical capital, a unit increase in its supply generates a unit increase in demand: households must buy securities *pro rata* to protect relative wealth positions: if the government increases the rate at which it hands out cash to members of the economy by one pound, financing the additional transfers by debt sales, flow demand for government debt automatically increases by one pound. The market for public debt achieves a metastable equilibrium.

5.1.1 Pseudo-thrift

Societies with huge public sector borrowing requirements – because of massive government transfer (including interest payments) – may look exceptionally thrifty. But they are not: savings financing transfers, returned to the government by bond purchases, do *not* map into accumulation of real wealth. Thus Canadians and Italians – and indeed Russians, in a twist developed in (1986, Chapter 8) – look thriftier than Americans, but have nothing to show for their pseudo-thrift. And economies whose governments make huge unproductive purchases financed by internal debt flotation are also pseudo-thrifty. Dennis Robertson put it well: 'the most important form of unproductive lacking in modern times consists of the transfer of spending power to governments . . . [It] results in the provision of Imaginary Capital' (1926/1932, p. 45).

Section 5.4 distinguishes effects of public purchases of real goods and services from those of transfers, Two principal comparisons are made. One distinguishes effects of lump-sum changes in annual rates of public spending from those of changes in the *proportion* of national product absorbed by the public sector. The other distinguishes effects of proportionate changes in public spending in tax-finance régimes from those in bond-finance ones; an unexpected free-rider phenomenon crops up.

* * *

Tobin, Modigliani *et al.* perceive public debt phenomena very differently from Barro. The upshot provokes queries about the very nature of society. 'Their' agents are less obsessed with their progeny and sometimes seek to 'beat the game', as I should think even Chicago economists do. And the experimental work of Modigliani and Jappelli (1988) finds the classical hypothesis inconsistent with the data.

5.2 SOME STYLIZED HISTORY

Consider an economy like that of the United States *circa* 1790, when Alexander Hamilton was promoting his Bank and Assumption plans during Washington's first administration (see (1988)).

In a financially primitive economy, most assets are held directly. And the great bulk of debt instruments are commercial (trade) acceptances; bankers' acceptances and bank bills are rare. In principle, creation of a liquid asset with universal currency would then be socially productive. For example, life-cycle savings and bequest modalities are then better served: see Modigliani (1986) and Samuelson (1958).

Say the government indeed supplies (perhaps inconvertible) paper that becomes a useful monetary contrivance. Its utility is *institutional*: the contrivance of monetary exchange has been wonderfully productive, but increments to the mass of money do not further promote the institution's utility – a point taken by Jefferson but sometimes overlooked by the putatively more astute Franklin and Hamilton. This result sharply contrasts with the one obtained for oranges or steel – although law and economics show that institutional structures affect economic performance in all directions. And a corollary point is crucial. Since the supply of liquidity services can be costlessly augmented, efficiency requires a *nil* convenience yield at the margin.

The nil marginal convenience yield result maps into a positive definite real stock, extracted from a functional relationship between marginal yield and real stocks.

In a competitive equilibrium associated with a social optimum, holders of *any* financial asset obtain the 'mercantile rate of profit'. So the claim's issuer must obtain a yield from resources bought with the proceeds of his IOU equal to the mercantile rate of profit.

Picking up the thread of the stylized history, now that its logical foundations are in place, the government, or Crown, may refurbish palaces, fight wars, etc. with the proceeds of its sales of paper; or it may rebate seigneurage profits through imperial donatives, tax cuts, etc. Alternatively it will set up a national savings bank in order to float its paper. The bank may become a vast financial intermediary whose highly liquid liabilities are traded in thick markets.

5.2.1 Purposes Served by the New Contrivance

Early in the history, land is entailed (as by statutes of primogeniture) and prohibition of slavery suffices to make human capital illiquid. Nor can consumption streams be reshaped by dealings in real assets. This is accomplished only through dealings in government debt: e.g. government debt may be sold by aged holders to young ones, enabling the aged to sustain living standards otherwise undermined by deterioration of their human capital. Operating in parallel, middle-aged agents divert income streams into securities purchased from aged vendors. As for *bequest* motivation (*pace* Modigliani?), men wanting to build estates, but not wanting to acquire businesses for reluctant or incompetent children, accumulate and bequeath government stock.

Maintenance of a family's *status quo* requires it to increase its government stock holdings *pari passu* with others, whether or not debt service is financed by taxation. Demand for government stock increases one-for-one with supply. In the hallucinatory upshot, funds slosh around in a closed circuit as debt stocks accumulate and are automatically absorbed. Accumulation of the paper without limit is quite consistent with a stationary state in the real domain. Is some fiendishly clever misanthrope behind all this? If so, her name is Social Democracy.

5.2.2 Evolution of Private Sector Dealing Towards Liquidity of Private Paper: the Italian Example

In the history's next phase, the private sector develops competitively viable instruments. And the history takes an Italian twist: growing sophistication of Italian asset markets, and the modalities of 1992 and beyond, will work to increase the liquidity of Italian private issue. Is the prognosis for Italian government debt dark then? The answer is congested. Chapter 2 and the Coda to Chapter 5 lead to sombre conclusions in the context of either an institutionalized or laissez-faire European monetary régime. But a 'new-classical' analysis of a notionally closed Italian economy on a lira standard has a surprisingly anodyne upshot. This is why.

In a closed new-classical economy, the *net* stock of government debt is identically *zero*: your holdings are our burden. If each of one million identical agents buys \$1m of government debt, everyone's *net* position is as before: each gross position is increased by \$1m; each debt burden is increased by $\$(10)^{12} / (10^6) = \$10^6$. Each must acquire assets to discharge the burden of others' holdings. So long as the yield of government stock is competitive, government debt issue stimulates demand for purchases of debt 1:1. A complete (*closed-economy*) pseudo-process is put into place.

But once liquidity premia vanish, it may *still* behove the government to abandon the debt field. Then even naïve agents will perceive deficits as taxes.

Remark

Productive activities of the public sector have been elided to promote a pure financial analysis. The productive activities of the public sector should be subjected to micro-analysis used for the private sector, up to a point: Chapter 4 shows that, in the new art of central banking, there is a trade-off between micro-efficiency of public sector action and open-market policy, deployed in real asset markets in the innovated economy.

5.3 SOME THEORY OF PSEUDO-PROCESSES

5.3.1 The Government of a Closed Stationary State Plays Social Democratic Politics

Initially transfers, positive and negative, are nil in a crudely stationary economy.

$$C = 1{,}000 = \text{GDP} = \text{GNP} = \text{Disposable Income} \tag{5.1}$$

Now the Government puts itself into play. It permanently finances transfers of \$100 per annum by debt sales; and it sells debt to pay interest on debt. Bonds are simply devices for maintaining equilibrated relative wealth positions.

The arithmetic is bizarre, but not unpleasant (see Sargent and Wallace, 1981). It is feasible for the process's activity level to increase without limit; public debt may attain *any* level.

In discrete terms, the volume of public debt at $t = n$ is

$$100(1+r)^n + 100(1+r)^{n-1} + \ldots + 100(1+r) = x(n) \tag{5.2}$$

$$x(n) = 100[(1+r)^n + (1+r)^{n-1} + \ldots + (1+r)] = 100[\textstyle\sum_1^n (1+r)^t] \tag{5.2a}$$

In continuous terms,

$$Dx = 100 + rx \tag{5.3}$$

$$Dx/x = 100/x + r \tag{5.3a}$$

$$D(\log x) = (100/x) + r \tag{5.3b}$$

$$\log x = (r + 100/x)t \tag{5.3c}$$

$$x = e^{(r + 100/x)t} \tag{5.3d}$$

The system is not well defined at the moment of (Big Bang) creation. At that moment the growth rate is infinite. Ours is a very brief history of time. And S. Zambelli points out that equations (5.3c) and (5.3d) are transcendentals . . . One seeks the sum of all principal that has ever been issued plus cumulated compound interest.

Happily the problem's simple economics drowns its potential mathematical horrors. Each unit of debt engenders one of *anti-debt* of equal and opposite economic force. The system is meta-stable: all that matters to Ricardo–Barro agents is one's relative standing. (The argument is on all fours with my burden-of-the-money-supply analysis in 1968, Chapter 13 and 1986, Chapter 9.)

The economy's real state continues to be described by

$$Y = C = 1{,}000 \tag{5.4}$$

along with equation (5.3), describing its public debt evolution. Of course, the algebraic sum of public debt and anti-debt is identically *zero*.

$$x^* = 0 \tag{5.5}$$

for all t, where x^* = debt *cum* anti-debt.

Coda to Section 5.3.1

Following Branson (1979/1989, pp. 454–5), we analyse the proportion borne by public debt to real output and capital in the long run.

$$\zeta_t = \delta y_0 e^{\varrho t} \tag{5.6}$$

where: ζ_t is the deficit at data t; δ is the proportion borne by the deficit to income; ϱ is the secular growth rate of the real economy; and y_0 is an initial condition on output.

The cumulant of public debt issue, x_t, is to be evaluated at $t = T$.

$$x_t = \delta y_0 \mid (e^{\varrho t})/\varrho|_0^T = (\delta y_0) \mathbin{/} \varrho)\ (e^{\varrho t} - 1) \tag{5.7}$$

$$x_t/y_t = (\delta/\varrho)[1-(1/e^{\varrho T})] \rightarrow \delta/\varrho \text{ as } T \rightarrow \infty \tag{5.8}$$

Each value of δ maps into a limiting x/y value; and the controlling function increases monotonically. The agents of the economy must be prepared to hold portfolios obeying this result. Finally, the analysis relates interest rates to the technique of production rather than to the secular growth rate.

5.3.2 Thrift Illusion

(a) *Government Outlays are Confined to Bond-financed Transfers*

Disposable income is to increase by an amount equal to the annualized transfer flow and is also pumped up by interest receipts. And, in the new-classical drill, all transfers are automatically accommodated by 'defensive' government bond purchases. 'Agents' may congratulate themselves on their virtuous thrift, blaming America, or something more immanent, for the failure of saving to lead to real wealth formation.

Section 5.5 shows that in Italy and Canada huge government transfers are readily accommodated by private saving: both economies are pseudo-thrifty. (Remember we are not concerned, here, with finance of state controlled productive activities.)

(b) *Government Purchases* (G) *are Bond-financed*

The national product accounts of closed economies A and B are described by Table 5.1. (In Barro's 1984, terms, government purchases are not to be substitutable for private ones and are not to contribute to productive possibilities.)

A's saving rate appears to be twice as high as B's; but the difference is illusory.

Table 5.1 Illusory savings rate differentials

	C		I		G		Y	
A	1,000	+	100	+	100	=	1,200	$S(A) = 200$
B	1,100	+	100	+	0	=	1,200	$S(B) = 100$

5.3.3 The Issue Joined: Accounting For The American and Other Public Sector Borrowing Requirements

Consider Table 5.2.

Purchases are over-financed, as they are in the United States. So far as we have gone, debt issues (equal to 4 per cent of GNP) will be automatically absorbed *ad infinitum*; and surely do not directly drain

Table 5.2 Partial tax finance of government transfers and purchases

	Proportions of GDP × 100%
Government purchases	8%
Positive transfers	8
Taxation	12
Debt sales	4

lendable resources, which are, after all, enhanced (nominally) 1:1 by the transfers.

There *is* over-absorption potential in the economy's *open* mode: say that aliens absorb half the debt sales. But over-absorption cannot be a function of the finance mode of government purchases *cum* net transfers; it *is* one of aggregate purchases, public and private, relative to gross national product.

Remark

The British government has been running a surplus, retiring debt with the proceeds. Along lines so far explored, pseudo-saving declines correspondingly.

Over-funding is an interesting notion that dwells at the interface of money and public finance. Thus the British government may sell debt even if it runs a surplus: cf sales of *tap stock*. The reader will easily work out *under-funding* for herself.

5.3.4 The Keynesian Counter-argument

The proposition that debt finance of government expenditures is irrelevant for real economic action is highly controversial. Keynesian and other economists are not as sanguine as Barro about *homo-sapien* benevolence. The agents of the counter-theory look for opportunities to increase consumption regardless of effects on their progeny; in my (1986) imagery, they are grasshoppers, not ants.[1] Transfers from the government afford agents the opportunity to make consumption expenditures otherwise blocked by constraints on their borrowing.[2] Indirect crowding out occurs: real interest rates must increase so that investment flotations are choked off and foreign investment, dual to the trade deficit, is attracted. (If elasticities of substitution are *very* high, interest rates need not increase.) In the counter-theory, positive transfers create an opportunity for profligacy that is promptly seized. See Tobin (1980, Chapter 3), as well as Modigliani and Jappelli (1988).[3]

5.4 EFFECTS OF CHANGES IN REAL GOVERNMENT PURCHASES ON CAPITAL ACCUMULATION IN A CLOSED ECONOMY

(Chapter 7 (1989a) supplies an open-economy version of this problem.)

In what follows, government purchases are not to substitute for private purchases. Nor do government purchases affect production possibilities. Productive public sector activities are hived off: the analysis must be embellished to explain the French or Italian economies, for example.

It was shown in Chapters 2–4 that the successor to monetary authorities in innovated economies must possess a portfolio of real assets if the innovated authority is to play in the economy. A principal feature of the new art of central banking hinges on transformation of the asset sets deployed.)

5.4.1 A Lump-sum Increase in Annualized Government Purchases

The limit point of capital accumulation is invariant against the *level* of government purchases. A lump-sum increase in annualized government purchases is like a natural disaster that wipes out some human and non-human capital but does not change secular production possibilities. More formally, the upshot is equivalent to a change in an initial condition of a classic differential equation paradigm: the absorbing state of a stable process is invariant against choice of initial condition.

Consider the following rather simplistic scenario. Where an economy's *per capita* stock of (all inclusive) capital is denoted K, the law governing capital accumulation is

$$\dot{K} = f(K-\bar{K}) \qquad f(0) = 0; f'(\quad) < 0 \tag{5.9}$$

The process converges on $\bar{K}$ invariantly against selection of the initial condition. (Kelsey, 1988, points out that 'chaotic processes are highly sensitive to initial conditions'. This is as it should be: economics is concerned with the flux of action of biological agents.)

Two remarks are in order.

1. The problem of section 5.4.1 should be modelled so that terms of transformation in production and consumption are invariant against shocks (transformed into changes in initial conditions in the discussion).
2. The following illustration supplies more economic intuition. An economy may be described by Knight's Crusonia plant model: the plant grows at 5 per cent p.a.; the plant can be consumed – portions not consumed grow at 5 per cent p.a. Say that the economy is in a steady state. Now the government appropriates 100 units p.a. of product, using these tax proceeds to fund an endless resistance to something in a faraway place. It is as if 2,000 units of 'plant' suddenly disappeared. Equilibrium will be restored, in time, if equation (5.9) describes the economy's underlying law of motion; in the new equilibrium, 2,000 more units of Crusonia plant will be permanently in place. So to speak, the *net* stock of Crusonia plant is an invariant in the long run.

(a) *Choice of Finance Mode*

Integrating the discussion with that of Section 5.3, consider choice of *financement*. If the 100 unit p.a. product diversion (cf Friedman's deficits that are taxes) is financed by debt sales, and even if finance charges are also financed by debt sales, the debt/anti-debt paradigm assures that all required finance is supplied automatically.

(b) *How is the Welfare Cost of the Government's Resource Appropriation Properly Measured?*

Once equilibrium is regained, the economy's consumption is restored, along with other crude 'macro'-measures of what Dennis Robertson called Ecfare. Welfare loss is embedded in the abstinence required to expand *gross* capital stock by 2,000 units. In a subtler model, endowed with a programming structure instead of a mechanistic law of motion, intergenerational tussle can be made quite sharp. Parents, obsessed with their children's comfort, and that of their children's children, etc. sharply curtail their consumption at once: equilibrium is promptly restored. Less benevolent living adults may initiate a slow dragging adjustment sequence. (In an open economy, capital can be restored by foreign borrowing; selfish contemporary adults can sustain their consumption, leaving their progeny with a foreign debt burden.)

5.4.2 The Proportion of Output Unproductively Absorbed by the Public Sector Increases

Invariance properties, obtained relative to the stipulation that taxes are extracted as proportionate income taxes, now dissipate. Consult the following glossary.

Glossary

r = the rate of interest (there are no risk or liquidity premia)
τ = the proportion of income absorbed by the government
i = the proportion of output absorbed by investment expenditure

(a) *The Simple Algebra of a Taxation Régime*

Equation (5.10) organizes the discussion.

$$(r-\tau) = f(i) - \tau = \Phi(1-i-\tau) \tag{5.10}$$

In equilibrium, the after-tax rate of interest must equal the marginal after-tax rate of return on investment, which must in turn equal the rate of time preference.

Barro *et al.* anticipate distorting effects of income taxation; they carefully specify lump-sum taxation. Tobin (1980, Chapter 3) explains why this is *so* important; and lump-sum taxation is tacitly specified above. Under proportional income taxation, income streams purchased by abstinence are taxed, but consumption is not: one pays taxes on the earnings of assets acquired with income that has been taxed. See equation (5.11), extracted from equation 5.10.

$$f(i) - \tau = \Phi(1-i-\tau) \tag{5.11}$$

$$f'(\ ) + (\partial\Phi/\partial i)di = 1 - (\partial\Phi/\partial\tau)d\tau \tag{5.12}$$

$$f'(\ ) = (-);\ \partial\Phi/\partial i = (-);\ \partial\Phi/\partial\tau = (-) \tag{5.12a}$$

$$di/d\tau = (+)/(-) = (-) \tag{5.13}$$

(b) *The Simple Algebra and Not-so-simple Economics of a Debt Finance Régime*

Under a debt finance régime, if an additional unit of capital is created, government purchases will increase by τr units p.a.: an incremental perpetuity of τr units p.a. has thus been created. It becomes necessary for the agents of the economy to reduce their consumption by τr units p.a. (i.e., a notional level of potential consumption is reduced).

If there were but a single agent, the specifications just installed seem quite adequate. But, in reality, there is an interesting externality or free-rider effect. True, my accumulation of an extra unit of capital imposes a 'bond burden' of τr on the economy; but, where α_j is my share of aggregate wealth in equilibrium, the burden on *me* is only $\alpha_j \tau r$. So the *perceived* fall in the marginal efficiency of investment is greater under a tax finance than under a bond finance régime. Efficiency is promoted by bond finance – to this extent.

Interpolation

There is no *collective* motive to buy bonds. *Individuals* buy bonds because bonds defend them against the individually perceived burden of the pseudo-wealth embodied in aggregate bond holdings.

If pseudo-wealth is perceived as true wealth, government bond issue entails a quasi-crowding out effect. See Tobin (1980, Chapter 3) and Modigliani (1986).

(c) *The Not-so-simple Economics of Debt Finance*

The economic rationale is controlled by the anti-debt concept developed in section 5.3. Government debt accumulated by others imposes a burden on me and indeed threatens me. If bond holders collectively convert their holdings into goods, and I do not have sufficient asset holdings, I suffer a loss when the government exercises its tax powers and redeems its bonds. The argument's economics are embedded in the non-empty core of a game; the core contains an equilibrium set of relative wealth values.

The argument just completed is further advanced if debt is convertible into commodities, say via the Aureus. And it is congested if excess supply causes debt to be at least partially extinguished by depreciation of its value, measured in goods.

A Segue Between Sections 5.4 and 5.5

Once the economy is saturated with liquidity, so that liquidity premia vanish, monetary properties of public debt also vanish; better, monetary properties are then quite uniformly distributed among many assets.

5.5 DESCRIPTIVE MATERIALS

(Figure 5.1 is supplied on p. 114 and Figure 5.2, along with Table 5.3, supplied on pp. 115–16.)

5.5.1 Comments on Figures 5.1 and 5.2 and Table 5.3

1. The highly divergent public debt paths contrast sharply with much narrower spreads in real performance data. So the data support Chapter conclusion that public debt evolutions are predominantly reflections of pseudo-processes, significant only in a quasi-monetary domain, not a real one.
2. Italian and Canadian data illustrate the 'democratic politics and pseudo thrift' theme of section 5.3 – a remark evoking two further comments.

   (a) The real upshot is often misperceived in Canada where many think that the service of internal public sector debt absorbs real resources and that Canadians are exceptionally thrifty. In truth, the huge Canadian transfer payments, however misguided, do not absorb real resources; and Canadians' purchases of their government's securities are but pseudo-thrifty.
   (b) Italians share Canadian misperceptions, but ongoing European developments cast up intriguing complexities for Italians that need not now trouble Canadians. Thus Chapter 2 shows that, if Italian debt were converted into obligations not dischargable by the Italian printing press, Italian stability would be threatened. (Cf the dénouement of an extended ECU, let alone an Aureus, standard.) Would 'Brussels' assume the debt?[4] Would the fragile Italian polity withstand a drastic reduction in transfers or a switch from debt to tax finance – let alone both? Is it politically feasible for the Italian government to liquidate a substantial part of its enormous real asset holdings? Virtual convertibility of the lira transforms a pseudo-problem into a perplexing real one.

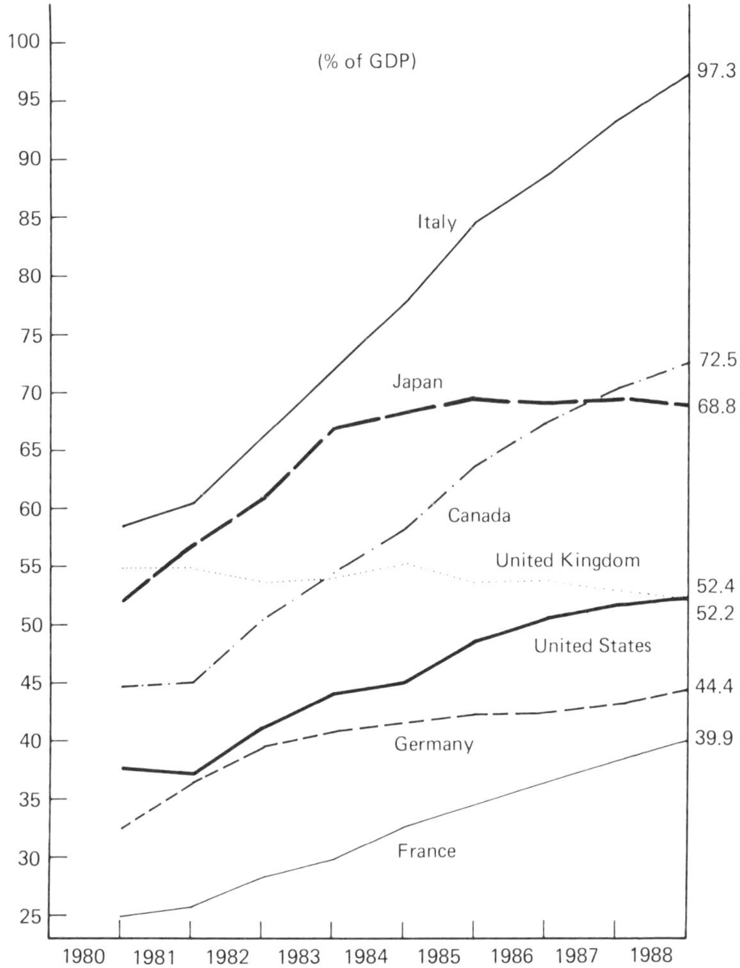

Figure 5.1 Public debt of main OECD countries (OECD, *Economic Outlook*; Bank of Italy, *Economic Bulletin* (October 1987); Banca Commerciale Italiana data)

Source: Banca Commerciale Italiana, *Monetary Trends*, 36 (February 1988) p. 6

3. The theory of Chapter 5 makes as little of British debt retirement as of higher American public sector borrowing requirements – so long as debt is sold to residents.

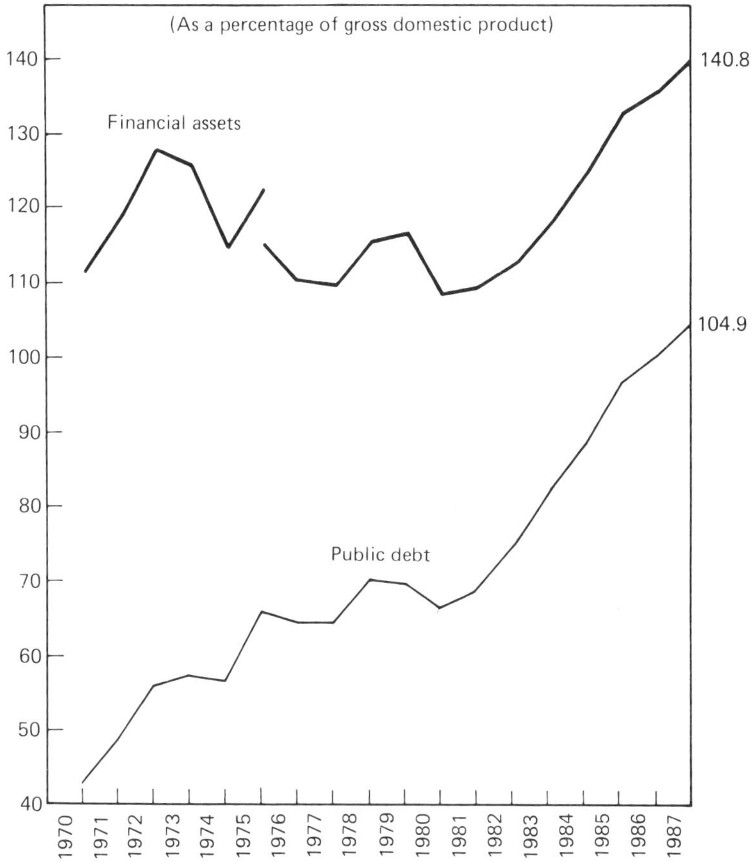

Figure 5.2 Public debt and financial assets (Italy, 1970–87)

Source: Banca Commerciale Italiana, *Monetary Trends*, 37 (July 1988) p.

Notes for Figure 5.2

1. *Financial assets*: domestic financial assets of the economy excluding shares (end-period amounts) and including liquid assets, bankers' acceptances, other deposits and interest-bearing paper, medium- and long-term securities and other assets. The forecast figure for end-1987 has been obtained from the Bank of Italy, *Economic Bulletin*, 7 (October 1986).
2. *Public debt*: amount of the public sector's domestic debt: it includes medium and long term securities and BOT sold on the market, BOT used for reserve requirements, postal deposits, loans of credit institutions, other domestic borrowings and debts with Bank of Italy-Foreign Exchange Office. The end-1987 projection is based on the government forecasts for the States sector borrowing requirement.

Table 5.3 Ratio of public debt to total financial assets

Countries	*1975*	*1980*	*1986*
United States	34.8	32.0	36.2
Japan	14.6	28.1	30.0
Germany	22.6	24.8	27.5
France	24.7	24.4	30.2[1]
United Kingdom	52.8	44.8	32.7[1]
Italy	43.8	52.1	62.9
Canada	44.5	38.3	49.4

Note:
1. The figure given is for 1985.
Source:
Banca Commerciale Italiana, *Monetary Trends*, 37 (July 1988).

5.5.2 Comments on Figure 5.3 (p. 117)

The spectacular *total debt* path replicates material already displayed. The divergence of the interest payments and non-interest borrowing requirement paths is especially interesting: so long as Italian debt is inconvertible, the Italian public debt problem is more amenable to monetary than to fiscal analysis.

The theory implies that the stock of Italian public debt is essentially a monetary one; and Italy is not alone! This remark gains transparency when money yields interest, as it does in Italy (see Modigliani, 1986). There are at least two corollary implications.

1. We are taken far along the path of Wallace's (1983) legal restrictions theory: exchange of public debt for money, in central bank open-market operations, looks more like exchanges of 10 dollar bills for (two) 5 dollar ones.
2. Implicitly diffuse definitions of *money* imply that monetarist-like inflation forecasts are subject to massive errors.

Coda to Chapter 5: A More Formal Analysis Linking Chapters 2 and 5

The control variable is the tax financed proportion of public expenditure. The analysis is in two stages. The first stage determines the equilibrium portion borne by public debt holdings to real wealth. The second stage determines the tax rate relative to the rate of return on

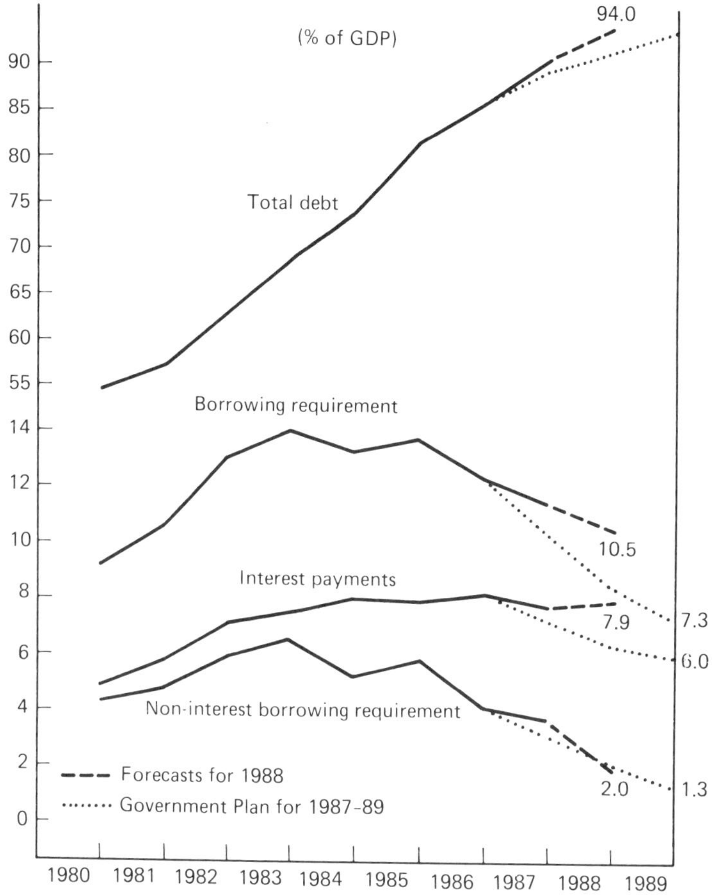

Figure 5.3 Trend of Italian public finances: provisional figures for 1987 and forecasts for 1988 compared with projections contained in the Government plan for 1987–9

Source: Banca Commerciale Italiana, *Monetary Trends*, 36 (February 1988) p. 3

Notes for Figure 5.3

1. The items refer to the State sector. The ratios to GDP have been calculated using new series of national accounts both for provisional figures and projections. Therefore the level of the ratios is different from that indicated in the Government Plan, where it was based on old series of GDP.

2. *Sources*:
   1987 provisional figures: Treasury's Quarterly Report on borrowing requirement (December 1987) and Economic Bulletin, Bank of Italy (October 1987).
   1988 forecasts: Financial Bill and Economic Bulletin, Bank of Italy (October 1987).
   Government Plan for 1987–89: 'Targets and Instruments of Budget Policy in the Three Years 1987–89', document submitted by the Treasury in agreement with the Budget and Finance Ministers in June 1986.

capital so that public debt grows at the same rate as real wealth.

In Italy, the equilibrium ratio borne by real public debt to real wealth may be exceptionally high; will it remain so when private debt markets are greatly deepened and broadened? In any case, once the equilibrium level, however high, is attained, and then exceeded, Italian freedom of action will be as harshly constrained as any – unless a command economy is installed, with dismal consequences of other sorts.

As for the second stage, equation (5.14) is an identity:

$$\Delta D = r^*D + \delta \tag{5.14}$$

The change in debt stock is equal to interest payments on existing principal plus fresh principal (δ), if $\tau = 0$. And, in equilibrium $\Delta D/D = \varrho$, where ϱ is the real rate of aggregate economic growth. So

$$\delta/D = \varrho - r^* \tag{5.15}$$

Reinterpret equation (5.15) in the following way. If the interest rate equals the growth rate, interest can be paid from borrowings – but no fresh principal can be floated in equilibrium. If the growth rate exceeds the interest rate, some fresh principal can be floated. If the interest rate exceeds the growth rate, tax finance is mandated. Then no fresh principal can be floated; and some interest must be paid from tax revenues.

(a) *Instability*

The system may be unstable. Stipulate that it is initially in moving equilibrium; and that the equilibrium ratio of public debt to real wealth falls so that there is initial excess supply of public debt. The ECU price of the lira will fall; and, if expectations are elastic, the required interest rate on lira bonds increases. See the following dynamic system.

$$\dot{v} = f(q) \tag{5.16}$$

$$\dot{q} = \phi[E(v)] \tag{5.17}$$

Therefore,

$$D^2v = \psi(Dv) \quad \psi'(0) > 0 \tag{5.18}$$

Glossary

v = the ECU price of the lira
q = excess demand for public debt

Stability can be preserved if, when v is falling undesirably, the tax rate increases and real assets (see IRI) are offered for public debt. Then the stock of public debt falls when it is in excess supply.

(b) *A Corollary Problem*

Preferences may shift away from lira-based debt and towards ECU assets. If the stock of lira-based debt falls when in excess supply, the solution of the corollary problem is promoted. IRI assets may be offered for lire. And discounts on lire assets encourage foreigners to offer ECU for them in this illustration of a truly new art of central banking.

Entrenchment of an ECU standard in Italy makes it easier to support the lira against ECU to the extent that real Italian assets are then better substitutes for ECU-based assets. (And the Italian public sector controls vast real asset stocks.)

On net though, entrenchment of an ECU standard for private Italian transactions will probably finally spoil the market for lira-denominated debt in excess of stocks required for 'ECU reserves'. Eventually, lira-denominated debt will be transformed into ECU-denominated debt. Correlative modalities include the following.

1. Huge sales of public sector assets for lira debt, much reducing the stock of lira debt, while enlarging the economy's private sector, will occur.
2. Guaranties of ECU-equivalent returns on existing lira-

denominated debt will be backed by the state's taxing power.
3. The public finances will finally accept an ECU standard discipline.[5]

Notes and References

1. As for 'ants vs grasshoppers', see (1986, pp. 120–1), for an analysis based on Buchanan (1958). Say that a war is financed by bond sales. Wartime ants reduce their consumption expenditures and buy bonds; their heirs' taxes for defrayal of debt service are financed by their bond income. Wartime grasshoppers sustain their consumption; they do not buy bonds; their progeny will reap the whirlwind (Hosea 8:7). The capitalized burden of following-generation grasshoppers is equal, and opposite in sign, to the capitalized value of the following-generation ant inheritance. And following-generation grasshoppers may support policies reckoned to melt their debt burden.
2. The text describes a process analogous to exploitation of public borrowing by consumers, thus enabled, *de facto*, to borrow at the public sector's interest rate. See Tobin (1980, Chapter 3).

   Agent *A* has a mediocre credit rating and wants to finance purchase of a consumer durable. The government is borrowing heavily; and, like other fiat issuers in closed economies, has a good credit rating (unlike Caesar; see Chapter 10). Ricardo-Barro logic impels an agent seeking to maintain the *status quo ante* to buy securities, thus anticipating incremental tax obligations for defrayal of debt service. But Agent *A* abandons the *status quo ante* and buys a durable instead of a bond. Her subsequent tax burden is precisely equivalent to interest cost at the government's borrowing rate.
3. See Modigliani and Jappelli (1988). In the English version, they write,

   > The Ricardian proposition, which predicts no relationship between deficits and interest rates is not supported by the data. On the contrary, in the context of the Italian economy, the deficits have played quite a significant rôle in increasing interest rates.
   >
   > Modigliani and Jappelli (1988, p. 32)

4. There are striking analogies running from prospective problems in consolidating Italian and other public debt into a pan-European one to American experience *circa* 1790, I describe *assumption* in Burstein (1988: cf 'Alexander Hamilton'). Some of the states were encumbered by huge debts; others were virtually debt-free.
5. Parallel monetary adaptations include the following. *Au fin* large transactions may clear through the agency of pan-European clearers whose members' reserves are real assets, including shares in companies. (Again, there is vigorous debate in Italy about whether banks should be merged

with industrial companies. *Au fin* they will be.) Small-valued transactions might, at the end of an evolutionary process, be discharged by a 'coinage' issued by a pan-European institution or by a number of privately owned pan-European institutions. The upshot is a dwarf image of the behemoth proposed in 1989 by M. Delors, Lord Cockfield, M. Valéry Giscard d'Estaing, Dr Masera, *et al.*

Part II
Money and Trade Cycles Over Two Millennia: Retrospective and Prospective Views of Central Banking

6 Preliminaries: Physical and Monetary (?) Foundations of Cyclical Action

6.1 PHYSICAL BACKGROUND

Underlying concepts include interference, diffraction, intrinsic and forced oscillation and resonance. For economics, wave interference is commandingly important – especially wave cancellation. Physical and economic processes are quite comparable from a wave mechanical standpoint. Steady-state response, along with transients, are a good example: see Feynman *et al.* (1963, I, pp. 21–6 and Chapter 24).

Feynman's discussion of forced harmonic oscillation, i.e. external driving forces, is especially illuminating (see 1963, I, pp. 21–5). Thus consider a second-order differential equation.

$$mD^2x = -kx + F(t) \tag{6.1}$$

The driving force may be at frequencies different from those of the intrinsic oscillations (see Allen, 1967). Frequencies and amplitudes of resulting oscillations readily differ massively from those of intrinsic ones.

Interpolation

The *energy* of a wave – cf kinetic and potential energy – is important for physics. But *energy* has not been exploited in economics, which indeed may be alien to it. Impressionistic economic exploitation of *energy* concerns mechanisms driven by vibration of *animal spirits* 'impacting' on industrial employment, investment, etc.; and vibration in 'the' taste for leisure is a motor force in supply-side-oriented theory.

* * *

Continuing discussion of equation (6.1), consider *resonance*, the reciprocal of cancellation and especially important for a theory of economic control subject to informational insufficiency and stochastic shock. (I report on resonance in 1986, 1988 and 1989a).

> If we adjust the frequency of the force to be 'in time' with the natural frequency, then we should get an enormous displacement . . . [If the frequencies are identical] it should oscillate at an infinite amplitude.
>
> Feynman (1963, I, pp. 21–6)

Interference is important for study of economic fluctuations – and indeed possibilities of coincidence of peaks and troughs of wave-like emanations, together with interference, have been deeply probed in economics. Waves cancel as well as amplify each other. In the upshot economic time series often defy systematic explanation.

See Feynman (1963, I, Chapter 29, especially pp. 29–35ff and I, Chapter 30). His Chapter 30 concerns diffraction – i.e., interference generated by *n* oscillators. Feynman shows that interference/diffraction phenomena are vital for the quantum theory. Nor is the algebra of waves commensurate with ordinary algebra. (See Feynman, 1963, Chapters 37 and 38, largely repeated in 1965, III, Chapters 1 and 2).

6.1.1 Two Economic Applications of the Physical Background

1. *Rational expectations.* Physics-based, more or less mechanical, models of economic fluctuations typically contradict rational expectations: opportunities for profitable exploitation should be seized; cycles in prices, including exchange rates, are often untenable for correct analysis. (Granted, fluctuations in say manufacturing employment may not be exploitable even if correctly forecast; see Robertson, 1926/1932, exhaustively discussed in Chapter 10, for a closely related analysis.)
2. *A more subtle interference model.* (see Feynman, 1963, I, pp. 48–3). The 'more subtle' model evokes, or invokes, Austrian economics. Feynman suggests drawing

> a vector of length A_1 rotating at frequency ω_1 to represent one of the waves in the complex plane. We draw another vector of length A_2, going around at frequency ω_2, to represent the second wave . . . If the frequencies are slightly different, the two complex vectors go around at different speeds . . . We see that A_2, is turning slowly away from A_1, and so the amplitude we

> get by adding the two is first strong, and then, as it opens out, when it gets to the 180° relative position, the resultant gets particularly weak and so on. As the vectors go around, the amplitude of the sum vector gets bigger and smaller and the intensity thus pulsates.
>
> Feynman (1963, I, pp. 48–3)

Economic equivalents include crop yields and strengths of demand for key exports. And the 'amplitude of the sum vector' may translate into the proportion of resources devoted to capital formation or into the *period of production*.

6.2 MONETARY BACKGROUND

The monetary theory of Part II is for the most part more orthodox and more narrowly focused than that of the wider-ranging Part I. Not only is Part II mostly confined to 'money, finance and cycles'; its job is to keep close touch with mainstream literature, not to supplant it. Part II is as much concerned with where we have been as with where we are going.

Most of the monetary theory of Part II flows from Chapter 3: cf extended Bank rate theory. If Part II's message can be formulated in a phrase, it is this: Financial intermediaries buy and sell paper; their action concerns supply of liquidity (for a fee), not real capital formation. MAs, able to override competitive market performance, may impose transient real effects that sometimes induce fairly regular vibration. But even these tenuous potentials evaporate beyond the banking principle – when the economy is saturated with liquidity so that there is no market for paper *per se*; then the sphere of MA action contracts, disappearing in the limit.

A correct analysis pivots on distinctions of money from credit and accounts for interest on money in open economies.

Turn to the orthodox model of the transmission of monetary impulses to outputs, relative prices and the general price level. Flexible interest on money is ignored. And the economy is, for practical purposes, closed. Taking up open market purchases by the central bank, yields of open-market securities fall, at impact, to the extent necessary to induce agents to substitute monetary balances for security holdings. *Real* yields of securities fall.

Substitution effects radiate out: prices of assets *en général* rise; and bank lending and investment are stimulated. The theory emphasizes new bank lending, neglecting exchanges of 'old' securities for claims on financial intermediaries. The resulting stimulus to aggregate demand boosts output and prices to degrees dependent on how full employment was to start with. The orthodox scenario, enhanced by rational expectations, culminates in theorems of invariance of real action against expected monetary change; and in more problematical invariance against unexpected monetary change.

6.2.1 Innovations in Theory

Paradigms based on 'interest on money' pivot on *spreads*. And spreads in competitive financial intermediary models are cost-based. The trigger mechanism of the old scenario is dismantled: no substitution effect automatically induces plans to change monetary balances in the wake of open-market operations.

In the upshot, monetary policy is geared to a generic Bank rate mechanism so that changes in volumes of bank mediation are the prime vehicle for achieving money growth targets (which have lost most of their importance); and 'money' appears to be chasing prices even when monetary underpinnings of changes in inflation are identified. Furthermore, elasticities of substitution between money (however defined) and other financial assets (liabilities) become so high, when money flexibly yields interest, that no more can be read into changes in money growth than from switches between pale green and slightly paler green asparagus.

Interpolations

Chapter 3 draws sharp distinctions, as did Keynes, between deployment of Bank rate as a money growth control device (however flawed) and as a means of influencing a spectrum, of whatever width, of real rates of interest. The latter modality turns classical economics on its head; yields on paper govern yields on real assets! The knotty problems intrinsic to a theory of inverse causality of this Wicksellian sort are swept away in the theory of an innovated economy in which securitization (taking the economy beyond the banking principle), tabular standards and a perfected giro are put into place. Then paper assets as such cannot obtain a yield; and the economy is saturated with liquidity. The classical principles of the day before yesterday rule the economy of the day after tomorrow.

Next, open-market operations in closed economies in which whatever is called money flexibly yields interest are assessed.

High elasticities of substitution among financial assets ensure that the public are readily induced to change the textures of their portfolios; the corollary is that effects on prices and outputs may be nil. And the notionally competitive banking (or financial intermediary) industry behaves like a constant cost competitive industry: it readily alters its activity level at a cost-based spread. *And* changes in volumes of intermediation are readily accomplished through acquisitions or dispositions of old securities. Monetary analysis plays out on a featureless (hyper) plane.

Now Bank rate comes in; see Chapter 3. Stimulus is supplied to borrowers to apply for fresh loans at (initially) lower *real* interest rates. (Higher rates are analysed symmetrically.) And lower rates over a wide spectrum of paper can be brought about by the stroke of a pen. That done, agents find it attractive to plan to convert 'paper' assets (like government debt) into 'real' ones. The flow rate of money offers for commodities, real estate, shares, etc. increases. There is excess supply of 'paper', including the portion assigned to 'money'. Paper depreciates relative to goods.

* * *

When money flexibly yields interest, monetary accounts are effectively indexed. So demand for real monetary balances is then invariant against the profile of inflation; and demand for nominal monetary balances increases *pari passu* with inflation. Money demand is driven by price behaviour. If money supply should evolve in a closed loop (so that it is driven by feedback), inflation potential is open-ended. Chapter 3 shows that operators of Bank rate control procedures may easily stumble into this snare.

Equation (6.2) describes price acceleration as a function of base money growth.

$$D\pi = f[D(m)] \qquad f'(0) > 0; f(0) = 0 \tag{6.2}$$

where π is the inflation rate and m the rate of growth of the monetary base. Unless appropriate controls are installed, the process is unstable.

It is easy to see how the dynamic relationship of equation (6.2) kicks in if interest rates are temporarily depressed by higher monetary growth – or by proclamation of lower Bank rate. Since all paper linked to money depreciates *pari passu* with it, excess supply of a variegated mass of securities, linked by very high elasticities of substitution, is provoked; and may be accompanied by excess demand for goods.

The channel of causality is ill-defined. Assume that the MA is known to be targeting a higher rate of inflation; and is known to be able to hit the target. Inflation will increase at once *à la* Sargent and Wallace (1981). The plausibility of exploitation of the direct channel induces higher inflation, validated on the feedback channel, since demand for additional nominal balances is elastically accommodated by the MA.

6.2.2 The *Modus Vivendi* of Bank Rate Encore

(See Chapter 3.)

Along lines indelibly associated with Wicksell, economists typically conclude that deviation of market from 'natural' (real) Bank rate influences money growth and, less plausibly, growth of real output.[1] But the money supply facet of the analysis has been improperly specified. It has been assumed that perhaps rapidly increasing monetary infusions are readily absorbed by a public who do not see that the yields of such balances may become negative as inflation cumulates. Rational portfolio management requires that real monetary balances *fall*. Nor is it explained why rational agents should trade real assets, whose own yields are stable or improving, for monetary ones whose yields are inferior and deteriorating; the critical arbitrage condition elucidated by Keynes (1936, Chapter 17) is violated.

Another important point tends to be neglected. In continuous equilibrium, higher nominal Bank rate maps into higher inflation; and lower nominal Bank rate with lower inflation (see Chapter 3).

What is more, when money flexibly yields interest, higher Bank rate entails a higher intrinsic growth rate of money supply. And finance requirements for interest-sensitive obligations *in situ* increase. Net demand for finance may increase as a direct consequence of higher Bank rate: increased interest obligation may exceed, and indeed swamp out, cancelled *financements*. (And we have seen that money is elastically supplied on terms defined by Bank rate in this régime.) But the controlling functional relation is not smooth. At 'low' levels of Bank rate, changes in Bank rate do not affect finance costs on initial balances as much as at 'high' levels. At low Bank rate levels, higher Bank rate is more apt to cut back money growth than at high ones. (Think of the huge disparity between an initial finance burden based on 16 per cent Bank rate and one based on 3 per cent Bank rate.) At the least, given the immensity of Bank rate-sensitive positions, it is plausible that positive effects on finance requirements of a rise in Bank rate should exceed contractionary effects on money growth of cancelled borrowing plans.

Finally, Chapter 3 explains that a force speciously like cost push is apt to negate the real impact of a rise in Bank rate. More or less competitive firms, confronted with perhaps massively higher finance charges, will surely test the water by raising prices so that validated price increases leave real rates of return intact. (The analysis pivots on Ricardo's required rate of profit.) A ratchet process may induce spiralling Bank rate *and* inflation.

6.3 INTRODUCING THE OPEN ECONOMY

Business-cycle potential is feeble in open economies; transient excess absorption is accommodated by a transiently negative trade balance; transient deficiency of absorption maps into a more positive trade balance, etc. And an open economy's sources of finance span the globe so that real interest rates are substantially exogenous for a small open economy.

Capital markets have been in close touch for a long time. Thus, in the nineteenth century, if America enjoyed a trade surplus, trade bills would be financed in New York instead of London – see Temin (1969) for a penetrating description of the state of play in the *ante-bellum* American economy.

6.4 FINANCE AND INDUSTRY; LIQUIDITY CRISES; MA INDUCTION OF CYCLES

6.4.1 Finance and Industry

Centre on *balance sheets*. Those of banks are famously precarious. The social contribution of bank lending lies in the illiquidity of the paper they buy (take back). And the social utility of their 'money creation' is based on the liquidity of their liabilities. Slumps induce vulnerable banks to dun creditors for payment as clients' cash flows deteriorate during slumps. And much working capital is financed by short borrowing from banks and other financial intermediaries. Furthermore merchants *et al.* both take and extend vast sums of book credit. There are substantial disruptive possibilities; latent pressures for forced liquidation are readily activated.

6.4.2 Liquidity Crises

This sub-section is an exception to the rule of Part II: it concerns the overall utility of the MA, not just its potential for induction of cyclical motion. A principal topic in central banking theory concerns the efficacy of official intervention during crises of liquidity; and crises of liquidity are important in monetary history, going back at least as far as Tiberius's intervention in AD 33 (see Chapters 8 and 10).

Crisis analytics are sharply discontinuous. It is not a matter of parametric modulation. Rather portfolio managers, perhaps reacting to a number of massive bankruptices, may exigently want to transform their portfolios *now*. The uneasy mathematical foundation for the study of this sort of economic pathology lies in catastrophe theory; and Professor Kindleberger keenly analyses bubbles, and ensuing panics, more informally.

The banking system is a mere intermediary. Fluctuations in volumes of its assets concern volumes of intermediation, not fresh real lending; banks do not supply real resources. So most of the force generated by vibration of liquidity preference is dissipated by its effects on liquidity premia – reflected by vibration in spreads obtained by intermediaries. True, a dramatic discontinuity in liquidity preference is not amenable to this schematization.

There are at least two reasons for hypothesizing that liquidity preference vibrations do not induce real action unless the process 'falls off the table'. The first becomes obvious when spectra of interest rates replace *the* interest rate: then, when liquidity preference 'smoothly' intensifies, intermediaries' spreads widen, stifling demand and inducing increased supply of liquid assets (cf claims against intermediaries). American examples, mostly drawn from 1863–1914, illuminate the *second reason*. The flaws of the National Banking system, founded in 1863, explain much of the data.

(The 1930–3 American experience is left to students of catastrophe

theory. Ours is a study of fairly regular vibratic
systems, *not* of discontinuities.)

Lloyd Mints (1945) explained, along lines further develop
Friedman and Schwartz (1963), how the National Banking System
flawed reserve system led to erratic vibration of the quantity of money, induced by fluctuation of preferences for claims against New York banks versus claims against country banks. Or erratic vibration could be induced by effects on New York banks of trade balance fluctuations or switches in international asset portfolios. The (inverted) pyramidal system amplified disturbances on active feedback channels.

6.4.3 Monetary Authority (MA) Induction of Cycles

Perhaps laissez-faire (free) banking would have outperformed the system *en vigeur*. Perhaps not. It suffices here to show how stabilization initiatives, then or now, are likely to induce cyclical behaviour in *any* milieu. The controlling logic, elegantly developed by Phillips and Goodwin, is explained by Allen (1958, 1967) in his conspectus of stabilization schemae. The coarsest depiction of differential equations makes this crystal clear. Lags (and/or delays) in data collection and processing, implementation of programmes, responses of affected systems to programmed stimuli, etc. mandate higher order differential equations: eigenvalues are typically complex. While it is necessary to develop non-linear formulations – see limit-cycles and 'strange attractors' – to make the underlying concepts empirically operational, the cyclical properties of elementary formulations persist. Even successful stabilization programmes induce cyclical motion: see especially Allen (1967, pp. 350–62) and Phillips (1954), glossed by Allen (1967).

Monetary theories of the cycle, like that of Irving Fisher or Keynes (1930: *Credit Cycles*) are easily translated into terms tenable for the rubric, 'MA induction of Cycles'. In the canonical script, the banking system, with the connivance of the MA (who may be the prime mover) grants massive credits to industrialists, thus enabled to impose *lacking* on the public (see Chapter 9). The structure of production is distorted in an 'Austrian' way. Lengthened periods of production may be unsustainable. And contraction of over-extended banks induces a crisis, etc.

Many other examples can be supplied. In 1930, Keynes entertainingly limned a *bismuth/castor-oil cycle* in which castor oil is supplied to an agent(!) who has been in a slump, so to speak, but is well on the way to recovery. A boom ensues. Bismuth is prescribed just as the system's strong homeostatic (recuperative) powers are generating appropriate retro-action. Etc. Friedman's 'formal analysis' (1951/1953) obtains a similar result via an incisive analysis of variance. And in 1986 and 1988, inspired by Allen's (1967) discussion of *resonance*, I suggested a wave-mechanical counterpart to Friedman's set-up: the forced vibration leads to a composite vibration whose frequency, amplitude, etc. differ from corresponding properties of the intrinsic vibration. And, since the energy imparted by the 'stabilizing' authority is apt to be more coherent than that playing out in the private economy, possibilities for fairly well ordered cyclical action are enhanced.

Finally, recall the conspectus, supplied in Chapter 3, of Poole's (1970) system. An MA, committed to defence of a (real) rate of interest in place before a surge in animal spirits, operates procyclically, promoting a boom that would otherwise spontaneously abort as liquidity dries up. And the same authority sells securities in the open market to prevent interest rates from falling in natural response to lower demand for finance in the wake of a sag in animal spirits. The authority intensifies a slump that might correct itself if it generated an excess of liquidity (see the *finance* discussion of Chapter 9).

(The authority's instruction to the open-market operator will be expressed nominally. And political pressures may impose 'money illusion' on the authority: for politicians the natural rate of interest is always lower than the market rate.)

6.5 FINAL REMARKS

The closed-model paradigms just explored do not survive open-economy analysis. In open economies, transient trade deficits and surpluses replace excess and slack absorption episodes. And capital inflows and outflows preclude cyclical pulsation; finance from abroad supplements local finance or, if need be, local sources of finance find vents abroad. Textures of local asset portfolios are readily altered by external transactions: undesired influxes of liquidity are easily switched out via purchases of less liquid assets, including Euro-market securities. And this is an old story. In the nineteenth century finance activity moved towards London from New York when base money flowed into London; and *vice versa* when say the American trade balance became more positive. Temin (1969) supplies a number of gripping examples; and see Chapter 8.

The hypothesis that MA behaviour induces cyclical action is further enhanced by study of IMF/World Bank action. Infusions of credit are followed by belt-tightening drills as borrowers experience debt service difficulty. And there is more. An economy responsive to Gnomic advice by international institutions sensitizes itself to its trade balance the way an economy with slender reserves obeying the rule of the Currency School is sensitized to *its* trade balance. If Economy *E*'s trade balance surges into the black, perhaps because of a positive shock to demand for its exports, the Gnomes tell it to pour more fuel on the fire and become a locomotive for growth. If its trade balance goes into the red because of a negative shock to export demand, the Gnomes tell it to enforce Draconian cuts, to tighten its belt, to be Responsible. The Gnomes distill a defunct economic doctrine in which changes in effective demand carry the burden of balance of payments adjustment. So there is still more to tell. Go back to the explanation, at the beginning of this chapter, of how diffraction (in a sense, incoherence) contributes to better aggregate economic behaviour, while coherence of impulses received by the economy can lead to disastrous climaxes such as resonance. An economy whose incoherence (in a wave-mechanical sense) assures that its intrinsic vibration is slight may shudder convulsively (economists say 'become subject to strong dysfunctional vibration') if the 'radiation' it receives becomes more coherent – especially if the 'radiation' is governed by improper economic theory. Thus Friedman (1951/1953) shows that 'dysfunction' is inevitable if too much stabilization effort is supplied by an authority.

The argument can be organized differently. As I explained in (1988, Chapter 2), the constitution of liberty (see Hayek, 1960) may require a level of disorder (in the sense of entropic degradation or incoherent radiation) unsightly to tyrants, who may be well-meaning, grey *fonctionnaires*.

More mundanely, a generic description of central bank action plausibly entails a fairly regular cycle of dilation and contraction, bringing us close to the outer edge of a domain carved out by Milton Friedman.

Appendix: Stabilization and Cyclicality

PRELIMINARY DISCUSSION

The principal subject of Chapter 6 can be further developed by a quite formal analysis.

Responses of agents of the economy to shocks or decisive changes in data will be highly diffracted, partly because there will be only a weak consensus about what is going on; but controlling authorities will act coherently, in the way that laser-light is coherent. So it is plausible that the vibrations of an unregulated system will be erratic. And we now insert the puzzle's final piece: the action of a controlling authority necessarily *lags* stimuli, setting up oscillatory effects along familiar classically-mathematical lines of development. A stylized exposé by R. G. D. Allen fixes these ideas.

A SIMPLIFIED ALGEBRAIC EXPOSÉ

(See Allen (1967, pp. 350–63). He relies heavily on Phillips (1954, 1957), especially on the 1954 reference.)

> All investment is included in autonomous demand. The model involves the multiplier, but not the acceleration principle. (Allen, 1967, p. 353).

And the following trick is performed: the origin is transformed so that variables are *deviations* from equilibrium values. *And* the deviation of autonomous expenditure (A) is to be *negative*.

The Variables

Demand $= Z = C - A + G = cY - A + G$ (A is an absolute value)

Output $= [1/(TD + 1)]Z$: $DY = (1/T)(Z - Y)$

T defines the length of the output lag. If $T = 2$ years, output responds to excess demand (which may be negative): then output's annualized rate of adaptation is ½ that of the excess.

The Natural (Unregulated) System

$$TDY + sY + A = 0 \qquad (s = 1 - c) \tag{A6.1}$$

$$Y = -A/s\,(1 - e^{-\gamma t}) \qquad (\gamma = s/T > 0) \tag{A6.2}$$

The natural Phillips–Allen system does not oscillate.

In life, unregulated systems react to random shocks. And agents are unlikely to know, or to even think they know, what is going on; it is preposterous that they should seriously forecast the future of the macro-economy. But, since '*Z*' bounces about unpredictably, output fluctuations may look cyclical: stochastic processes often generate pseudo-cyclical patterns. What is important is that the result's deterministic component is non-cyclical.

Proportional Stabilization Policy

Where τ is the time constant of a simple exponential lag 'between the formulation of policy *P* and its effect on demand, G' (Allen, 1967, p. 352) and *P* is described by $P = \alpha\,(-Y)$ – where *Y* is *not* an absolute value(!) – the *second order* differential equation of the controlled system is

$$\tau T D^2 Y + (T + s\tau)\, DY + (s + \alpha)\, Y + A \qquad \text{(A6.3)}$$

It is quite plausible that 'regulation introduces a cycle into the path of output which was not there before regulation' (Allen, 1967, p. 354)

How The Analysis is Affected by Intrusion of A Multiplier–Accelerator Model

Allen (1967) takes up a multiplier–accelerator model at p. 356. It is a much harder nut to crack than the multiplier model. But its upshot is exceptionally salient for us (and indeed Professor Allen puts its capsulation into bold type):

> A mixed proportional and integral stabilization policy, applied to a multiplier–accelerator system after an initial fall in demand, succeeds in correcting fully for the deficiency in demand but at the cost of increased oscillation. (Allen, 1967, p. 361).

He goes on to point out that, 'in the typical situation, the unregulated system has a mildly explosive oscillation in output. A more explosive cycle is left in the system on regulation with a mixed proportional and integral stabilization policy' (Allen, 1967, p. 361). True, *derivative stabilization* is able to blot out induced oscillation. Under derivative stabilization, government purchases (to this extent) are governed by the dynamic law $P = \alpha\,(-DY)$.

Two comments are called for.

1. Derivative stabilization – the concept owes to Phillips (1954) – entails *instantaneous* response by the authorities to departure of output from its equilibrium path. It cannot be surprising that derivative stabilization, eliding lagged response, central to cyclical induction, may cancel oscillations. *And* derivative stabilization is infeasible.

2. Allen cites other obstacles to effective cancellation of oscillations in output – in the context of Phillips's stylized model.

> Even so, only simple exponential lags have been used in the models. A more realistic lag, particularly in the investment function, would be of double or triple exponential form. Phillips shows that both the *existence* of various lags, and the particular *form* taken for each, have considerable and sometimes critical effects on the outcome [citing Phillips, 1957] . . . Multiple lags tend to increase the oscillations left after regulation on the proportional and integral policies and to make the task of derivative policy, in ironing them out, so much the harder (Allen 1967, p. 362).

HOW WICKSELL–POOLE MONETARY AUTHORITIES INDUCE CYCLICAL ACTION (OR WORSE)

Take the evolution of the own rate of return on real assets as autonomous for monetary analysis. And the acceleration of *nominal* aggregate output (ϱ) is to be a function of the deviation of the *real* market-rate (r) from the (real) natural-rate of interest (π).

$$\dot{\varrho} = f(\pi - r) = f(x) \quad [x = \pi - r; f(0) = 0] \tag{A6.4}$$

Under a régime of *open-loop* monetary policy, r evolves substantially independently of x. Then the banking system is not a player in cyclical processes. But, under *closed-loop* control, and in particular under an active (vs an adaptive) Bank-rate régime (see Chapter 3), the banking system (*cum* MA) – monetary authority is important indeed. Then, if the MA displays strong inertia, so that r is sustained on an interval on which it has been 'shocked', the upshot is pro-cyclical; as ϱ increases, the MA pumps more reserves into the banking system to hold down r. Homeostasis is blocked. And in due course the emergency cord (as on a train) will be yanked. The upshot may be a strong, if erratic, oscillation.

Equation (A6.5) describes a Bank-rate régime.

$$\dot{r} = \phi(\varrho) \qquad \phi' > 0 \tag{A6.5}$$

Linearizing,

$$\dot{\varrho} = a(\pi - r) \tag{A6.6}$$

$$\dot{r} = \mu\varrho \tag{A6.7}$$

Write $\pi - r = x$. Using equations (A6.6) and (A6.7),

$$\dot{\varrho} = 0 + ax \tag{A6.8}$$

$$\text{Trace} = 0$$
$$\text{DET} = -\mu a$$

$$\dot{r} = \mu\varrho + 0 \tag{A6.9}$$

For $\mu < 0$, noting that $a > 0$, the system exhibits saddlepoint instability (or stability, as you may). Nor is this specification absurd: an MA committed to 'stabilizing' *nominal* interest rates (perhaps because of irresistable political pressure) imposes $\mu < 0$(!).

For $\mu > 0$, the system's phase portrait is a circle. Then real Bank rate and nominal-income acceleration are thrust into a fixed orbit around their 'normal' values. This possibility symbolizes the ultimate futility of orthodox stabilization-notions.

Remark

Peter Skott, who has made a number of valuable criticisms of an earlier draft, writes that the portrait is an ellipse. The exhausted author replied that a circle, after all, is a degenerate ellipse!

Note

1. Professor Hayek is among the 'Wicksellians'. Even a casual reading of his *Monetary Theory and the Trade Cycle* (1933/1966) makes that obvious. I explain in this book, and in my 1988 one, why I disagree with Professor Hayek, whom I keenly admire. But perhaps the gap between Wicksellian and Ricardian positions (including mine) can be spanned. Booms may frequently be triggered by abnormally-high multiples for earnings streams in asset markets (i.e. by abnormally-high p/e factors); and such episodes may typically induce abnormally low p/e factors when over-optimism collapses, when greed is replaced by fear. My point is that such positions are unlikely to hinge on the banking system (see Chapter 7 below). Still, a skeleton of a market-rate/natural-rate hypothesis *does* survive the analysis I prefer.

7 Implications of Empirical Properties of a Hypothetical Open Economy

7.1 DATA CHANGES IN AN OPEN ECONOMY

The implications of a menu of plausible changes in data in an open economy for trade/business fluctuations are inconsistent with systemic cyclical motion; and surely with *monetary* motivation of cyclical motion.

7.1.1 An Open Economy

Trade is normally to be balanced. GNP may be roughly equal to GDP: about 20 per cent of GDP is claimed by foreign investors, and is balanced by our revenues from holdings abroad. Exports/imports normally are 35 per cent of GDP. The properly calculated savings rate (encompassing company saving) is 8 per cent. Real monetary stocks are equal to 5 per cent of real wealth, but are excluded from perceived social wealth. Government purchases of goods and services may normally absorb 20 per cent of GDP; as well as 20 per cent of imports. Adding in transfers, including interest on public debt, government expenditures are 40 per cent of GDP. And the public sector borrowing requirement (PSBR) is normally 3 per cent of GDP.

7.1.2 Some Rather Large Changes in Data

Changes in demand for monetary stocks are easily accommodated by small changes in relative interest rates. Or Euro-dollars or foreign currencies may be obtained, along with cover: necessary adjustments in securities prices and yields are indiscernible: huge global markets effortlessly ingest these transactions. Increased asset purchases by our central bank (assumed to offer claims against itself satisfiable by its fiat issue) may be harder to brush off; but it is implausible that such transactions should affect real yields obtainable on a global network.

Say that the savings rate increases by one quarter, to 10 per cent; and that half of savings are company savings. And company saving increases 1:1 with planned capital expenditures: cf retained earnings. Five-eighths of the gap is closed this way (cf 1.25/2.00 = 5/8).

Household savings concern consumer durable acquisitions as well as 'paper'. And the consumer durable idea is quite diffuse. One may build up chess and music skills – purchasing books, discs and instruments as well as personal instruction; or gardens may be landscaped. Say that such plans absorb 0.35/2.00 of the initial gap, leaving a gap to be filled in equal to 0.4 per cent of GNP. The mortage market will absorb enough savings to bring provisionally explained absorption of savings to 9.75/10.00 of total planned savings. There remains a shortfall of aggregate demand, in a simple Keynesian sense, of 0.25 per cent of GDP – probably insignificant statistically. This may require an improvement in the trade balance of (0.25) ÷ (35) × 100 per cent, approximately 0.7 per cent, less than onequarter of 1 per cent of GDP.

Now consider a *50* per cent decline in planned capital formation: capital formation is to decline to 4 per cent, from 8 per cent, of initial GDP. But this suggests lower company saving on reasoning parallel with the argument just above. Allowing for the companion increase in disposable income (cf higher dividends; the underlying consumption theory is very coarse), the aggregate demand shortfall is cut to 2 per cent of initial GDP. A shift in the durability of household expenditure may close the gap by another one-half of 1 per cent. (Consumer expenditure *must* be distinguished from consumption.)

Reflecting on the putative shift in durability of household expenditures, a surprisingly large portion of household saving imitates Robinson Crusoe's: decisions to save are substantially ones to spend on durables; decisions to reduce fresh accumulation are to that extent ones to reduce saving, and are accomplished by switching expenditure towards less durable products.

So the shortfall in aggregate demand is cut to 1.5 per cent of GDP.

The mortgage market becomes easier as flows of financial saving seek outlets (or sellers of 'old' assets to savers look for outlets for sales proceeds). The mortgage market's fringe of unsatisfied borrowers may become accommodated, cutting the aggregate demand gap to 1.25 per cent of initial GDP.

A combination of import substitution with more exporting of an order of magnitude of 1.25/35, accomplished if exports alone increase by 3.7 per cent, looks feasible – cutting the shortfall to 1.2 per cent of GDP.

Our capital goods industries will actively seek foreign orders, while making price concessions encouraging domestic planners to 'front load' capital spending programmes. Residual pressure of the massive contraction of the propensity to invest is miniscule.

Keynesian potentials for business fluctuations in open economies seem insubstantial. We must look elsewhere.

7.2 POTENTIAL CYCLICAL ACTION

First consider some ideas organized around variance/covariance matrices. How heavy a load can be borne by the coordinative mechanisms? Thus if demand shifts between sectors are typically erratically large, substantial numbers may be laid off without being reabsorbed elsewhere for some time, forcing the unemployed to cut back spending. And there may be sharp falls in profits of the capital goods sector if accumulation programmes are curtailed in favour of planned liquid asset accumulation and foreign investment, while price, and other, rigidities, in the foreign trade sector may block offsetting stimuli. But perturbations of this sort *large enough to drive business cycles* (as against isolated episodes) seem implausible.

Now consider small open economies (SOEs). Shifts in demands for a SOE's exports easily explain fluctuations in its well-being: if terms of trade shift adversely, planters cut back offers to the service sector, etc. The transmission process is quite transparent, but it lies outside the domain of either monetary motivation or the multiplier-accelerator.

7.2.1 Monetary/Fiscal Sources of Real Fluctuations(?)

So far possibilities for systemic business fluctuations look flimsy. Only the SOE survives as a candidate; and the results squeezed out of it pivot on *real* trade theory (and are well supported by data generated by the nineteenth-century American economy). We now probe more deeply into potential monetary/financial sources of that portion of trade fluctuation that cannot be explained by factors such as vibration of export demand.

The first scenario pivots on *credit*; monetary residues are not critical. An economy's saving rate may increase on an interval on which investment prospects look rosy. Savings readily flow into new, sometimes grandiose, projects. Substantial portions of required finance are loan capital, much of it from abroad: trade deficits incident to new construction, and higher consumption of sectors benefiting from intensified demand, are readily financed. And some wages shoot up.

7.2.2 Expectations are Falsified!

Many agents, responding to sudden collapse of estimated net asset positions, drastically cut back consumption and postpone expenditures on durables. Some fail financially; and their failures may sink their creditors. The economy must reconstitute itself, cutting out segments that have gone dead. And the chastened economy may be burdened by heavy foreign debt.

Reconstruction and reconstitution confront inertia. And the banking system, contributing heavily to the upswing, is likely both to exacerbate the downswing and impede recovery: its efforts to contract its credit may lead to fear of chain bankruptcies, if not to the real thing. And weakened balance sheets stimulate demand for and contract the supply of intermediation. Lenders will seek gilts; debtors will siphon off receipts into debt retirement. Foreigners too will shy away: bridging finance is repelled, not attracted; financial feedback channels amplify contractive forces. It is a short step to disorganization of goods markets.

Specializing the argument to a closed economy, envisage an expansion of the industrial sector that has attracted savings flows, probably through bank mediation. Profit margins plausibly increase; and non-industrial sectors plausibly experience drains of available inputs. Attempts to replenish such drains, leading to higher factor prices, induce incremental *effort*. And interest rates increase – as will equity prices, if the episode is triggered by expectations of markedly higher net income streams (expectations that may not be justified). True, in an open economy, capital inflow deters higher interest rates, especially if aliens share fevered expectations.

(The industrial sector does not justify the confidence inducing its expansion; much investment proves misplaced. Share prices fall. There are failures. Banks may become shaky. Many who made commitments to the industrial sector, *comme* capitalists or specialized workers, cannot fulfill plans to buy goods and services.)

Now write a comparable script for an *open economy*. Trade deficits accompany initial capital inflow. And prices of complementary domestic resources increase. But the projects prove duds. The economy is left with a debt overhang. Restoration of financial equilibrium requires that terms of trade worsen until necessary capital outflow (debt repayment), dual to trade surpluses, is generated. 'Excess debt' must be discharged.

Crises are typically provoked by financial, not monetary, factors. Balance sheet deterioration and/or widespread pressure for debt liquidation may constrict the arteries of financial circulation. As firms are paid by clients, they divert resulting credits to their creditors. Nor do creditors, dunning for payment, plan to relend inflows. If creditors are *banks*, there is an incidental fall, perhaps a large one, in monetary balances. Resulting free falls of prices further damage debtors' balance sheets . . . The script has points in common with the American crash *circa* 1931.[1]

Closing up discussion of *crises in open economies*, foreign creditors can be as exigent, and as susceptible to panic, as domestic ones. But contraction normally engenders spontaneous forces working to improve the trade balance and to induce concomitant inflows of *liquides* – perhaps subject to long lags. If the process confines itself to well-marked bounds, it is easy to glimpse the financial counterpart to cyclical patterns of aftershocks of real quakes in properly open economies.

7.2.3 How Plausible are the Scripts?

The charts and tables assembled in section 7.3 suggest that natural vibration around trend lines dominates other sources of data change. And damping looks very strong indeed. Economies appear to evolve staidly, unless their governments turn to wild play.

What is the proper role of the MA in further damping spontaneous vibration? It is subsumed by the proposition that the MA's field of action is *paper*: the MA neither absorbs nor supplies real resources; it directly operates on quasi-monetary government securities. The supreme riddle of macro-economics is wrapped in the enigma controlling interaction of official operations in paper assets (obligating the issuer to pay paper printed on the state's presses and strictly barren otherwise) with immense, complex real processes, associated, in proper economic theory, with own yields. Much of what passes for Keynesian economics, and all the economics of the bourse, the press and the politicians, claims that the paper shuffle dominates the economy studied more soberly by micro-economic theorists.

7.3 STUDY OF SOME DATA

(See especially Governors of the Federal Reserve System, Washington, DC, Federal Reserve *Bulletin*, 74 (12), (December 1988), *Viz*. Financial and Business Statistics, Federal Reserve *Bulletin*, 1988, pp. A1–A69.)

Consider orders of magnitude of Federal Reserve credit, changes in Federal Reserve credit, base money, nominal GNP, etc.

These are some of the conclusions drawn from Table 7.1 (based on Table 1.21, Federal Reserve *Bulletin* 1988, p. A13). The contribution of the banking system to credit taken and changes in credit taken is modest even if open-economy potential is ignored. Furthermore, high elasticities of substitution between say IBM and Citicorp paper imply that much expansion and contraction of bank balance sheets results from substitution of bank liabilities (non-bank liabilities) for non-bank (bank) ones. Such dilation and contraction may not mirror 'real action'. Thus see the huge financements of leveraged buyouts (LBOs) – paper shuffles in which banks often are pivotal.

Continuing analysis may attractively evolve along the following lines. Take net bank lending as an annualized flow. Then extract the trend from the data, obtaining deviations of bank lending from trend – doubtless highly positively covariant with comparable money growth statistics.

Table 7.1 US money stock, bank assets and GNP (December 1987)

Variables		*$bn*
M2	*Money stock*	2,901
L	*Money stock*	4,327
Loans and securities of US commercial banks		2,223
US GNP (from Table 2.16, p. A51) 1987		4,526.7

Source:
Federal Reserve *Bulletin*, 74 (12) (December 1988).

(Over short intervals, small deviations generate huge annualized flow-rates. Cf a 1 per cent contraction in total bank lending accomplished over one week. This imparts a truly massive shock to the markets.)

Compare resulting orders of magnitude with those of GDP, for example, and deviations from *its* trend. The upshot seems devastating for the work of Dennis Robertson and the earlier J. M. Keynes: their work relies on strong effects on prices, profits, investment expenditures, etc. of deviations from trend of bank lending (see Chapter 3 and, especially, Chapter 9).

Tables 7.2 and 7.3 supply more substantial data; and confirm the initial conjecture that changes in bank data cannot account for much of the vibration in prices and outputs that is observed.

Table 7.4 (albeit sketchily) evokes the ease with which expansion and dilation of domestic sources of credit is offset by foreign borrowing and lending in open economies. Not only are changes in bank lending dwarfed; so is domestic financial mediation in general (albeit not so consummately).

Table 7.2 Funds raised in US credit markets ($bn)

	1985	*1986*	*1987*	*1988 (1H extrapolated)*
1 Total net borrowing by domestic non-financial sectors	846.3	830.6	680.6	695.3
2 Raised by US Government	223.6	215.0	143.8	156.9
5 Raised by domestic non-financial sectors	622.7	615.6	536.7	538.4
31 Total net borrowing by financial sectors	198.3	297.2	285.2	218.8
32 US government-related part of line 31	101.5	178.1	168.3	106.1

Source:
Federal Reserve *Bulletin*, 74 (12) (December 1988) Table 1.57, p. 442.

Notes:
1. The table's lines are numbered to facilitate ready reference to the Federal Reserve *Bulletin*, Table 1.57.
2. Line 31 entails a double count: some of these fundings were placed abroad. Federal Reserve *Bulletin*, Table 1.58, p. A43, the source of Table 7.3 below, confirms this conjecture.

Table 7.3 Direct and indirect sources of funds to credit markets

		1983	*1984*	*1985*	*1986*	*1987*	*1988 (H2 extrapolated)*
1	Total advances in credit markets to domestic non-financial users	546.8	750.8	846.3	830.6	680.6	695.5
10	Advances to foreign borrowers	23.7	57.9	62.3	97.8	62.5	129.4
	Private financial intermediation						
20	Credit market funds advanced by private financial institutions	394.7	581.0	569.8	746.3	552.7	590.5
21	Commercial bank component of line 20	144.3	168.9	186.3	194.8	136.3	153.8
21a	First differences: line 21: (1984) − (1983) = 24.6	–	24.6	17.4	8.5	−58.5	17.5
	Private domestic non-financial investors						
33	Direct lending	150.9	169.2	282.9	86.9	176.8	104.5
39	Deposits and currency	227.8	325.4	220.9	285.0	162.0	206.3
47	Line 33 + line 39	378.7	494.6	503.8	372.0	338.8	310.8
1a	First differences: line 1	–	204.0	95.5	−15.7	−150.0	14.9
21a	Line 21a repeated	–	24.6	17.4	8.5	−58.5	17.5

Source:
Federal Reserve *Bulletin*, 74 (12) (December 1988) Table 1.58, p. A43.

Table 7.4 US international transactions ($US bn)

		1985	*1986*	*1987*
1	Current account balance	−115.1	−138.8	−154.0
11	Change in US government assets, other than official reserve assets (increase = (–))	−2.8	−2.0	1.2
12	Change in US government official reserve assets (increase = (–))	−3.9	0.3	9.1
22	Change in foreign official assets in the US (increase = (+))	−1.2	35.5	45.0
28	Change in foreign private assets in the US (increase = (+))	131.1	185.7	166.5

Sources:
Federal Reserve *Bulletin*, 74 (12) (December 1988) Table 3.10, p. A53; Table 3.21, p. A62.

Figures 7.1, 7.2 and 7.3, based on Banca Commerciale Italiana materials, solidify the argument.

Figure 7.2 emphatically shows that bank balance sheets are but modestly important in the global scheme of things; and are becoming less and less important. Indeed the BCI work understates the *total financial asset* variable: enormous Euro-market positions are *not* encompassed. And the materials do not directly show how easy it is for credit flows to be reoriented across the global network, counter-acting modest domestic pressures described by Tables 7.1, 7.2 and 7.3.

Figure 7.3 tells the dramatic Italian story: as the Italian financial sector rapidly becomes highly sophisticated, Banca d'Italia must needs lose its grip on relevant financial magnitudes. And then there is the Year of Europe, 1992.

7.4 CONCLUDING REMARKS, BASED ON THE DISPLAYED DATA

Wicksellians, Marshall, Keynes (in the *Treatise*), Robertson *et al.* rely heavily on the dual to bank money expansion, i.e. bank credit expansion, as a motor driving financial influence on the real economy. Irving Fisher's work supplies another example: cf his monetary theory of the trade cycle, exposited by Makinen (1977) and by Friedman and Schwartz (1982, Chapter 10). The data sharply rebuke efforts to put expansion and contraction of bank credit up front; and indeed discourage reliance on aggregate domestic credit flow changes to explain important fluctuations. For one thing, the open economy induces the equivalent of wave cancellation. (See Chapters 3, 6 and 9).

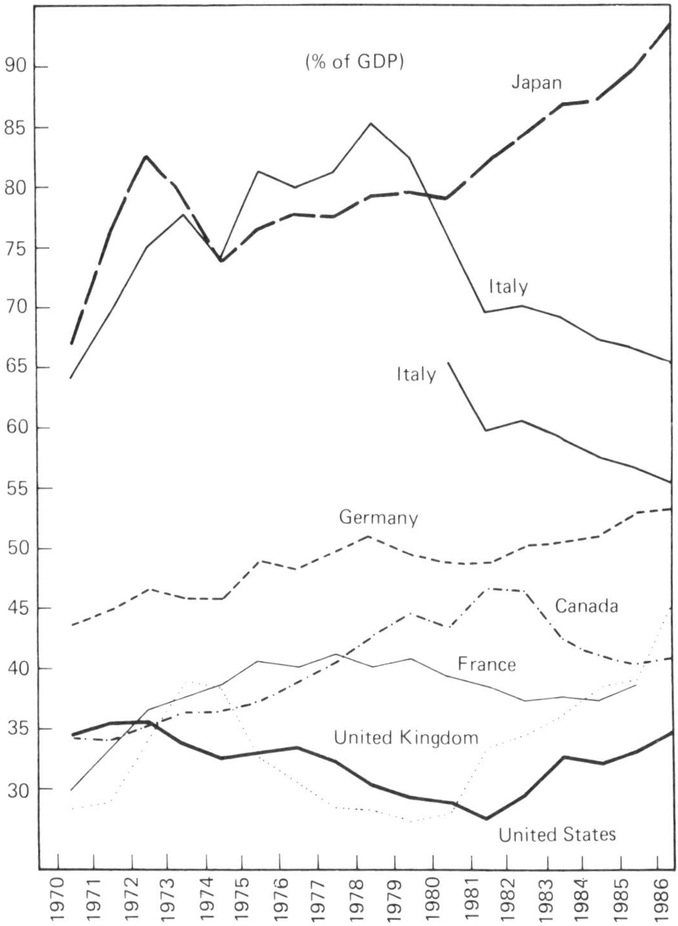

Figure 7.1 Bank deposits as a ratio of GDP: an international comparison

Source: Banca Commerciale Italiana, *Monetary Trends*, 37 (July 1988) Figure 4, p. 8

Notes for Figure 7.1

1. *Source*: Calculations based on data from IMF, International Financial Statistics.
2. *United States*: American commercial banks, Edge Act corporations and branches of foreign banks; *Japan*: all banks, Sogo banks, Shinkin banks, Norinchukin Bank and Shoko Chukin Bank; *Italy*: commercial banks; *Germany*: consolidated data on commercial banks, state banks, regional and local banks, private banks, specialized banks, savings banks, cooperative banks, mortgage banks, postal banking system and supra-regional

credit institutions; *Canada*: chartered banks (discontinuity of statistics in 1981); *France*: consolidated data on registered banks, banking establishments, people's banks, Banque Française du Commerce Extérieur, National Agricultural Credit Bank and mutual credit banks (discontinuity of statistics in 1977); *United Kingdom*: U.K. monetary sector (discontinuity of statistics in 1975, in 1981 and in 1983).

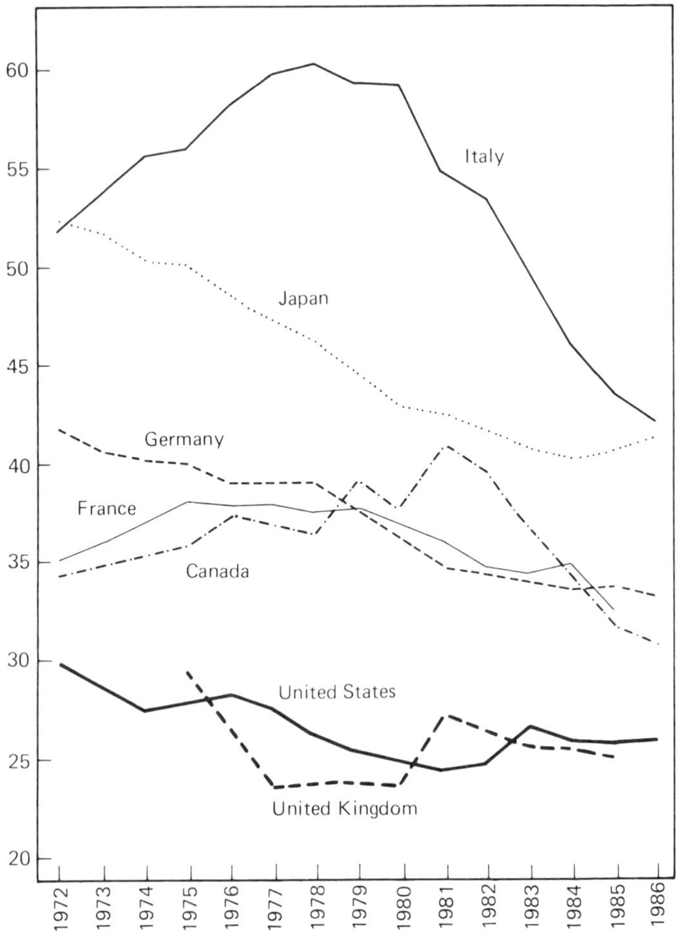

Figure 7.2 Ratio of bank deposits to financial assets: an international comparison — converted to %

Source: Banca Commerciale Italiana, *Monetary Trends*, 37 (July 1988, Figure 7, p. 13)

Notes for Figure 7.2

1. *Bank Deposits*: IMF, *International Financial Statistics* (source).
2. *Financial Assets*: domestic, excludes shares.

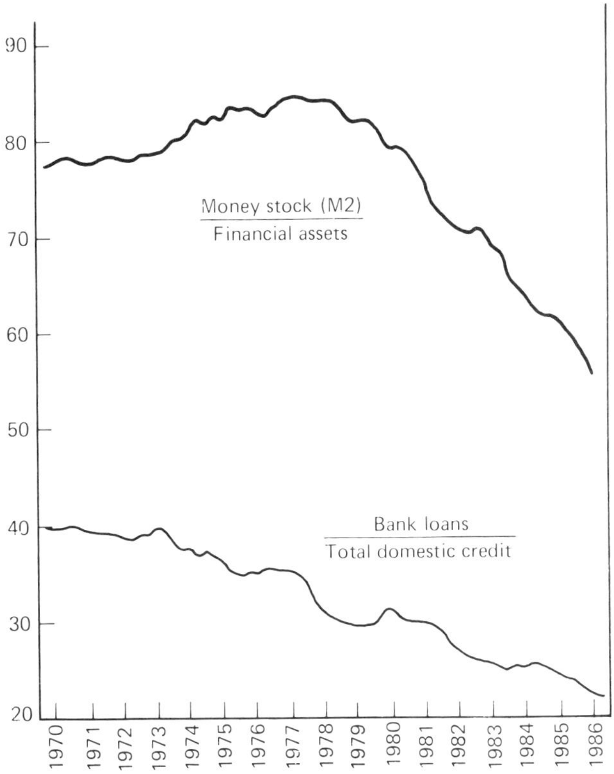

Figure 7.3 Money (M2) and bank loans in relation to total financial flows (Italy, 1970–86) — converted to %

Source: Banca Commerciale Italiana, *Monetary Trends*, 37 (July 1988, Figure 3, p. 7)

Notes for Figure 7.3

The ratios are calculated from seasonally adjusted data.

1. *Financial Assets* are those of the non-state sector: domestic shares are excluded.
2. *Bank loans* include both lire and foreign currency loans.

Note

1. The text's story entails an interesting problem in *finance* in the special sense of the word studied in Chapter 9. Consider mechanics of a *finance* perplex corollary to the text.

   Install a lag – it can be short – between an agent's expenditures on inputs and receipts from sales of outputs fabricated from the inputs. And return to the script in which aggregate expenditures contract so that producers' expectations are disappointed. The most pessimistic producers lose the least. And all losses must be *financed*. Nor need attempts to reduce indebtedness succeed overall (see Chapter 9). This is all that needs to happen to block *that*. Each firm reckons to divert part of its proceeds into debt repayment, imposing losses on others; and households, flogged on by dunning banks, try to reduce debt in the same way. Output declines cumulatively – and indeed aggregate debt *may* fall as working capital shrinks.

8 Some Theory of Innovated Open Financial Networks

The theory incorporates ongoing denationalization of money; and along one of its azimuths, fully developed in Chapter 2, fluctuations in values of national currencies are a mere sideshow: see the extended ECU standard. And it explains how Euro-market dealings may continuously reconstruct virtual currency positions so that switches in asset preferences are accommodated by balance sheet reconstruction – through the agency of dealers, including 'speculators'.

Consider a general portfolio analysis in an amorphous financial space in which whatever is *money* is operationally indistinguishable from many other financial substances. There is a telling analogy to securities market action. Forward and futures transactions, together with options writing, affect virtual supplies independently of the firm's board, comparable to a central bank. Spontaneous market action swamps out or offsets official policy and freely crosses national borders, often with unobservable effects. What if a real British asset is monetized by purchase of an option to put the asset for a stated quantity of US dollars? Or a big London bank may alter its loan portfolio in order to offset an open short position in US dollars (USD) created by accommodation to a global increase in demand for USD sensitive positions. Or consider this. Financial houses o'er the world can satisfy increased French demand for liquidity: options may be written, virtually guaranteeing French franc indemnification of French holders; and indemnification may be *virtual*: payments media may be foreign currency equivalents to French Franc-denominated amounts. And banks may raise capital by selling equities in France.

So ongoing innovations sap the ability of central banks to control credit flows and money supply within their jurisdictions. Banks anywhere can issue *A*-dollar monetary liabilities for borrowers' notes; covering resulting open positions by selling securities, including their shares, in *A*'s security markets. Nor is that all. Gigantic multinational companies (MNCs) will in time go into banking overtly;

they are quasi-bankers now, as I explained in (1986, chapter 11). Their obligations are backed by vast global holdings, including highly liquid receivables; their global dealings create natural hedges. When these ideas are taken beyond the banking principle, all possibilities for recognizably monetary sources of business fluctuation dissipate.

8.1 SPECIALIZATIONS OF THE THEORY

8.1.1 Effects of Changes in 'Local' Base Money Growth

Consider the aftermath of a spurt in growth of *B*-dollar base money. Increases in 'local' money supply incited by base money growth will be spontaneously countered, at least in part. Options entitling holders to *E*-dollar payments will run off without being replaced or will be closed out prematurely. The following transaction, not entailing deals in underlying stocks, is revealing. Holders of options to put assets for *E*-dollars will trade them for options to put assets for *i*-dollars, thus extinguishing the *E*-dollar puts.

This conclusion can be reached slightly differently. Whatever are called *monetary* *E*-dollar-denominated assets comprise a small, perhaps miniscule, part of the proper domain of discourse; and distinctions of monetary from non-monetary subsets may be chimerical when all assets flexibly yield interest. Nor is that all. Say that virtual monetary stocks (selected Euro-currency holdings, *E*-dollars or equivalents to *E*-dollars, etc.) are initially equal in mass to conventionally-defined *E*-dollar monetary stocks. Say that these stocks have been growing at 10 per cent p.a. The MA steps up growth of 'conventional' stocks to 15 per cent. If virtual money stocks now increase at only 5 per cent, the aggregate expansion rate stays put.

8.1.2 Innovated Response to Asset Preference Shifts

In the theory, increased liquidity preference of agents of the *j*th economy is accommodated by small increases in spreads obtainable by agents (anywhere) prepared to sell liquid *j*-dollar-denominated (or guaranteed) claims (perhaps against themselves) for illiquid ones. The settlement medium is immaterial.

The market's responses may defy conventional analysis: put options may be written on i-dollar assets held by agents of the jth economy, perhaps monetizing their assets in a j-dollar measure. Or i-economy agents may purchase calls on j-dollar assets, simultaneously buying put options entitling them to convert j-dollar profits (or, if they stand for delivery, proceeds of security sales) into i-dollars on stated terms. Speculators easily absorb resulting pressure.

In a small open economy, in which agents may mostly hold foreign currency, changes in liquidity preferences are accommodated by switches within (x_{ij}), a vector of i-dollar securities held by j-agents $(i = 1, 2, \ldots, j-1, j+1, \ldots)$.

8.1.3 Deepening the Security Market: Example

(a) *Applying the Theory*

A company's cost of capital may be measured by the price of its shares relative to its 'true' earnings potential – ignoring subtleties mandated by Modigliani and Miller: the proper *res* is the value of the company's capital, however financed. And the share price is sensitive to autonomous speculative motions capable of producing bubbles or implosions.

As for the *supply of shares*,

1. The supply of shares is responsive to *demand*: demand vibrations affect new issue, in part *via* changes in debt/equity ratios.
2. Forward and futures transactions, together with options writing, affect virtual supplies independently of the actions of the firm's board, comparable to a central bank.
3. If the supply of stock (cf the *underlying commodity*) increases, the equilibrium share price plausibly falls. But, as in monetary models, quasi-issue may be negatively correlated with the supply of underlying shares. (We elide disposition of proceeds of stock sales.)

Consider two corollaries to point 3. (1) Projecting the analysis onto open-economy theory, j-dollar securities may be issued by the rth authority or agent. Positive and negative position will be taken across the whole spectrum of 'issue' so that each agent's balance sheet displays a hodge-podge of 'denominations'. (2) An increase in supply of underlying stock makes it easier to sustain short positions: danger of delivery squeeze is abated.

(b) *Financial Denationalization*

The representative agent contracts for liabilities (obtains 'resources') in various measures and arranges for cover like agents with short commodity positions. The underlying stock includes government debt as well as central bank liabilities: delivery squeeze peril is exiguous. So monetary authorities cannot exercise control over the volumes of locally-denominated liquid assets (liabilities) in their jurisdictions.

In the model, banks' assets and liabilities are written up in any number of monies of account. True, *E*-dollar obligations of *E*-banks may be preferred: *E*-banks are apt to have privileged access to *E*'s central bank. But Lloyds Bank can obtain overdraft facility from Chase (perhaps as part of a swap) so that it can surely meet US dollar demands on sight. In the upshot, the stock of money in Economy *E* cannot be properly defined in terms of liquid liabilities of selected *E* institutions, expressed in *E*-dollars.

(c) *Currency Competition*

Currency competition – or, better, competition between metrics – is pervasive in the theory – and will be in life. Why 'competition between *metrics*'? Debts expressed in the *i*th metric (money of account) can be discharged by *j*-dollar tenders; an economy can be *i*-dollarized without switching to the *i*-dollar as a payments medium. The upshot shatters aspirations of monetary authorities to manage their currencies: e.g., liquid holdings in the *k*th economy cannot properly be assigned an exclusive *k*-dollar metric; and options dealings transform apparent *k*-dollar holdings into virtual *j*-dollar ones in ways that cannot be tracked.

(d) *Quasi-banking*

(See 1986, Chapter 11.)

Banking functions become distributed over a continuous field rather than clustering at nodes. But quasi-banks imitate the banks of orthodox theory in distorting their balance sheets in order to supply liquidity services (for a fee). Again, the monetary dimension of financial intermediation crumbles beyond the banking principle.

Options markets illustrate quasi-banking. *B* can monetize *A*'s assets, in any measure, by selling *A* a put option. The option has at least two central implications. (1) Money supply is then ill-defined even in closed economies. (2) In an innovated open economy, agents' operations cannot be properly assorted by 'economy of origin'. For one thing, options and futures contracts need not be settled in any particular currency: a *j*-dollar option contract may be settled by an *i*-dollar tender, or by a cocktail-tender.

(e) *Applying the Quasi-banking Model: Money and Finance Evolve on a Featureless Plane*

Say that there is a basic shift of currency preferences against the *E*-dollar.

The Orthodox Scenario Specialists must take in stock (of *E*-dollars). They will lower the price (in an *i*-dollar measure) they are prepared to pay for *E*-dollars; they will widen buy–sell spreads for *E*-dollar transactions.

The Innovated Scenario Say that demand shifts towards *i*-dollar assets. Under quasi-banking, the effective supply of highly liquid *E*-dollar assets correspondingly shrinks, with some adjustment of spreads. And an increase in the supply of 'conventional' *E*-dollars induces contraction of *E*-dollar options writing; just as contraction of supplies of *E*-dollar monetary balances, however defined, stimulates quasi-issue.

(*De facto* reserve stocks far exceed conventional monetary bases. Government debt and high quality company securities, including readily marketable shares, are viable quasi-banking reserves.)

Quasi-banking in Future/Beyond the Banking Principle A proper theory of an innovated economy may elide banks. Once regulatory obstructions are cleared away, issuers of short-term liquid obligations do not expand and contract their balance sheets in discrete steps, responding to intermittent official stimuli; instead they continuously expand and contract in profit seeking response to stimuli received from the market. Money supply evolves in a closed loop. And *securitization* makes a wide gamut of assets indistinguishable from a monetary standpoint: compound claims to *many* mortgages are as intrinsically liquid as a claim against a fully reserved (and so a fictional) intermediary.

(f) *Financial Denationalization Encore*

In an open *j*th economy, various *i*-dollar claims ($i \neq j$) freely circulate alongside *j*-dollar ones; metrics are freely elected. Hayek (1976) shows that governments, jealous of seigneurage profits, systematically obstruct spontaneous evolution of monetary modalities, including denationalization of money, so as to stimulate demand for official money.

In the theory's economy, French francs may be borrowed in the form of French 'currency'; and the proceeds directly injected into the British economy. The loan may be repayable in a variety of currencies. Convex combinations of *n* basic vectors are admissable; *n* currencies discharge debt cast up in any number of metrical combinations. A debt denominated in *j*-dollars need not be discharged by a *j*-dollar tender. Nor need currency baskets in the *j*th economy contain *j*-dollars. Mappings from official action to fluctuations in output, and in other important variables, become very faint. And its is worth repeating that conventional measurements of stocks of *j*-dollars are then deceiving. Holders of *j*-dollars may have *i*-dollar guaranties. They may have bought up options; *j*-dollar holdings may be subordinated to strategies keyed on the *i*-dollar. In the limit, *j*-dollar holdings of '*j*' residents may be open-valued on a *j*-dollar scale and fixed on an *i*-dollar one.

(g) *Speculative and Other Private Sector Intervention in the Money Supply Process*

Perhaps the supply of *j*-dollar-denominated monetary assets – e.g., treasury currency and selected bank liabilities – is less than demand. Wider spreads induce options writers elastically to supply enlarged stocks of monetized *j*-dollar assets – i.e., to write options virtually monetizing a variety of stocks in a *j*-dollar metric. If there has been a *once-over* shift in asset preferences, agents forming expectations rationally, may demand wider spreads as their portfolios become distended. But a bubble will not form: the preference shift is understood to be once and for all. In the innovated model, virtual money supply is endogenous in open and closed systems.

8.2 A PRECIS OF THE THEORY

8.2.1 Money Supply

The 'supply side' of the analysis is amorphous. Portfolio switches are induced by miniscule changes in spreads; elasticities of substitution are high. So energy released by asset preference shifts and central bank action is mostly absorbed within the global financial sector; it does not escape into 'real economic space'. Furthermore the *supply of money* cannot be operationally defined under fully innovated conditions.

8.2.2 The Upshot for the Open Economy

Disequilibrium in *any* asset market may affect balances of payments; and valid channels of influence of asset market shifts or shocks on the real economy include the following.

1. Autonomous speculation many induce foreign exchange rate vibrations, leading to correlated vibration of terms of trade.
2. Net global excess demand for (excess supply of) *j*-dollar-denominated assets may also transmit to terms of trade.
3. Vibrations of real asset preferences (for assets across economies) may communicate to trade balances primarily via effects on terms of trade.

In the theory, free market processes swamp out official sector monetary actions and freely cross national borders, often with unobservable effects. A British purchaser of a put option may monetize a real British asset in a US dollar measure; French franc positions may be converted into virtual Swiss francs by options deals.

Innovations break down the fibre of nationalized money. In the upshot, central banks merely make ripples on surfaces of lakes made up of underlying stocks including government debt. Quantities of monetary, or monetized, assets evolve from spontaneous free market dealing. Since *B* can monetize *A*'s asset in any measure by selling *A* a put option (etc.) monetary disequilibrium is corrected by changes in writers' portfolios in the innovated economy.

8.3 EXEMPLIFICATION OF THE THEORY

8.3.1 The First Example

Bank Alpha sells medium or long-term debentures (unsecured obligations) for *A*-dollars, committing itself to pay *A*-dollar consideration equivalent to a stated ECU-denominated quantity on maturity. The *A*-dollar proceeds are invested in *A*-dollar denominated paper.

So Bank Alpha's book is skewed. It may lay off its ECU exposure by buying options to put *A*-dollar assets for ECU equivalents. Bank Alpha does not seek foreign currency, however; only cover.

8.3.2 A Related Example

Sellers of securities to the *A* central bank deposit the proceeds (central bank drafts) with *A* banks in exchange for ECU-guaranteed claims. If *A* banks buy *A*-dollar assets with the proceeds, their foreign exchange books are unbalanced; so they may lay off the fresh exposure by making options deals. Or they may seek to buy ECU-sensitized securities, offering *A*-dollar bank drafts. Acceptors of such offers may seek to lay off *their* incremental *A*-dollar exposure. Or *A* banks may offer higher deposit rates, enabling them to acquire ECU-sensitized securities: securities dealers will plan to hold higher yielding *A*-dollar deposits, acquired by selling ECU-sensitized securities.

8.3.3 An Assortment of Further Illustrations of the Theory

1. Aliens wish to increase their USD-sensitive positions. Barclays Bank may 'issue' dollar-linked paper. Such issue creates an open short position in American dollars. So the bank may increase lending on which repayment is keyed on the USD; an example is sterling loans calling for repayment in sterling equal in value to a stated USD-denominated amount on the due date. Or it may buy put options, effectively 'dollarizing' some of its assets. Changes in demand for USD thus trigger effects not registered by monetary statistics.

1.1 British banks transform some sterling liability, some of which may be monetary, into USD liability, so to speak at the stroke of a pen. From a portfolio balance standpoint, the banks are now too long sterling and too short USD. They can redeem equity by selling debt, correcting excessive length on the sterling side. And they can lengthen their USD positions by selling equity for USD . . . So far as we have gone, nothing need happen to the dollar/sterling rate.

1.2 Under laissez-faire, British depositors may want to reduce sterling claims in favour of dollar ones. So British banks convert such claims into ones redeemable in USD or in sterling on a guaranteed USD-equivalent basis. Liquid American securities qualify as reserves.

It may be attractive to capitalize the new banking business: since claims can be floated with an attractive spread (due to intensified demand for dollars), 'seigneurage profit' can be capitalized. In the simplest case, British houses will sell shares in the United States.

2. A bank anywhere can 'issue' monetary liabilities in *E*-dollars, covering them by selling long securities, including its shares, in *E*-land, acquiring *E*-dollar assets with the proceeds. *E*-land residents will have simply shifted the structure of their equity holdings – buying obligations of financial intermediaries (reckoned as non-monetary if the institution does not belong to the *E*-land clearing house). In the upshot the influence of the *E*-land central bank on 'its' economy is diluted.

3. Japanese investors acquire vast quantities of American assets, including cheques drawn on American banks, from Japanese exporters. The dollar claims may be sold for ECU-denominated obligations even if they are to be discharged by USD tenders (in an ECU measure). Banks may raise capital by selling shares and long bonds in Britain, Italy, Germany, etc. until their books are evened up.

4. French companies may demand more liquidity. The *liquides* may be denominated in French francs. Guaranties (to indemnify in French franc equivalents) are given by banks everywhere. The banks may raise capital by selling equities in France (a key notion in the study). Or French companies may either make long loans to the banking institutions or sell puts to French agents seeking to increase their liquidity

Beyond the banking principle, the menu of virtually liquid assets is *huge*; economies are saturated with liquidity so that, obviously, it need not be imported.

(Strictly saturation requires that the giro work frictionlessly and asset markets are perfect. It is but a limit point, a useful reference state.)

5. What if Englishmen want to assure dollar values of their assets so that they are left only with risk intrinsic to property ownership? A Belgravia property owner may buy put options. Sellers have shorted the dollar; but they may have vast dollar-sensitized holdings (the options may be sold by IBM or Eastman Kodak).

   (The risks are generated stochastically. One cannot *insure* against falls in sterling the market believes are going to happen. One might then seek a sucker, but not an insurer.)

6. The following instances embellish the theme, *interaction of industrial/commercial with financial modalities*. Label financial counterparts, or duals, to industrial/commercial situations (*F*), and the latter (*I*).

(*I*.1) A European company sells in the United States and buys materials and factor services elsewhere. The company is typically long dollars.
(*F*.1) The company issues dollar-denominated debt, thus balancing its exposure to the dollar.
(*I*.2) A British company regularly imports from the United States. It typically owes dollars.
(*F*.2) The company raises Euro-sterling capital, investing the proceeds in dollars or dollar-guaranteed assets – shortening its sterling position and lengthening its dollar one.
(*F*.3) USA-Ajax floats a huge DM Eurobond issue.
(*I*.3) USA-Ajax diverts its sales towards Germany and switches assets towards investment in German companies or in positions covariant with the DM. Proper evaluation of an agent's *n*-dimensional financial position encompasses her *global* position, including currency-sensitivity of the sort posed by typically selling for DM and buying in a FF metric.
(*F*.4) British portfolio managers (indeed all agents are portfolio managers) seek to increase their dollar exposure.
(*I*.4) British exporters invoice in dollars and retain proceeds in dollar-sensitive forms. (This may put some pressure on the pound, although the British do *not* plan to increase their *monetary* dollar positions.) In an outlying case, Britain could

become 'dollarized' to a degree; it could become attractive to bill *British* clients in dollars. The payments medium would probably be sterling; the nominal quantity of sterling required to satisfy a British debt becomes open, and the dollar equivalent closed.

8.3.4 Concluding Illustration of the Theory

Focus now on implications of the theory for the ability of central banks to control credit flows within their jurisdictions.

The Banque de France, instructed by the Minstre des Finances, seeks to damp down (or choke off) credit flows. Citicorp may barge in. And these are some of the properties of the ambient innovated financial environment. *Non*-central banks may make swaps like those between central banks so that they finesse risks of having to redeem liabilities to make alien tenders at short notice; cf swaps between Citicorp and Lloyds Bank. Not that such risks are compellingly important: underlying stocks include mountains of government debt, high-quality corporate bonds and debentures, etc. And in future Citicorp, and many others, will be fully-fledged players on foreign giros. (In the meanwhile, accounts chequeable in France are readily swapped for liquid short-term Citicorp liabilities. There is an analogy to *sweeping* permitting American bank accounts not *de jure* chequeable to be debt-discharge vehicles *de facto*.

Continuing the script, Citicorp massively increases its French lending. It may raise capital in France. Français effectively sell stock to Citicorp for Citicorp shares. Citicorp invests the proceeds of sales of its shares in French franc securities markets – evening up its book.

8.3.5 Generalization of the Illustrations

One principal new idea concerns how a bank anywhere can 'issue' monetary liabilities in *E*-dollars, covering resulting risk by selling long securities, including its shares, in *E* security markets, evening up *E*-dollar exposure on its books. Residents of Economy *E* simply alter the texture of their collective equity portfolio; *inter alia* they buy non-monetary obligations of financial intermediaries.

Another new idea concerns ways in which options and related modalities create and wipe out virtual monetary positions in ways statisticians cannot hope to track.

Implications for the robustness of central bank control are harshly negative. Even now central bankers exercise tenuous, if not exiguous, control over credit emission only through Regulation buttressed by the state. Even now the concept of *money*, as an operationally measurable magnitude, is exiguous. How then can 'money' drive the business cycle?

8.4 SOME FOLLOW-UP MATERIAL

1. *MNCs beyond central banking* IBM's balance sheet is titanic. One envisages link-ups between banks and industrial companies leading to utile buttressing of bank balance sheets. (Chapter 2 discusses the Italian debate over such link-ups.) Or, along vaguely nineteenth-century lines, IBM might conduct banking, or quasi-banking, operations, accepting drafts on itself by way of granting credit. Obligations would be backed by its vast global holdings, some almost perfectly liquid.
2. *Alien banks intrude on the MA domestic control efforts* Barclays Bank easily attracts Italian funds by paying over the market for deposits and lending out placements as they flow in. Attempts by Banca d'Italia to restrain lending are sharply impeded.

   Comparable closed-economy countervailance is well known; but operations in Euro-currency markets, scattered o'er the world, are often impossible to monitor.
3. *Underlying stocks* Analogies to forward markets in commodities are very attractive. Divorce of positions in actual (underlying) stocks from options positions, for example, is complete: recall how a Belgravia real estate holder sensitizes his position to the dollar.
4. *Acquiring Cover* Banks can probably obtain cover more cheaply through options deals than equity and long-debt sales. And the nature of the exposure being covered is ill-understood; the controlling logic follows.

When Chase 'dollarizes' a Dutch position, it is *not* betting against the dollar. Forecastable events in efficient markets are fully reflected in existing quotations (including those for forward dealing); cover is sought only relative to unforeseeable events. So when holders of vast amounts of dollar-sensitive assets sell put options to holders of non-dollar assets who seek to make their holdings more dollar-sensitive, they are *not* selling the dollar short. They are slightly reducing their positive sensitivity to a more or less random increase in the dollar rate(s), for a price. So stochastic properties of portfolios relative to alternative mixes of currency-sensitivity are highly mutable – with dire implications for prospects of effective control by central banks.

8.5 FINAL GENERALIZATIONS BASED ON THE THEORY

The theory implies that general price levels, as now conceived, may be indeterminate. And the drastic diminution of the rôle of monetary authority implied by the theory further reduces monetary motivation of cycles in business activity: after all MAs have been shown to be the prime monetary movers of such fluctuation.

8.5.1 Behaviour of the General Price Level

The study shows that the virtual quantity of money is not feasibly measurable: no proper '*M*' is operationally definable. Monetary theories of general price levels become empty; and tabular standards more interesting, especially since received notions of the general price level are based on an inept choice of measure (see Chapter 2).

8.5.2 Free Banking and Our Theory

Our conclusions are now to be passed through a prism supplied by Kurt Schuler (1988). Schuler and his sources fail to attain the theoretical pinnacle neared by Wallace (1983) because they fail to see that 'choice of measure' is different from 'choice of money'. They confuse money of account (ontologically equivalent to tons and metres) with *property*, a subset of which may be called *money*. One does not own a yard; one owns financial substances, as one owns a yard of cloth. Upon choice of measure being properly solved, as it is in an extensive tabular standard, entitlements of creditors are unambiguously *real*; *stability of the general price level* reduces to the degree of depreciation or appreciation of various financial substances.

Schuler *et al.*, in the wake of Hayek (1976), centre on competing currencies, including private ones. And, since obstructions to competition are massive, and the concept's feasibility arguable, the resulting literature has not led to a clear result, especially since contributors tend to be obsessed with *privatization*, pro and con. It suffices to refocus the argument the way Einaudi (1937) does to obtain clear-cut results of the sort displayed in Chapter 2. Our rubric is 'MAs and Business Fluctuations Redux'.

8.5.3 MAs and Business Fluctuations Redux

(See Chapters 6 and 9 for quite exhaustive study of cyclical effects of MA action.)

The theory exhibited by Chapter 8 so diminishes the rôle of monetary authorities that it is pointless to search for niggling pro-cyclical consequences of MA action in its context. But two loose ends are usefully tied up in Chapter 8. One, concerning the nagging perplex of potential crises of liquidity as far back as the reign of Tiberius (in AD 33), is consigned to a note to Chapter 8. The other is extracted from the *Free vs Official Reserve Management* controversy largely tangential to this study. Our interest is in possibilities of perturbation induced by MA action even if such action is utile overall.

> Selgin (1988) answers a question that has long nagged free-banking theorists: can free banks acting in unison imitate a central banking system and inflate? He shows [*sic*?] that they cannot because all would suffer a greater chance of losing reserves and going bankrupt, even if the system as a whole does not lose reserves. Under central banking, however, a single entity controls all the ultimate reserves of the system . . . Diffuse ownership of reserves under free banking allows the clearing system to generate signals (namely reserve losses or gains) that inform banks whether the public's desire to hold their liabilities is increasing or decreasing. Central banks, in common with other kinds of central planning, lack such information and hence are prone to make big mistakes instead of just the little ones that entrepreneurs in a free market often do . . . This thesis is an application to banking of the Austrian School argument about the difficulty inherent in socialist economic calculation.
>
> Schuler (1988, p. 10)

Chapter 11 shows that this reasoning is strained. More importantly here, we would wish that Schuler centred instead on departure of the (real) rate of interest for money from the 'natural' own rate of return on physical capital – critical for 'Austrian' monetary cycle theory. Monetary authorities provoke such disparities; spontaneous competitive action of banks compels their interest rates to trail the evolution of the cost of capital quite passively. It is not possible for a competitive banking system to induce systematic cyclical action; such a banking system would, of course, receive stimuli that it might convert into pulses inducing pro-cyclical action – but it would not be an active agent. Monetary theories of the business cycle must needs be theories of MA action.

The style of Schuler's argument admirably suits our purposes: he argues, in essence, that the very coherence of centralized control may make it ineffective. The extract can be restructured so that it is an exercise in *diffraction*, characteristic of spontaneous economic action and blocking cyclical potential. (True, a spontaneous system is theoretically capable of resonating: even if cycles are virtually impossible, *crises* may occur.)

Note to Chapter 8: A Crisis of Liquidity in Ancient Rome

(See Chapter 10.)

According to Robert Graves, the emperor Tiberius was neurasthenic in the monetary sphere too.

> The informers about this time began to accuse wealthy men of charging more than the legal interest on loans . . . A deputation went to [Tiberius] and pleaded that everyone should be allowed a year and a half to adjust his private finances to conform with the letter of the law, and Tiberius as a great favour granted the request. The result was that all debts were at once called in, and this caused a great shortage of current cash. Tiberius's great idle hoards of gold and silver in the Treasury had been responsible for forcing up the rate of interest in the first place [*sic!*?] and now there was a great financial panic and land-values fell to nothing. Tiberius was eventually forced to relieve the situation by lending the bankers one million gold pieces of public money, without interest, to pay out to borrowers in exchange for securities in land.
>
> Robert Graves, *I Claudius* (London: Penguin, 1953, pp. 314–15), first published in 1934

Reflecting on Graves's (the emperor Claudius's) account, it appears that the emperor unwittingly provoked a crisis he was able to cope with because he anticipated Bagehot's reserve principle. For Schuler this is a mixed bag.

Reducing the substance of Graves's account to the turgid economics of our day, Crown policy called for financial surpluses without corresponding open-market purchases. The policy is said to have drained the liquidity of the private sector, pushing up interest rates. In principle, trade could have been depressed: proceeds could have persistently fallen short of expectations as recipients of payments sought to improve their balance sheets – an anachronous rationale without empirical support; Chapter 10 shows that immense non-monetary precious metal hoards made global shortages of money unlikely even if prices were sticky.

Finley's (1985) account is more favourable to the emperor.

> [A] rather mysterious outbreak occurred in the city of Rome in AD 33, under Tiberius. This crisis, according to a very brief but not very lucid account of Tacitus (*Annals*, 6.16–17) began with a popular outcry against widespread irregularities by the moneylenders, to which they again responded by calling in their loans, again threatening the landed holdings of many respectable men. The emperor intervened with an interest-free loan of one hundred million sesterces for worthy debtors and the excitement soon died down. Tiberius's concern was for 'those whose *dignitas et fama* were threatened'; so was Cicero's in his furious denunciation . . . of debt-relief measures . . . They are an attack on property and the propertied classes . . . but he knows nothing about a threat to economic growth or to the economy, except for the rudimentary . . . observation . . . that more money is loaned [when] the collection of debts is not threatened by demagogic interference.
>
> Finley (1985, p. 143)

(Finley cites Rodewald (1976) and Crawford (1970).)

The upshot of Finley's account is also a mixed bag for the free banking school. Cicero's sound comment that demogogic interference is the very stuff of interventionist financial policy is supportive. On the other hand, a panic seems to have been aborted by timely official action. *Confidence*, that bromide of City men through the ages and the *raison d'être* of close liaison between the City and the Bank, looks important.

9 Banking Policy and Economic Fluctuations

9.1 PRELIMINARY REMARKS

(Chapters 3 and 9 are linked.)

After a preliminary conspectus, Dennis Robertson's *Banking Policy and the Price Level* (1926/1932) is studied from a particular slant. Robertson, like Wicksell, fails to explain satisfactorily how the banking system crams huge dollops of new 'notes' down the economy's gullet. He fails to develop properly the monetary process dual to his forced saving (induced lacking) one.

Although Robertson's banking system is somehow able to redirect resource flows, it has an ancillary rôle in his theory. *Banking Policy*'s is a *real* theory of economic fluctuations – rooted in the work of Marshall and Mill; cf reciprocal demand, decreasing costs (increasing returns) and lumpiness-and-indivisibility (clarified by Knight).

This is Robertson's slant. There is an intrinsic trade-off between price volatility (induced by monetary volatility) and fluctuating faults in the structure of capital. The economy's spontaneous action cannot smoothly adjust capital commitments to the requirements of a continuously optimal capital structure. The regulators of the banking system should mend this fault.

Robertson's model is closed; and this is probably a fatal flaw. And the schema's monetary/credit processes evolve in a closed loop: the monetary authority continuously responds to perceived faults in the structure of capital and, less overtly, to imbalances of aggregate supply and demand.

Banking action and business fluctuations are studied from a better-known angle in Section 9.3. Schuler (1988) reflects what seems to be the strong consensus that the principal impact of central bank action on the real economy results from disparity of market from natural rates of interest – presumably real ones. It soon becomes apparent that this consensus is flawed: Wicksell explicitly assumes that the weird behaviour of his banking system does not influence the own rate of return on real capital or Thornton's *mercantile rate of profit*.[1] Wicksell's theory looks more like a theory of price behaviour *pur et simple* the longer one studies it. This makes our job harder: the hypothesis – that the principal source of systematic monetary influence on the real economy lies in the volatility of monetary authorities – lies close to the surface of the rejected consensus. Candour requires that the gambit be rejected and support be found elsewhere.

9.1.1 A Preliminary Conspectus

What do banks really do? They are *not* primarily real savings intermediaries. They offer their paper for higher-yielding, less liquid paper, living on a *spread*. True, in a régime of equilibrium growth, bank balance sheets expand along with real capital and output. But there is no proper sense in which banks finance such growth: they simply expand their collections of paper: their function has been to supply liquidity, not capital.

Chapter 8 shows that the aggregate balance sheet of banks *cum* virtual banks expands and contracts in response to demand in an environment in which elasticities of substitution are very high. Nor is it surprising that elasticities are so high in a global economy in which banks *propre* are distinct mostly because they are regulated, as many Euro-banks, and other virtual banks, are not.

An episode in which banks notably increase their issue on their own initiative should find bank spreads narrowed and their paper yielding relatively more. Yet in Wicksell's scenario, and in the work influenced by him, massive increases in issue accompany deteriorated yields of bank paper. This flaw is to be cured. We begin by critically reflecting on the standard scenario for monetary authority (MA) induced disjunction of market from natural rate, resulting in putative cumulative expansion of issue, forced saving (or induced lacking), torsion on the structure of capital (e.g., unnatural lengthening of the period of production), etc.

The banks, following the MA, offer to trade at lower interest rates. It is commonly assumed that this will drag down the real cost of capital. But it is more plausible that the prime effect should be to reduce the volume of real intermediation. Since banks are quite insignificant as collectors of real savings (as Chapter 7 shows) it seems absurd that bank action should affect the real cost of capital: if anything, the flow of real resources seeking placement is contracted by the banks' putative action. It is more plausible to follow Ricardo and stipulate that real interest rates should be substantially invariant against such action. What is more, non-bank intermediaries, or banks disobedient to the MA, can profitably attract resources and lend them to deficit spending units by trading at higher rates of interest: there is excess demand for real lendable resources at the lower rates imposed by *diktat*.

In 1817 Ricardo pointed out that the banking system cannot regulate the hire price of a product it does not produce. Banks buy and sell paper. True, expenditures of primary purchases of bank paper can, in principle, be financed by sales of bank paper to claimants to real resources. But why should a putative 'abstainer' increase his bank paper holdings, on less favourable terms, when he can make direct loans on better terms – or can buy the paper of virtual banks on better terms?

When financial institutions offer higher prices for real assets, simultaneously pricing their paper to yield less, they *do* induce offers of paper by agents *planning* to sell paper to banks and to trade bank paper for goods. But they do *not* induce increased demand to *hold* their paper. Quite to the contrary!

The process may induce a higher depreciation rate of bank paper against goods; and Wicksell can be read as saying little more than that. Nor need real rates of interest offered by financial intermediaries be affected. Primary borrowers, disappointed by their inability to obtain real resources at bargain rates, will offer higher ones. Financial intermediaries will profitably break ranks and trade at higher interest rates.

The equilibrium hire price of a real resource should be substantially invariant against manipulation of the own rate of a paper asset.

Remark

A competitive banking industry cannot generate Wicksell's problem. In competitive banking equilibrium, deposit rate shadows the autonomously evolving 'mercantile rate of profit'. (In a competitive banking industry all claims flexibly yield interest; and differentials are cost-based.)

9.2 ROBERTSON'S BANKING POLICY AND THE PRICE LEVEL (1926/1932)

This passage links up Robertson's work with ours.

> The conclusion of certain writers [viz. Lavington and Cassel] that it is the unambiguous duty of the bank to render itself the agent for the procural of just so much Short Lacking that the level of prices is

> kept stable seems to rest on too easy an assumption of the fulfilment of economic harmonies. In short periods of rapid change, the incompatibility between a banking-policy designed to secure appropriate additions to the quantity of circulating capital may . . . become a serious source of trouble.
>
> Robertson (1926/1932, p. 58)

Robertson claims that there are sufficient degrees of freedom for *any* banking policy to smooth out price wrinkles *and* deviations from appropriate additions to the stock of circulating capital.

What are the devices of banking policy? What is the paradigmatic structure in which the devices are nested? It becomes clear that the latter is a set of variations on the forced saving theme; and that the pivotal device is forcing of bank issue on a strangely passive public who automatically soak up monetary issue obliviously to a foreseeable future. This is perplexing: Robertson anticipated rational expectations more than any writer of his time known to me.

Robertson's monetary theory flows from Chapter 5 of *Banking Policy*, 'The Kinds of Saving'. 'A man is lacking if during a given period he consumes less than the value of his current economic output' (p. 41). And there is a troublesome threefold distinction 'between Lacking which is Spontaneous . . . Automatic . . . and Induced.' (p. 47). Extended quotation is necessary to explain these key ideas, absolutely central for monetary theories of fluctuations of real economic action.

> Spontaneous Lacking corresponds . . . to Saving . . . The definition of Automatic Lacking must be approached indirectly. Automatic *Stinting* occurs whenever an increase in the stream of money directed on to the market prevents certain persons from consuming goods which they would otherwise have consumed. One cause of Automatic Stinting is a decision . . . of certain persons to reduce their money holdings . . . to dis-hoard; another is the *expenditure of newly created money* (emphasis supplied) whether by the Government or private persons. Either of these processes brings on to the market an additional daily stream of money which competes with the main daily stream of money for the daily stream of marketable goods . . . and thus deprives the residue of the public from consumption which they would otherwise have enjoyed. Automatic *Stinting* involves Automatic *Lacking* when, but only when, the consumption of those who undergo it is reduced

> both below what they intended and below the value of their current output . . . Their opposites may be called Automatic Splashing and Automatic Dis-Lacking
>
> If all members of the public simultaneously dishoarded . . . on balance neither Lacking nor Dis-Lacking [need] be done by anyone. Conversely, if all members of the public increased their Hoarding . . . the real income of each might suffer no diminution; for the intended Lacking involved in his spontaneous Hoarding might be exactly cancelled by the Automatic Splashing in which the Spontaneous Hoarding of his neighbours enabled him to indulge.

The neutrality described by the above paragraph is the sort obtained under rational expectations: knowledgeable, proficient agents stay abreast of events, and each other. Thus net automatic lacking hinges on forecast errors.

> Induced Lacking occurs when the same process that imposes Automatic Lacking on certain people having also reduced the real value of their money stocks [*violà*! The inflation tax] these people hold money off the market, and refrain from consuming to the full value of their current output, in order to bring the real value of their money stocks up again to what they regard as an appropriate level. Thus Induced Lacking differs from Automatic Lacking, in being voluntary and designed; but resembles it, and differs from Spontaneous Lacking, in being the direct result of an increase in the stream of money directed on to the market. For some purposes it is convenient to group together Automatic and Induced Lacking as Imposed Lacking . . . The privation imposed on the public by an ordinary process of inflation consists partly of Automatic and partly of Induced Lacking.

Automatic Lacking reflects transient disequilibrium: there is excess demand in goods markets; bank borrowers, freshly supplied with bank issue, hive off output unsuccessfully bid for by others.

Induced Lacking is a measured response to deterioration in values of real cash balances incident to price rises.

> Induced Dis-Lacking occurs when the same process which confers Automatic Dis-Lacking on certain people having also raised the real value of their money stocks, these people . . . consume more than the value of their current output, in order to bring the real

value of their money stocks down again to what they regard as an appropriate level.

Robertson (1926/1932, pp. 47–50)

These ideas are put into play in Robertson's Chapter 6, 'Short Lacking in the Trade Cycle', pp. 71ff. We shall show, in a précis of the *real* background of Robertson's theory, how he concludes that 'the fundamental feature of the upward swing of a trade cycle is a large and discontinuous increase in the demand for Short Lacking, occurring as an essential preliminary to an expansion of output' (p. 71). But the supply of spontaneous lacking is insufficiently elastic 'to cope with such pronounced and discontinuous increases in demand . . . The responsibility for meeting them rests entirely upon the banking system' (p. 72).

The sequel falls promptly into place. The banking system forces lacking through an inflationary process, so that the goals of price stability and optimal fluctuations in industrial activity *are* incompatible. And in the downswing, undesirable contraction of what came to be called *aggregate demand* is countered by dislacking.

Interpolations

1. Robertson contributes a beautiful passage on inflation. 'The internal mechanics so to speak of a process of inflation are almost as hard to visualize as those of the atom and seem to require the same kind of hypothesis of discontinuous motion' (note 1, p. 49).
2. Robertson seems *d'accord* with our view of what banks really do; and oblivious to its harshly negative implications for bank influence on real output, even in closed systems. He writes,

> the key to the whole matter is that the 'command over capital' conferred on the borrower by an additional bank loan is in reality provided not by the owner of the deposit in which the new loan eventuates but by some other money-holder who refrains, whether spontaneously or under pressure, from consuming the full value of his current output.

The upshot is devastating for the theory when money flexibly yields interest so that the inflation tax, or Robertson's equivalent to it, cannot be collected. And what is to prevent foresighted agents, able to post collateral, from taking out 'counter loans' in order to preempt automatic lacking? (Again, 'interest on money' blocks induced lacking.) When these pieces are put into play, Robertson's modalities seem impotent; they seem to do little more than promote dysfunctional volatility in money supply.

3. Robertson's model supports the idea that MA structures are the sources of monetary contribution to fluctuations in real economic action. Thus the inelasticity of spontaneous lacking, so central to his theory, goes far to block industrial fluctuations. The monetary authority steps in to generate a hopefully benign fluctuation in output at the cost of concomitant price fluctuation.

   Robertson posits that certain vibrations in real prospects, importantly augmented by lumpiness and indivisibility in production, call for humped investment if dynamic efficiency is to be preserved. But inelasticity of spontaneous lacking shuts off much of this potential vibration – save for MA intervention.

9.2.1 Resumption of the Gloss of *Banking Policy*:

(a) *Primitive Overshooting Scenarios*

Robertson shows, with considerable panache, that amplification by the MA of vibrations in real prospects, overcoming inelasticity of spontaneous lacking, or dis-Lacking, imparts mostly malignant *secondary* vibration to the system. This secondary vibration comprises a set of fluctuations that is surely a product of official action. *Banking Policy* elaborates a schema harnessing the action of the MA to real vibrations otherwise blocked by inelasticity of spontaneous lacking.

Robertson organizes a difficult exposition with exceptional clarity.

> It is argued . . . that, taking for granted the existing state of man's command over economic forces, and also the general organization of capitalist society, certain considerable and discontinuous expansions of industrial output must be regarded as socially beneficial. [But] owing to the double function of the banking system as a creator of currency and a procuror of Short Lacking, it will not as a rule be possible for such expansions to be made except to the accompaniment of a certain rise in the price level. But . . . the expansion of industrial output is liable to be carried beyond the point justified by the underlying conditions of utility and cost; the demand for Short Lacking is likely to be inflated out of proportion to the expansion of industrial output . . . [It] is the duty of the

> banking system . . . to prevent or check these *secondary* phenomena of trade expansion – if necessary by churlishness in meeting the increased demands for Short Lacking. If the banking system once loses control of the situation [it may be unable] to extract from the public . . . the Short Lacking required to maintain the current or projected volume of output . . . Once this state of affairs is reached, the only remedy the banking system can apply is to enforce a drastic reduction in the demand for Short Lacking through the liquidation of stocks of goods and the curtailment of swollen productive capacities . . . The traditional English policy of breaking so far as possible the violence of the fall may be against the general interest rate, since it may only . . . maintain an unduly distended demand for Short Lacking.
>
> Robertson (1926/1932, pp. 78–80)

The autonomously cyclical behaviour of Robertson's banking system is especially interesting for at least two reasons. (1) His description of malignant secondary vibration, induced by the MA, carries more conviction than that of the banking system puffing wind into the sails of the primary vibration. (2) Important political-economic implications flow from the prime scenario in which the MA intervenes to pump up the supply of lacking and finds it has supplied undesired impetus to the system, leading to overshooting. The forcing term describing MA 'corrective' action induces cyclical behaviour; and the forced oscillation may have a larger amplitude than the intrinsic one.

Now consider *Dis-Lacking*. It is induced by a decline in the price level, pushing cash balances above desired levels (and not to be confused with the egregious real balance effect). Robertson is oddly complacent about the possibility that the banking system will intensify a recession, while he recognizes that it might be possible to offset excessive use of force (see Chapter 3, section 3.4).

> It would seem to be the duty of the banking system to acquiesce in the primary fall of the price level . . . and to resist the secondary fall in such wise as to stimulate the demand for Short Lacking through a restoration of the optimal scale of output and length of the production period . . . It is likely to prove harder for the banking system to check the uneconomic fall in prices than to restrain an uneconomic rise . . . [There] may be *no* rate of money interest in excess of zero which will stimulte an unwilling [bor-

rower]. Secondly, a policy of direct limitation of bank loans has no counterpart in a period of falling prices.

Robertson (1926/1932, pp. 80–1)

9.2.2 How Secondary Demand for Short Lacking May be Provoked: Overshooting

(See Robertson, 1926/1932, pp. 72–7.)

1. Although it is possible for the representative entrepreneur to finance increased costs of circulating capital replacement caused by a higher price level from his augmented receipts, 'it is at least as likely that instead of doing so he will increase his personal consumption or his permanent investment, and will apply to the bank for an increased money loan to cover his trade expenses' (p. 73). Additional lacking by the public must sustain an increase in the capital base: in moving equilibrium, circulating capital requirements are satisfied from increased output, but there is a *finance* problem on the traverse to higher output or a faster growth plateau. (Cf below: Keynes translates the argument into more refined terms – and then reaches a horrid conclusion.)
2. Speculative motivation, and indeed effects of rational foresight, further impel demand for bank loans (in an expansionary episode), leading, in Robertson's theory, to additional Automatic and induced lacking. For one thing, the (Böhm–Bawerkian) period of production lengthens, since 'merchants become more anxious to hold goods in store instead of bringing them quickly on the market' (p. 75). And the consuming public is tempted to dishoard:

   > If prices are expected to go on rising, people tend to hurry on with the purchase of [durable] goods of which the exact moment of purchase can be varied within pretty wide limits.
   >
   > Robertson (1926/1932, p. 75)

   A feedback channel is activated when prices are accelerated by expansions of bank lending if the supply of reserves to the banking system is elastic – importantly because of the banks' dual rôle as a creator of currency and procuror of short lacking. Price rises tempt borrowers to borrow all the more. Should not Robertson step back from this precipice and opt for open-loop control? He does not.

9.2.3 Modalities for Coping With Secondary Vibrations

(See especially Robertson (1926/1932, pp. 76–80).)

A Preliminary Remark

Friedman's 'Formal Analysis' (1951/1953) yields sumptuous possibilities for real world monetary authorities, groping in twilight, if not inky darkness, to impose roughly cyclical fluctuation on an economy whose natural motion is heavily damped (see Chapter 6). The MA, misreading some transient positive indicator as a signal to provoke Additional lacking, may accelerate central bank credit, leading to price acceleration it later feels compelled to damp down by decelerating its credit. Etc. And the process is exacerbated if the MA is sensitive to the yawping of politicians and 'investment bankers'. It is easy to build cycles propelled by plausible, if dysfunctional, action of monetary authorities in a stochastic economic universe in which parameters are not accurately measured.

* * *

Robertson, a dévot of closed-loop control, advocated an active Bank rate policy.

> The most obvious weapon at the disposal of the banking system for mitigating the rise in the price level is of course the manipulation of its money rates of interest.
>
> Robertson (1926/1932, p. 76)

One of this book's principal themes is that active Bank rate policies are apt to fail. (See Chapter 3.)

Robertson suggests that a rise in Bank rate, leading to 'higher interest for money', works in three ways. 'First, a rise in the rate of interest allowed to depositors diminishes the temptation to Dishoard, and thereby diminishes the aggregate amount of Imposed Lacking consequential on a given addition of money loans' (pp. 76–7). So saving is encouraged. But this result pivots on interest for money ruling the roost: if the own rate of return on real assets evolves autonomously relative to 'interest for money', higher Bank rate leads merely to an expansion in the volume of mediation. Secondly, higher interest rates encourage entrepreneurs to keep their circulating capital topped up by ploughing back (retaining) earnings instead of spending them. The second effect is a variation of the 'stimulus to saving' theme – and is to be appraised sceptically for the same reasons. Thirdly, higher interest rates are to deter demand for loans 'to procure new increments of Circulating Capital' (p. 77).

9.2.4 The Banking System's Second Weapon

'The second weapon at the disposal of the banking system [the MA] is the sale of government securities' (p. 77). Robertson correctly characterizes purchase of government debt (tacitly not the debt of productive public sector entities) as Unproductive Lacking. Only the government's taxable capacity makes such holdings valuable. In any case, if higher yields induce the public to substitute public debt holdings for consumption (for example), aggregate demand pressure is reduced. And banks may increase their lending, hiving off holdings of government debt to the public.

Robertson's analysis of the banking system's second weapon is incomplete. He does not exploit the blazing contradiction between price stability and overshooting of accumulation of circulating capital so close to the argument's surface. A reshuffle of government debt, accompanying an increase in spontaneous lacking, is non-inflationary – but the period of production is unduly lengthened. Of course, if the underlying pressures lead to an inflationary blow-off, the secondary, undesirable, increase in real circulating capital is averted. (Robertson may have forgotten that the immediate issue concerns *secondary* accumulation, not the beneficent primary thrust towards increased accumulation.)

9.2.5 The Banking System's Third Weapon

'The third weapon at the disposal of the banking system is direct limitation, by rationing or other means, of the quantity of new money loans' (pp. 77–8). The 'third weapon' is nugatory in an innovated economy. Chapter 7 explains why: a 'local' banking system typically supplies much too small a portion of total credit taken for control of the subset of financial intermediaries directly regulated by the MA to map into effective control of credit flows. Furthermore, elasticities of substitution, especially on an open-economy network, are very high.

9.2.6 Concluding Comments on Regulation in Robertson's System: Induced Cycles

The theory developed in Chapter 8 implies that in a modern open economy systemic possibilities for cyclical real economic action are slight. What pass for cycles are little more than irregular pulses with stochastic sources. A corollary implication is this. To the extent a system is closed, feeble intrinsic cycles may be 'regularized' and amplified by MA interventions. Robertson offers an example, if perhaps unwittingly. Recall his recognition that, in a primitive *resonance* paradigm, the MA may lose control so that, in a desperate effort to regain its grip, it will, 'enforce a drastic reduction in the demand for Short Lacking'. He deeply probes this chilling admission in chapter 6, §6 of *Banking Policy*. He sees that it is hard for the MA to identify the processes it dimply perceives: is accumulation or decumulation of inventories *voluntary*? So MA intervention programmes are (statistically) expected to increase variances of the processes they impinge upon; or to boost amplitudes (as per resonance theory).

Ironically Robertson's stabilization programme's fatal flaw is discovered in his prescient (1926) *ex-ante/ex-post* formulation of inventory movements *à la* Stockholm School theory.

> What is significant is not the actual magnitude of stocks at different dates, but their magnitude in relation to the Short Lacking demanded by merchants and speculators, and made available through the banking-system and otherwise, for carrying them. The trend of stocks, taken by itself, does not constitute an intelligible guide to banking policy.
>
> Robertson (1926/1932, pp. 82–3)

In particular, stocks (inventories) may fall off during booms because the supply of finance is insufficient: 'there are already difficulties in eliciting requisite supplies of Short Lacking' (pp. 82–3). Or aggregate demand may exceed its expected level, draining inventories. In either case, investment exceeds saving in the terminology of the *Treatise* or of Robertson's later work. Or, along supply-side lines, inventories may be falling because 'there are technical obstacles in the way of a continued expansion of industrial output' (p. 83), so that stocks are run down as orders flow in at rates exceeding output. As for downturns,

> An increase in stocks during the first stage of the depression indicates that the demand for and supply of Short Lacking is being artificially sustained . . . An increase of stocks during the latter stages of depression indicates that production has not succeeded in adjusting itself to the collapse . . . in the demand for and supply of Short Lacking; while a diminution of stocks at this stage indicates that, for good or evil, readjustment of the scale of output has been effected.
>
> Robertson (1926/1932, p. 83)

Robertson does not take the short step leading to abandonment of closed-loop monetary control. Instead he calls for a stabilization policy based on timely identification of turning points, a notoriously difficult, if not impossible, job: 'thus the trend of stocks . . . must be interpreted in the light of the phase that has been reached in the trade cycle' (p. 83). If the MA misses the downturning point, it will interpret inventory decumulation as a signal that Short Lacking is insufficient and/or that aggregate demand is overheated – when the economy's spontaneous action is appropriately adjusting stocks. If the MA misses the upturning point, it interprets a rise in stocks, based on solid evidence of impending stronger demand not yet available to statisticians, as a signal that the recession is deepening, so that involuntary inventory accumulating is intensifying. Nor is that all. An open economy's trade balance spontaneously accommodates demand/supply imbalances Robertson wants the MA to address. Robertson draws the wrong implications from his fine analysis:

> It is part of the duty of the banking system to promote at each phase of the cycle such a balance between the different kinds of production as to minimize this source of instability in the estimates made by the business world of the advantage of acquiring instruments.
>
> Robertson (1926/1932, p. 94)

9.2.7 The Real Foundations of Robertson's Theory

(Also see Robertson's *A Study of Industrial Fluctuations*, 1915.)

Robertson's is a *real* theory of economic fluctuation. Its monetary component is ancillary. It concerns his flawed theory of monetary control, adjusting the 'natural' ebb and flow of lacking, especially short lacking, to the solution of a tacit simplistic optimal control problem defined in 'real space'. Nor is the theory psychological: it is not rooted in fluctuations of confidence.

Interpolation

In the following passage Robertson both states his outlook and anticipates new-classical theories of fluctuation.

> I hold that far more weight must be attached [than is now fashionable] to certain *real*, as opposed to monetary or psychological, causes of fluctuation . . . I do not think it is even nearly true that if all business men always made, and acted upon, true judgments about their own self interest, industrial fluctuations of a fairly rhythmical character would disappear.
>
> Robertson (1926/1932, pp. 1, 3)

* * *

Robertson's is, roughly, a theory of *humped investment*: see his Chapter 4, 'Inappropriate Fluctuations of Output'. He calls 'attention to a fresh ambiguity in the conception of an appropriate or optimum scale of industrial output . . . [arising] from three closely-allied facts, all rooted in a single technical characteristic of modern industry – the necessity in many trades of using very large, expensive and durable instruments of production' (p. 35). Thus Marshallian *lumpiness and indivisibility*, central in Professor Knight's teaching. Robertson nicely illustrates the upshot:

> The underlying economic situation may justify an increase in productive capacity of 50 per cent; but technical considerations may impose a decision between 100 per cent or nothing . . . The optimum expansion of industrial output *relatively* to the exigencies of the technical situation may be much greater than the expansion of output which would be really appropriate in view of the underlying conditions of utility and cost.
>
> Robertson (1926/1932, p. 35)

Technical factors may mandate that an investment hump be followed by a quite lengthy period of depressed industrial investment expenditure.

In a closed economy, lacking must strictly imitate investment (broadly defined, as it should be). But the consumption of forward-looking consumers is quite 'stable'; spontaneous lacking does *not* strictly imitate investment. So Robertson proposes that, during an upswing of 'optimal' planned investment, the MA seek to compel lacking by inducing a surge in bank lending and its residue, money supply.

An open-economy version of the script, neglected by Robertson, calls for initial deterioration of the trade balance, readily financed abroad; American history up to the first world war shows how easy it is to attract foreign capital to profitable projects. Accommodating trade-balance fluctuations conveniently shadow fluctuations in finance-requirements in open Robertsonian economies.

(a) *Two Further 'Causes of Divergence Between Actual and Potential Output'*

Say that an industry consists of fifty identical firms. It is universally agreed that a permanent increase in demand will lead to a 10 per cent increase in industry output in a new equilibrium. An interesting rational expectations problem arises. If each forecasts that the others will follow optimal control paths while planning to maintain a 2 per cent share of industry output, each firm's forecast is correct. Otherwise forecasts are incorrect. There is a well-defined rational expectations equilibrium entailing humped investment: rational expectations do not repeal lumpiness and indivisibility.

If the implications of rational expectations are conflated with those of open-economy theory, sources of real fluctuation are confined to technical factors like lumpiness-and-indivisibility, mandating humped investment. Business-cycle theories pivoting on Error, followed by Revelation (of Error) – in closed systems so that valves controlling flows to and from alien economies are shut – are then discarded.

(b) *Robertson's Scenario for the Industry Just Studied*

> [It] is quite likely that each firm, regarding itself as a special protégé of Providence, and ignorant of the preparations that are being made by its neighbours, will provide, say, one-twentieth instead of its appropriate one-fiftieth of the appropriate increase in output, so that total output is increased by 25 per cent instead of by 10 per cent. The demands of each firm for new instruments of production will be correspondingly exaggerated, and the longer the new instruments take to construct, the more scope there is for

> miscalculation, and the greater will be the excess of the actual output of instruments over the output which is really appropriate . . . The more severe too will be the restriction ultimately necessary . . . to bring the rate of output down to the appropriate level [citing his *A Study of Industrial Fluctuations*, 1915, Part 1, Chapters 1 and 2].
>
> Robertson (1926/1932, pp. 37–8)

9.2.8 The Second Cause of Divergence Between Actual and Appropriate Output (pp. 38–9)

The 'second cause' divines innovations in economic theory that took root about fifty years later. Increases in prices received by producers are misperceived to be increases in local prices (in Barro's locution) instead of reflections of a higher general price level (i.e., one of many price increases. The 'second cause' entails supply-side economics. Output is expanded (or, conversely, contracted) in response to misunderstood price signals. When the signals are finally correctly read, output plans are reversed. But that is far from being all. Chapters 6's conspectus of physics foundations of the theory of economic fluctuation shows that, at any time, the (relative) price stimulus received by a producer is a composite of stimuli emitted far back in time. And wave addition is a curious process, replete with lively possibilities for *cancellation*. And there are *many* agents, each producing many products: the order of the commodity space is very high. *Then* take account of *interaction* of expectations: characteristically covariant relations of sweeps of mood changes – especially when each forecasts the forecasts of others – are apt to exacerbate possibilities for fluctuation, as Pigou pointed out:

> Apart altogether from the financial ties by which different business men are bound together, there exists among them a certain measure of psychological interdependence. A change in tone in one part of the business world diffuses itself, in a quite unreasoning manner, over other and wholly disconnected parts.
>
> A. C. Pigou (*Economics of Welfare*, 1st edn, p. 840, cited by Robertson, 1926/1932, p. 38)

Robertson succinctly summarizes his flawed deductions from the story for monetary policy. The flaw is no surprise: he writes at p. 4 of

Banking Policy that he believes firmly in credit control and not in monetary laissez-faire.

> Hence the alterations actually made in the scale of output tend to exceed the appropriate alterations; hence also that monetary policy which is most effective in bringing about quickly and without friction the appropriate alteration will also tend to *overshoot the mark* (emphasis supplied), and to be, unless kept well in control, the most fertile in the generation of error [!].
>
> Robertson (1926/1932, p. 39)

Interpolation

Chapters 2–4 show that choice of numéraire, or metric, has characteristically been inept, obstructing extraction of correct information from price signals: perhaps my relative price has increased; perhaps not. In a tabular régime, it is easy to read one's relative price. Milton Friedman's Nobel Lecture (1977) makes a related point: irregular inflation may make price signals so noisy that the economy contracts – so that there is a positively sloped Phillips curve (in inflation/unemployment space).

9.3 SUPPLEMENTARY MATERIALS FOR THE REAL FOUNDATIONS OF ROBERTSON'S THEORY

9.3.1 The Offer Curve

Robertson deploys the Mill–Marshall offer curve as early as p. 8 of *Banking Policy*. *Elasticity* is emphasized – especially in a preliminary analysis of a notionally non-monetary economy. The following excerpt displays confusion however: rational strategy for *concerted* group action is imposed on the uncoordinated actions of members of competitive groups: after all, the invisible hand of competition bars members of the same industry from congregating even for merriment and diversion.

> The effects upon a group's output of an alteration in the real demand price for its products depends on whether the elasticity of the group's demand for the commodities offered in exchange is greater or less than unity. If the former, a rise in the real demand

price for its products will furnish a rational inducement to expand output and a fall to restrict it; if the latter, the reverse will be the case.

Robertson (1926/1932, p. 13)

Say that 1,000 *X* are exchanged for 1,000 *Y*. Now 1,100 *Y* are offered: the price of *Y* has fallen 10 per cent. If demand for *Y* by the producers of *X* is inelastic, they will cut back production.

9.3.2 Consumer Durables

Consumer durables are crucial for correct macro-economic theory. For one thing, consumer durable accumulation accounts for a substantial portion of investment. For another, a proper theory of saving includes consumer durable accumulation or decumulation in its saving, or dissaving, concept. And the myriad yields, relating streams to sources, include those for consumer durable holdings. Finally, expenditures on durables must be sharply distinguished from consumption of their services. The time series for the latter is as well behaved as that for the former is erratic. Purchases of durables are easily postponed or accelerated. They readily contribute to economic fluctuations. And the ease with which they can be switched on or off makes it easier for increases in industrial investment to be supported or decreases to be offset – although, alas, changes in demand schedules for industrial and consumer durables are apt to be positively covariant.

9.3.3 Some Subtleties in the Theory of Saving

A Preliminary Comment

A decision to switch from watching films to buying clothes (or to watch films at home on one's VCR instead of going to the cinema) is one to increase one's properly-defined savings rate.

* * *

Look at the theory of saving from the point of view of Samuelson (1958); cf *overlapping generations*. If I buy books and tweed jackets and trade up to a more expensive car, I postpone my consumption *without* the social contrivance of money. I will carry depreciable durable stocks into my very old age, during which I let the stocks run down without replacement. Or I may, in high old age, sell my library, using the proceeds to borrow books, go to films, etc. In a moving equilibrium, the young buy durables from the old and sell services of durables to them.

In order finally to fix ideas, contemplate a hypothetical case in which all consumption is by the old. The old sell off durables as they go along. And the old, since they consume *all* services of durables, buy the services of the young's sources, financing service purchases by selling sources from their diminishing stocks to the young.

Remark

Banking Policy is not nuancé of consumer durable accumulation. This may explain why Robertson largely confines himself to 'the interest for money', ignoring the wide spectrum of yields linking values of expected service streams to asset prices.

* * *

A quite subtle theory of saving, mostly eliding money and finance, can be built up from these materials – and indeed Adam Smith went a long way in this direction (see 1989a, chapter 7).

Fairly large elasticities of substitution let small changes in relative yields induce appropriately large shifts in the composition of service flows. When humped investment in chemical and power plants is called for, lacking will promptly make finance available, even in closed economies: it need only become slightly more attractive to postpone landscaping projects, car-upgrading, piscine enlargement, etc. in favour of participation, directly or indirectly, in industrial investment. If yield changes are perceived to be temporary, elasticity of response is all the greater.

9.3.4 More on Life Cycle: Overlapping Generations Features of Consumer Durables Analysis

Consider a human one-horse shay who has inherited a collection of durables. He sustains steady lifetime consumption, before crumbling into dust. In Stage One, he saves; perhaps he acquires literary and chess skills – lacking building up human capital is important in a proper analysis. Postponement and 'rushing' in consumer durable programmes can offset or neutralize fluctuations in industrial propensities to invest. Sustaining consumption in Stage Two, when earned income decays, requires that these accumulations be drained off; the cars, refrigerators, etc. taken into Stage Two are run down. Or consider shares in source holding companies he may accumulate in Stage One. 'Durables as a social contrivance' is a more fructive theme than 'money as a social contrivance'.

Say that preferences shift so that the Young of the moment wish to shift to paper money; the Old are running down *whatever* they have accumulated but, perhaps responding to their heirs' tastes, may wish to transmit paper money instead of durables at death. Such a change in taste is a windfall for producers of paper money (doubtless including the Crown). They can acquire accumulated durables cheaply, sell paper on favourable terms for current goods and services, etc. (see Burstein, 1989a, Chapter 7).

Remark

In the resulting temporary equilibrium, real yields obtained by holding paper money fall. And prices of non-monetary sources fall relative to capitalizations of yields based on sales of the services of such sources. So pressure on the source production markets is reduced. Restoration of full equilibrium occurs when the appetite for paper is sated. In the meanwhile, wage declines restore the attractiveness of producing sources, and are reversed when the appetite for paper is sated.

These complex events may be too exiguous to measure. And, in secularly growing economies, 'lower rates of wage growth' is read for 'lower wages'.

9.4 A PROPOSED THEORY OF BANKING POLICY AND ECONOMIC FLUCTUATIONS

Theoretical reasoning supplements the rough empirical work of Chapter 7 in demonstrating the unimportance of banks for industrial fluctuations. Posit scallop-shaped supply curves of intermediary services: supply responds very elastically to demand, conforming to a well-defined spread. And in innovated systems demand for various paper is very elastic relative to yield differentials. *Sans* Regulation, debt clearing eligibility will be offered for a tiny yield discount; the complementary proposition is that clearers offer a wide variety of deposits – *joint* products are purchased.

The results just obtained imply that the size of the aggregate balance sheet of financial intermediaries may vibrate quite strongly without affecting the real economy; and 'shares' of component parts of intermediary balance sheets will vibrate still more strongly with still less real effect. What is more, it is highly plausible that the evolution of the real cost of capital becomes autonomous relative to the action of the financial sector and the MA: an autonomous base line is accompanied by some wavering in the intermediary paper line; that is all.

Possibilities for 'money driven' business fluctuation are more substantial in a still influential model in which a distinct subset of zero-yield (or perhaps fixed-yield) assets is alone eligible to clear off debt. Elasticities of substitution in supply and demand are low. Equilibrium requires that open-market interest rates respond strongly, if transiently, to changes in money base growth.

9.4.1 Collision of the Proposed Theory With Orthodox Models of Financial Mediation

Control of the banking system does not confer control of real expenditure flows. We showed that the empirical importance of the banking system is too slight for it to dominate financial system action; and that changes in the volume of financial mediation do not supply net credit to, or withdraw it from, the economy. For net real credit to be supplied by the financial system, it must float off fresh claims against itself that correspond with fresh lacking or abstinence by non-financial agents: mere substitution of indirect for direct ownership of real resources is irrelevant for the finance of new capital formation.

The argument is now to be pitched up so that it conforms to innovated modalities and goes beyond the banking principle: debt is to be cleared on a giro; the financial terrain is to be quite featureless.

In the innovated régime, any agent able to sell claims against herself can acquire credits flashing across the giro in favour of *X* by selling her paper to *X*. Nor can paper command a premium in an economy saturated with liquidity – although the credit-rating skills of intermediaries will continue to command a price.

In the old script, sellers of goods elect a temporary abode of purchasing power and, when the banking system expands its credit, discover they have been too slow to react. In the new script, sellers of goods for paper are as fast on the trigger as borrower-spenders. And holders of 'old paper' are prompt to defend against depreciation by borrowing themselves. In the nouveau régime, it is impossible to impose Lacking.

9.4.2 Coda to Section 9.4: Indexation; Tabular Standards

Indexation

If all accounts are indexed, agents stuck with depreciated paper are entitled to indemnification. Any Automatic Lacking is accompanied by a dragging force, *viz*. creation of property rights calling for indemnification of losses on financial assets.

The financial intermediary system in its turn will require indemnification. Primary borrowers will know that any inflation tax will be passed through to them; rational, forward-looking potential borrowers will know that they cannot pull a fast one, as they do in Irving Fisher's monetary theory of cycles. And rational expectations impart another twist. Agents who have not taken additional credit, and want to protect their purchasing plans, will speed up planned spending upon learning that they risk being forced into Saving (Lacking) by excess demand for goods (accompanied by supplies being held off the market by sellers expecting further price rises). Their indexed balances grow *pari passu* with inflation: they are automatically financed. And they can avert being crowded out by obtaining new lines of credit. The upshot translates into simple depreciation of paper claims, as does that of Wicksell's model.

Tabular Standards

Under an Aureus standard, expansion of financial intermediary balance sheets has no significant real effect *per se*. Market markers mark down Aureus prices of paper pouring onto the market. Aureus prices of goods and services barely twitch. See the discussion in Chapter 2 of effects of gold influxes when an economy is on a gold standard, contrasted with those when it is not.

9.5 ON FINANCE: AN INSTRUCTIVE EPISODE IN *DOGMENGESCHICHTE*

Bibliographical Note

Volumes XIII, XIV and XXIX of the *Collected Writings of J. M. Keynes* (*JMK*), including their fine indexes, are exceptionally important for what follows. Other pertinent sources are:

Keynes (1937a). reprinted in *JMK*, XIV, p. 201, cf. especially p. 208ff.
Keynes (1937b). reprinted in *JMK*, XIV, p. 215.
Keynes (1938). a rejoinder to Robertson (1937), reprinted in *JMK*, XIV, p. 229. (The important Keynes–Robertson correspondence on finance is reprinted in *JMK*, XIII, XIV and XXIX.)
Ohlin (1937). appearing in the March (p. 53) and June (p. 221) issues of the *Economic Journal* (EJ).
Robertson (1936).
Robertson (1937a). March and June issues of the *Economic Journal*.
Robertson (1937b).
Robertson (1937c).
Shaw (1938).
Shaw (1938/1979). see *JMK*, XXIX, p. 276.

9.5.1 What is 'Finance'?

The *finance* controversy need not have got off course. Keynes's initial description of the idea is a short step from assignment of the topic to 'real', not monetary, economics.

> Planned investment – i.e. investment *ex ante* – may have to secure its 'financial' provision *before* the investment takes place; that is to say, before the corresponding saving has taken place . . . There has, therefore, to be a technique to bridge this gap between the time when the *decision* to invest is taken and the time when the correlative investment and saving actually occur . . . Even if the entrepreneur avails himself of a finance provision which he has arranged beforehand . . . the market's commitments will be in excess of actual saving to date . . . If he accumulates a cash balance beforehand . . . then an accumulation of unexecuted or incompletely executed investment decisions may occasion for the time being a special demand for cash . . . Let us call this advance provision of cash the 'finance' required by the current decision to invest (emphasis supplied).
>
> J. M. Keynes, 'Alternative Theories of the Rate of Interest' (1937a) reprinted in *JMK*, XIV, pp. 207–8

Critique

Keynes does *not* take this short step.

> In a simplified schematism, designed to elucidate the essence of what is happening, but one which is, in fact, substantially representative of real life, one would assume that 'finance' is wholly supplied during the interregnum by the banks; and this is the explanation of why their policy is so important in determining the pace at which new investment can proceed. Dr Herbert Bab has suggested to me that one could regard the rate of interest as being determined by the interplay of the terms on which the public desires to become more or less liquid and those on which the banking system is ready to become more or less unliquid. This is, I think, an illuminating way of expressing the liquidity theory of the rate of interest; but particularly so within the field of finance.
>
> Keynes (1937/1973/1987, p. 219)

But 'finance' does not concern money: it would be scandalously inept for a company to put proceeds of anticipatory loans into barren cash. And banks are only marginally important here: the relevant 'money' markets are immense: their transactions volumes swamp out fresh bank lending.

The excerpt offers additional proof that, alas, Keynes is wholly committed to monetary theories of real rates of interest. For the soil of theory to remain fertile, the king must be slain.

When the *finance* problem is translated into the real domain, it meshes with the modern theory of consumption; and with jumps in data required by invisible events, e.g. changes in expectations so that conventional forecasting techniques break down; see Lucas (1976). Robertson supplied the required clue in 1926:

> It might be thought at first sight that an expansion of output due to lowered real costs . . . would not involve any preliminary increase in the demand for short lacking: since the Circulating Capital employed in the industry or group of industries in question, as measured in terms of the group's own products, automatically increases in proportion to the imminent increase of output . . . But if the demand for its products is elastic, the members of the group become at once entitled to a greater aggregate reward in terms of goods in general, which has to be advanced to them from the same source.

> The most obvious and important instance is the increased demand for Short Lacking to carry an exceptionally large harvest of a crop for which demand is elastic. [Perhaps months before the crop] enters into final consumption, the rest of the Community is called upon to advance by some means or other an increased aggregate real reward to the farming population. At the same time the industries which find in the increased harvest a rational justification for an increase in output . . . desire to expand their Circulating Capital; so that a double stream of increased demand for Short Lacking is directed on to the banking system [*sic*?].
>
> Robertson (1926/1932, p. 71, note 1)

Until its very end, the excerpt is a scintillating exercise in theory. The banking system, buying paper with paper and living off a spread, has little to do with the proper real resource problem. Thus contemplate a moneyless giro. Agents anticipating deficits obtain commitments backing sales of paper for giro credits (or, in an uninnovated system, cash balances). Proceeds will be invested in marketable paper (including flexibly interest yielding money). The matrix of claims is shuffled up, but banks are outside the loop . . . In an open economy the 'finance' phenomenon is unlikely to cause observable data changes. The proper problem is strikingly classical. Robertson's illustration can be framed by an 'advance' theory of wages (cf the *wages fund*). But there is an important difference between the classical analysis and ours. In the classical analysis, wage goods consist of last year's harvest – the economy lies in Northern Europe, not in Florida or California, where harvesting is continuous. The rhythm of antique agriculture disappears from modern formulations – in which real lacking develops in many channels, including the consumer durable one. And modern economies boil off *lacking* and *finance*.

9.6 ANOTHER FINANCE PROBLEM

This finance problem entails another tiresome controversy; and flows from Keynes's *Treatise*; and is entangled with the *liquidity preference/loanable funds feuilleton*. Does unregulated economic action promote lower real interest rates as slumps unfold; and higher ones as booms unfold?

The problem is usefully transformed into one in open-economy theory. Economy E comprises the entrepreneurs; Economy W, the workers. A slump due to excess of savings over investment leads to a trade deficit for *E* that must be *financed*. (The terminology is that of the *Treatise* and is associated with *another* bitter feud.)

So far as we have gone, there is no downward pressure on interest rates: *E*'s trade deficit leads to demand for credit 1:1 with the excess of savings over investment. Indeed key virtual interest rates may *increase*: thus costs of capital may increase as share prices crash 'irrationally'.

(Keynes, along with most others, assumes that relevant products are commercially produced goods so that, when there is excess supply, producers pile up undesired inventories or are unable to sell perishables at their supply prices. What about *services*? In a pure service economy, the equivalent to such disequilibrium is disparity of actual from anticipated proceeds, leading to contraction of planned outlays on goods and services. Rational expectations permit a weak equilibrium in which the economy contracts so that conditional plans are realized; but its activity levels are too low relative to a notional solution of a companion problem in welfare maximization.)

A stability problem emerges. Where x = excess demand for liquidity and $\dot{x} = f(x)$, is $f'(x) > 0$? The algebra limns liquidity crisis nexi studied by Professor Kindleberger.

Nor need 'the' interest rate fall if *E*'s excessive production is curtailed. Say that *E*'s production declines to the level of *effective demand* (cf the *General Theory*) so that entrepreneurs' proceeds are what they must expect them to be if they are to persist at that production level. Aggregate output may thus be merely adapted to a rate of interest determined exogenously to the model, as in Leijonhufvud's 'Wicksell Connection' (1981): as Keynes (1936) pointed out, a wide spectrum of interest rates may be 'natural' in this modelling.

So far only a bootstrap theory of interest has emerged: the rate of interest is what it is because that is what it is. But the classical/neoclassical theory of interest is determinate. Real rates of interest, linking values of service flows to source prices, nest in a rough moving equilibrium harmonizing real forces; and money is but a veil. These conclusions can be pitched up.

1. Chapter 2 shows that real economic behaviour is influenced by choice of measure. Thus the dynamics of displacement from equilibrium caused by fluctuations in liquidity preference or gold

production are very different under a gold standard than otherwise. And Chapter 2 shows that classical interest rate behaviour is easily extracted from a tabular standard. Thus the banking system's spread dissipates when the economy is saturated with liquidity.

2. In classical theory, in which the real dog wags a monetary tail that sometimes swats it, the monetary authority influences the liquidity premium obtained by 'money market' assets – short of innovations mandating elimination of liquidity premia. And the MA may cope with occasional disorganization of money markets, inevitably entailing real effects; think of Federal Reserve interventions in the Penn Central and Chrysler crises – and in the wake of the Crash of 19 October 1987. And the MA sometimes disrupts the money markets!

   In classical theory, real interest rates are determined by forces lying almost wholly outside the MA's field of action. So the day after tomorrow imitates the day before yesterday: elimination of liquidity premia beyond the banking principle and in innovated clearing systems allow only real forces to act on interest rates.

9.6.1 Spontaneous Yield Adjustment During Economic Fluctuations

It is plausible that fluctuations of multiples borne by share prices to current earnings are due more to fluctuations in earnings expectations (and to noise) than to fluctuations in real interest rates. Fluctuations of real interest rates are much less important for business-cycle theory than those of risk premia and earnings expectations. And this conclusion is embedded in the literature. Hawtrey's inventory-rooted trade-cycle theory has been rejected because changes in carrying costs weigh so little in the controlling calculus: if the price of copper is expected to increase by 1 per cent in a week, a 22 per cent p.a. cost of funds is not deterring.

(Of course, the cost of funds cannot be wholly irrelevant for real economic action.)

The spontaneous action of a *closed* economy is ambiguous for costs of funds over the business cycle; in an *open* economy, capital tends to be available quite elastically. In particular, two lines of theoretical development suggest that spontaneous pressures on interest rates are strongly damped over the cycle. One is drawn from consumption theory; the other from 'automatic stabilization'.

Forward-looking consumption is sustained near 'permanent' levels when disposable income falls, so that the supply of finance is diminished – and/or loan demand increases. To this extent, spontaneous action of a closed economy pushes up interest rates if there is a slump; and *vice versa* for a boom.

The Keynesian multiplier calculates the increase in output inducing a unit increase in leakage – offsetting a unit increase in autonomous spending. In a simple Keynesian analysis, increases in autonomous spending are self-financing – i.e., basically neutral for excess demand in credit markets. (In the standard drill there is upward pressure on interest rates because of increased demand for transactions balances due to higher effective (goods) demand.) In less simplistic Keynesian formulations, higher public spending and/or tax cuts directly entail higher interest rates: capital inflow, financing trade deficits, must be induced. And *vice versa* for contractive fiscal policy.

9.6.2 Historically Destabilizing Fiscal Policy

Granting that historic baseline public expenditure is much less than now, fiscal policy, before our time, was automatically *de*stabilizing. For one thing, governments were constrained to pay cash in advance; see Chapter 10. So government response to declining revenues during slumps was to slash spending and increase tax rates; while buoyant revenues during booms encouraged higher government purchases. (See Chapter 10 for an ancient analogy that proves factitious; and note the analogy to local authorities, and others who cannot print money, of the present day.)

Remark

Anglo-centrically, prior to Sir Robert Walpole, governments were not systematic players in loan markets; but their sporadic interventions were likely to be pro-cyclical. Indeed the chartering of the Bank of England nests in King William III's exigent need to finance the war against the Sun King.

9.6.3 Investment in Fixed and Working Capital Over the Cycle

Working capital requirements rise or fall with activity levels. At a given ratio of borrowed to total capital, demand for fresh credit falls with output to this extent – exerting downward pressure on interest rates. But three double-edged comments are mandated.

So long as output plans are based on over-optimistic expectations, firms must continue to finance 'trade deficits'.

Pessimism and fear may lead treasurers to seek lower levels of borrowed to total capital during slumps; and higher ones when sentiments reverse during booms. To this extent, supply falls in debt markets during slumps, but equity markets must digest more offerings. Effects on costs of capital are mixed.

Prudence may urge reduction of working capital ratios during slumps, reducing demand for credit to this extent – while perhaps provoking chain bankruptcies in disorganized credit markets, intensifying the slump and indeed producers' aggregate trade deficits.

* * *

The relationship between the volume of industrial production and fixed capital formation is more irregular than that between working capital and production. And the more forward-looking is investment, the more the analysis corresponds to the modern theory of consumption. Demand for funds then tends to be less sensitive to the cycle; interest rates behave less cyclically. And, of course, automatic stabilization of demand schedules reduces the amplitude of the business cycle.

A Further Remark on Forward-looking Behaviour and Real Cycles

The classical mathematical formulation of cyclical behaviour relies on higher-order differential equations and so on feedback – that is to say on lagged reaction or, alternatively, on expectations being adaptive. So if expectations are forward looking, traditional sources of cyclical action dissipate.

9.7 CODA TO CHAPTER 9: FROM WALTER BAGEHOT TO THE NEW ART OF CENTRAL BANKING

Chapter 9 is closed out with a capsulation of the relationship of the theory of this book to that of one of the subject's founder figures, Walter Bagehot (see Sayers, 1957).

Bagehot's *Lombard Street* does not concern MA control of real costs of capital; it is not all Wicksellian. Bagehot is concerned with two *drains*, internal and external. Internal drains ensued from attempts to convert assets into bank notes and other currency. Bagehot urged that, then, the Bank lend without stint.

So long as much dealing was financed by trade bills, so that there were lively possibilities for chain-linked bankruptcies, the internal drain rubric was capitally important. Debtors were obligated to pay official money and, as a practical matter, could discharge obligations with bank tenders. And the banks were in close liaison with the Bank of England: the Bank was able, if it was willing, to increase its fiduciary issue from time to time, dousing panics by lending without stint; the Bank was well placed to influence risk premia. But Bagehot did *not* suggest that the Bank seek to control the real yield of gilts through its influence over the terms on which 'member banks' offer to sell their paper for less liquid paper.

External drains put the Bank under Pressure. So long as the gold reserve was thin – and it was always thin – the Bank had to combat external drains by restricting its credit and sharply raising Bank rate in order to attract funds to London. (The Bank of France was *de facto* the very last lender of last resort for Britain: official bridging finance was readily available.)

There are inexact parallels between Bank response to external drains and purgative Bank rate (see Chapter 3). It suffices to say that the episodes studied by Bagehot were short lived and confined to the money market (Lombard Street). Secondary contractive effects of high Bank rate on the real economy could not cope with emergencies provoked by external drains.

Of course, 'high' Bank rate exerted transient contractive influence on the real economy. But the magnitude, frequency and phasing of such episodes remain up in the air. And the (provisional) thrust of this book, (and 1989a), is to play down the real impact of Bank rate.

9.8 RECAPITULATION OF THE BOOK'S THEORY OF MA INTERVENTION

Capsulating the book's theory of MA intervention, before treking far back in time, in Chapter 10, the evolution of real costs of capital is hypothesized to be substantially autonomous relative to MA action: the MA neither furnishes nor absorbs real resources. If banks offer to deal only at rates below the baseline real cost of capital (taking the theory very pure so that the real cost of capital is determined by the growth rate of Professor Knight's Crusonia plant), they will lose business. Nor can banks offer real terms better than say Thornton's mercantile rate of profit: they cannot transform pumpkins into glass coaches – although transient price rigidities can transform high nominal rates into correspondingly high real ones.

As for MA operations in government stock, see Friedman (1968) and the appendix to Chapter 14 of the *General Theory* (which I glossed in 1988). Government stock is no more attractive than bank paper at subnormal yields. True, both can float their paper at a premium so long as it yields unique liquidity services – so long as we have not gone beyond the banking principle. David Ricardo brilliantly explained these matters in 1817.[2]

Notes and References

1. Otto Steiger points out, in a letter, that Wicksell, in his *Lectures* (1906/1935, 2, p. 193), defines the real rate of profit as 'the *expected* yield on the newly created capital' (emphasis supplied). And he points out that Lindahl (1939) comments on this as well, albeit along different lines from those of Steiger and his collaborators. See Steiger (1987): *The New Palgrave*.

   What is important here is whether 'the expected yield on the newly created capital' evolves autonomously with respect to the money market rate. Wicksell *does* seem to specify such autonomy. The idea is best dissociated from monetary analysis.
2. Government paper can feasibly offer yields above the mercantile rate of profit if appropriately backed by the government's taxable capacity. The government's taxable capacity enables it to practise a pseudo-alchemy.

10 Some Classical Economics: Monetary Features of Trade Fluctuations in Ancient Rome

10.1 PRELIMINARY REMARKS

Much essential monetary theory is clarified by the ancient skeletal materials. And there is serendipity too. Finley's (1985) insistence that the imperial economy suffered from a chronic shortage of coin is of a piece with a widespread fallacy about eighteenth-century British North America, shared by Alexander Hamilton in his still admired Bank and Public Debt reports (see Burstein, 1988). Study of the ancient fragments, and their faulty analyses, helps establish that the principles of economics are adequately universal. And there may be an economy for which 'cash in advance' is tenable: that of ancient Rome.

10.1.1 Conceptual Background for Study of the Ancient Materials

Roman public works were as sophisticated as they were vast. But the empire's financial structure was primitive. Construction costs had to be defrayed in *coin*. So it may seem plausible that surges in investment (especially in public works) were quite strictly matched by infusions of precious metals – and huge treasures obtained in conquests did finance the fori of Julius Caesar (Gaul) and Trajan (see also his Basilica Ulpia, Dalmatia). A certain hypothesis is encouraged: *the pulse of Roman investment and/or inflation may have been governed by that of monetary expansion*. The hypothesis evokes analogies to imposed lacking or forced saving via expansion of financial sector lending or government-currency issue.

(a) *The Hypothesis is Unsuccessful*

The feeble, irregular pulse of the ancient economy's vibration does not seem to have been governed by monetary pulsation. Why? A number of decisively high elasticities permitted human and non-human resources to shift smoothly between sectors; and precious metals to move agilely between monetary and non-monetary stocks.

High elasticity of supply of common labour in ancient Rome has at least two sources. One is in the slave system. The elasticity of supply of chattel labour at any point on the imperial grid seems to have been substantial; and the sordid process controlling aggregate supply of slave labour responded strongly to reward. For one thing there was little race prejudice: slave status was widely conferred.

The other source lies in *panem et circenses* (bread and circuses). The Roman welfare state – supplying bread, oil, the variegated services of the baths, sometimes bloodily exciting entertainments, etc. – made leisure attractive and established a fairly generous safety net. The welfare system led to a large 'float' of free labour that could be enticed into construction activity at premium wages.

(Rents, including rents of ability, of skilled craftsmen fluctuated with demand. And the elasticity of supply of skilled effort was quite high. The state's welfare provision had little influence on the leisure margin of skilled craftsmen. Not only was their 'required' living standard substantially higher than that of common labourers: their life styles were less customary; their expenditures were more variable and more sensitive to the ebb and flow of economic opportunity.)

Non-monetary stocks of precious metals (including practical objects crafted from precious metals) much exceeded monetary stocks. The quantity of monetary gold and silver was determined by a convenience yield of non-monetary stocks exogenous to the 'money market'. So the purchasing power of gold and silver over goods in general was determined by the much larger non-monetary precious metal markets; quantities of monetary holdings floated up or down in response to an autonomous marginal criterion. Since precious metal objects were so prized, the purchasing power of full-weight coins (i.e., of unadulterated money) was high. The upshot, in eighteenth-century British North America as well as in Rome, is often confused with 'shortage of coin'.

(b) *Rome did not Face a Proper Inflation Problem*

The Crown's chronic inability to fund its often profligate expenditure led to chronic debasement of the coinage. The Roman emperors often sought to extract the equivalent to an inflation tax by debasing the coinage. Coins were reckoned by *tale*. So weights of gold or silver equivalents to Crown obligations were persistently cried down. Resulting depreciation entailed many of the appurtenances of inflation; but the purchasing power of precious metals, reckoned by *weight*, held up throughout.

So a quantity theory of money is consistent with qualitative explanation of currency depreciation: when coin is reckoned by *tale*, not weight, deterioration of the coinage increases the price of a well-defined quantum of gold or silver on a value scale on which the unit of measure is disjoint from 'weight' (see 1986, Chapter 1 and Chapter 2 above).

The scenario illuminates behaviour of present-day Caligulas and Neros – perhaps bourgeois politicians spinning out their days in revolving-door governments – who often succumb to the temptation to depreciate their paper currencies.

(c) *Organization of Chapter 10*

Chapter 10's materials are distributed among seven heads. (1) Labour supply. (2) Slavery and wage/price flexibility. (3) Absence of an idea of progress. (4) The simple financial structure of the Roman empire; (5) 'Cash in advance'. (6) Liquidity preference and non-monetary precious metal stocks. (7) Depreciation of the value of money in Roman times.

10.2 LABOUR SUPPLY

Until well into the eighteenth century, if not the middle of the nineteenth century, a stringent energy equation choked net Western productivity and doubtless contributed towards absence of an idea of progress. The prime sources of energy in the industrial sector, save for such heat sources as wood, were human and non-human livestock whose maintenance requirements absorbed much the greater part of gross output in ways described by closed Leontief systems. But Malthusian-like models do not define population limits for the imperial Roman economy: immediately controlling constraints were more military than Malthusian. If the Romans had acquired technologies permitting absolute military dominion over barbarians, so that German incursions into Gaul, for example, were definitively foreclosed, the economic size of the empire Hadrian sought to stabilize geographically would have outstripped actual results. If Roman generals had deployed regiments equipped with automatic weapons, the cost of deterrence would have fallen dramatically. Much more land could have been intensively cultivated within the boundaries of a secure empire.

'Wage funds' rigidly bounded labour force potentials at specific localities. Thus 'the imperial city of Rome lived on grain imported from Sicily, Spain, North Africa and Egypt'. (Finley, 1985, pp. 33–4). Static shipping and port technologies harshly constrained key supplies – as did dread of famine:

> In Antioch, during the famine of A.D. 362–63, it required the forcible intervention of the emperor Julian to have grain brought from two island districts of northern Syria, one fifty, the other a hundred miles away.
>
> Finley (1985, pp. 33–4)

Thus much for labour supply at a very high level of aggregation.

10.3 SLAVERY AND WAGE/PRICE FLEXIBILITY

(See especially Finley (1985, Chapter 3, pp. 62ff) and Nicholas (1962/1969, pp. 71–6). And remember that social and economic gradations were severely wide in ancient times.)

Hire prices of chattels, including live stock, reckon to be highly flexible. So, in principle, slave labour allocation obeys paradigms designed for more or less perfectly competitive markets; to the extent that masses of workers in the Roman empire were subjugated, highly flexible hire prices of human chattels might have substituted for the sticky wages of modern practice – so important for business-cycle theory over the last 150 years. What were the facts?

> Whenever we know of a private establishment, urban or rural, regularly employing the services of numbers of workmen whose status is identified, these were slaves. Enterprises hiring free men on even a semi-permanent basis are simply not to be found in the sources.
>
> Finley (1985, pp. 73–4)

The fragmentary evidence cannot support robust conclusions. But the fragments *do* support the hypothesis that supplies of labour were elastic at ancient margins. Surely slave cadres are more readily shunted about than free labour forces. And free common labour supply, available to support slave cadres, seems to have been quite elastic. (Free and slave workers seem to have worked together harmoniously and were not ethnically distinct.) Craftsmen services reckoned to be elastically supplied along lines modelled by the new classical macro-economics.

Remarks

Rewards received by chattels do not generally closely correspond to yields obtained by masters – although prize bulls may be lavishly provided for by profit maximizing owners (or cf the Empress of Blandings).

Finley (1985) supplies both an illuminating discussion and an extensive bibliography of slavery in the ancient world

10.4 ABSENCE OF AN IDEA OF PROGRESS

Finley comments interestingly on what Oswald Spengler calls the Apollonian World View.

> The Greeks and Romans inherited a considerable body of techniques and empirical knowledge, which they exploited well insofar as it suited their particular values, and to which they added the gear and the screw, the rotary mill and the water mill, glass-blowing, concrete, hollow bronze-casting, the lateen sail and a few more . . . But there were not many genuine inventions after the fourth or third century B.C. . . . We must remind ourselves time and again that the European experience since the late Middle Ages in technology, in the economy, and in the value system that accompanied them, was unique in history . . . Technical progress, economic growth, productivity, even efficiency have not been significant goals since the beginning of time. So long as an acceptable life-style could be maintained, however that was defined, other values held the stage.
>
> Finley (1985, pp. 146–7)

Finley may date the onset of the idea of material progress too early. Consider America. Although Benjamin Franklin, né 1706, went far to define a prudent materialism later celebrated in America, John Adams, né 1735, abhorred its values; nor did the Adamses enter the mercantile/financial mainstream until John's grandson, Charles Francis, married into the Brooks family. What is more, John Adams and other Founders planned to train gifted youths to become *optimates*: the New Republic was to emulate Plato's. (The concept was already embodied in France's *grands écoles*, later expanded by Napoleon I.) And all the Adamses, like Plato, favoured sumptuary laws. Thomas Jefferson, né 1743, was of the Enlightenment and looked towards progressive intellectual and moral human development. But he was at most ambivalent on the economic plane: his phantasies of the New Republic were pastoral, but not his practical policies; he deplored materialism and lived grandiosely. What is now thought of as the quintessentially American idea of material progress did not motivate the American revolution; and the *esprit* of the Founders was classical. True, Greed set in early: Tocqueville supplies copious examples – including the laments of the last surviving signer of the Declaration of Independence, Charles Carroll of Carrolltown (1737–1832).

Coda to Section 10.4 (Absence of an Idea of Progress)

Finley takes economics too far. After an interesting description of Roman indifference to harnessing energy and inventiveness to promote practical technology ('the contrast with the Royal Society in England is inescapable'), he suggests that the fall of Rome owed to neglect of prospects for economic efficiency. Referring to insufficiency of Roman means to resist growing Germanic and Persian incursions from the middle of the third century AD, he writes

> Nothing could be done to raise the productivity of the empire as a whole or to redistribute the load. For that a complete structural transformation would have been required.
>
> Finley (1985, p. 149)

I argue that military insufficiency is explained differently. True its origins were technological: the Romans failed to acquire destructive capability to offset effects of low birth rates and softening manners. Higher cultures are at a disadvantage in the brutish battle tactics that persisted well beyond Roman times. Roman advantages in discipline and conceptual thinking were bound to erode; and higher cultures are ill adapted to savage hand-to-hand combat.

A more successful imperial economy would have offered juicier targets: barbarous onslaughts would have unfolded at a faster pace. Rome would have fallen sooner. Edward Gibbon makes rather the same point, and anticipates Mr Gorbachev as well.

> we cannot be displeased that . . . an industrious people should be protected by those arts which survive and supply the decay of military virtue. Cannon and fortifications now form an impregnable barrier against Tartar horse; and Europe is secure from any future irruption of barbarians, since before they can conquer, they must cease to be barbarous. Their gradual advances in the science of war would always be accompanied, as we may learn from the example of Russia, with a proportionate improvement in the arts of peace and civil policy; and they themselves must deserve a place among the polished nations they subdue.
>
> Edward Gibbon, *Decline and Fall* (Penguin Classics edn, D. A. Saunders (ed), 1985, pp. 627–8)

10.5 THE SIMPLE FINANCIAL STRUCTURE OF THE ROMAN EMPIRE

There was a vast amount of personal lending on virtual call; and heightened specie preference, provoking calls, can in principle engender self-feeding implosive effects. But Section 10.6 shows that immense hoards of specie and non-monetary precious metal objects exerted strong damping influence. There was an immense mass of manoeuvre, albeit no centralizing principle. Roman emperors exerted little financial control; after all, they were subject to cash in advance.

10.5.1 Possibilities for Implosion

In an implosion induced by intensification of specie preference, agents hive off specie as they are paid so that others can no longer properly expect to obtain the volume of proceeds they must get to justify costs of production. The sequel feeds on itself: hoarding propensities intensify, partly because of expectations that prices will continue to fall.

10.5.2 Finley's Analysis of the Properties of Rome's Financial Structure

Finley discusses personal lending, and the apparent lack of much other lending, in the simple financial economy of ancient Rome in some depth.

> From one end of antiquity to another, one can easily count the known examples of borrowing on property for purposes of purchase or improvement. The mortgage was . . . a short-term personal loan designed [in the words of Sieveking (1933, p. 561)] 'to cover deficiencies in the supply of necessities occasioned generally by some emergency which has made unexpected demands on the resources of the borrower', not a deliberate device for raising money at a low rate in order to invest at a higher rate . . . Among men of property these demands were either familial (a dowry) or sumptuary or political . . . Sometimes such expenditures brought large returns . . . but they were in no sense returns on an investment in property. It is thus not surprising that there was neither a recognizable real-property market nor a profession of estate agent or dealer.
>
> Finley (1985, pp. 117–18)

The disjunction from modern concepts is less than Finley suggests: after all, one of Fisher's approximations to the theory of interest is confined to consumer loans; and in an approximate stationary state, net productive investment is nil, but intergenerational transfers and transactions like Sieveking's may entail vast volumes of gross transfers that look like consumer loans.

Finley correctly extracts a signally important implication from the rudimentary Roman financial structure: in ancient times too, financial forces did not contribute to real economic fluctuations; and in ancient times too 'money and finance' erratically fomented crises.

> Not only were the ups and downs in production always attributable to natural catastrophe or political troubles, not to cyclical crises, but so-called 'credit crises' turn out to have had the same roots, not

> in supply-and-demand operations in a normal 'money market'. Cicero was painfully aware of the effects of a sudden shortage of coin on interest rates and land prices; and Dio Cassius revealed similar awareness of the reverse when Augustus brought back the captured Egyptian treasure to Rome. [Still no ancient commentator] offers any reflections on what we may call long term movements, on the secular movement of prices.
>
> Finley (1985, p. 142)

But the secular movement of prices (say in a gold metric) seems trendless! See Nicolet (1971) and Finley's copious references, pp. 240–1.

Finley may be too rash: see Section 10.7. In other places, he correctly emphasizes highly elastic demand for specie and precious metal objects; as well the immensity of stocks of these substances. It is more plausible that the captured Egyptian treasure was tucked away into stocks so that it had little effect on interest rates and prices, *pace* my failed hypothesis.

At pp. 197ff, Finley reports massive attacks on his 'primitivist' position by Andreau (1977) and Thompson (1979, 1982). The heated debate is readily conflated with those over the proper rôle of financial institutions in economic development.

Interpolation

If the accumulation point of a real capital evolution is well defined, more sophisticated financial modalities contribute towards earlier attainment of an invariant wealth level. True, in the real world, the equilibrium volume of working capital accumulation depends on the adequacy of financial markets. Thus dead stock diminishes as loan markets become more efficient.

10.5.3 Finley's Analysis: Ancient Credit Crises

(See the Note to Chapter 8.)

Finley develops a rudimentary example of an ancient credit crisis following a military catastrophe at Ephesus: there was widespread, covariant effort to reduce positions to specie. Nor was the City innoculated against panic.

The civil war that brought Julius Caesar to power instilled a fear in

> Roman moneyed circles of a 'demagogic' measure to cancel debts. Interest rates were lowered by tribunes; creditors called in their loans; debtors were unable to pay; their land was seized and became a glut on the market, with coin literally running out.
>
> Finley (1985, p. 143)

He goes on to point up how crises entail spasmodic, self-feeding lurches in preferences. Yes! In an unstable variant, attempts to obtain specie increase excess demand for it as many debtors sink. And, as outlays fail to generate demand on return channels (as the spokes of Professor Knight's wheel of wealth are jammed) freer spenders get into still worse trouble. But for all that the Roman economy was *not* very prone to widespread or prolonged credit crises. One explanation pivots on Cicero's 'prescientific observation' that more money is loaned when debt collection is not threatened by demagogues: it was *not* for the most part. Another explanation pivots on huge stocks of non-monetary precious metals. It is elaborated on in Section 10.7 and is anticipated by Barsky and Summers (1988) and (1989a, Chapter 8).

10.6 'CASH IN ADVANCE'

The fabled power of Roman emperors stopped far short of that of nondescript bourgeois governments of the present day in the economic sphere: the emperor had to pay cash in advance.

The constraining force of 'cash in advance' was relaxed by at least two factors. One operated the way bank 'sweeping' erodes conventional definitions of aggregate transactions balances. The other pivots on a now-familiar situation, *viz.* the huge potential increments to the active monetary circulation that could be elastically put into play (holdings of non-monetary precious metals).

As for 'cash in advance' anciently,

> To begin with, the state was as tied as any private individual to hard cash on hand (occasionally to short term, often compulsory, loans). In the second century B.C. the affluent temple of Apollo at Delos stored both its own savings and those of the city-state of Delos in its divinely protected strong room, as the temple of Athens did in classical Athens.
>
> Finley (1985, p. 174)

He appends an important footnote to this paragraph: 'I refer here to coined money only, not to the infinitely larger quantity of uncoined treasure sterilized in this temple as in so many others'. (As for *sterilized*, Finley, like Alexander Hamilton and his mercantilist intellectual forebears, seems to think that money rains stimulate 'real' crops.)

Finley's continuing comments on stores of value at Delos are useful.

> The two treasuries were called the 'sacred chest' and the 'public chest', respectively, each consisting of a number of [clearly labelled] jars . . . The principle of cash in a strong box restricted Roman emperors just as closely . . . Sizes of [imperial] donatives were largely determined by the amounts available in the jars.
>
> Finley (1985, pp. 174–5)

Some of Finley's harshest criticisms of the Roman financial system flow from theory now passé. It is useful to evaluate his critique from a number of points of view; insight is gained into the history of Rome and the history of economics.

Having established (at p. 141, for example) that 'money was hard coin, mostly silver, and a fair amount of that was hoarded, in strong boxes, in the ground, often in banks as non-interest-bearing deposits', so that fiduciary money was barred (along with repeatedly endorsed negotiable instruments, important in British North America), Finley explains that there was massive money lending anciently, but that 'lenders were rigidly bound by the actual amount of cash at hand. There was no machinery for the *creation of credit* (emphasis supplied) through negotiable instruments. The complete absence of a public debt in this context is a meaningful indicator' (p. 174; see my Chapter 5 above).

We have repeatedly explained that financial intermediaries do *not* create real lendable resources. The incapacity of ancient banks to lend entailed the reform advocated by an earlier Chicago school; cf 100 per cent reserve banking. It probably contributed to stability; and the incapacity did not block creation of real lendable resources. The ancient system more plausibly anticipated salutary innovations than led to constipation of accumulation.

Perhaps the most rampant, and malignant, error in monetary theory has been confusion of money with credit. The ancient debt-discharge system relied on a mass of coin along lines that Presidents

Jefferson and Jackson wanted to install in the United States; and which, if adopted, would have elided the liaison of government with money power that Hamilton installed (see 'Alexander Hamilton', 1988). Still financial intermediation, separated from money creation, is fruitful; and the coarseness of the ancient financial intermediary system hampered accumulation of capital – or delayed attainment of the equivalent to a Ricardian stationary state.

Coda to Section 10.6: How the Emperor Claudius may have Eluded 'Cash in Advance' in Financing his Harbour at Ostia

'Cash in advance' is often a misleading rubric. Thus in future transactors not permitted to take more credit on the giro may acquire (for a fee) the power to tap another's account. From time to time, Caesar used more muscle to the same effect. Robert Graves's story about Claudius's *financement* of his harbour at Ostia may be true.

> 'But, Caesar, where's the money to come from,' he bleated like a sheep.
>
> . . .
>
> Within an hour I had the six richest corn-factors in the City before me. I frightened them.
>
> . . .
>
> [I told them] I wanted an immediate loan of one million gold pieces . . . which I would pay back as soon as the financial situation justified it.
>
> . . .
>
> The money was paid over within five days, and the works at Ostia began at once.
>
> Robert Graves, *Claudius the God* (1934/1954, p. 145)

10.7 LIQUIDITY PREFERENCE AND NON-MONETARY PRECIOUS METAL STOCKS

As the Roman empire transisted from the more ascetic purer republic (surely as idealized by Virgil), conspicuous consumption, encompassing potlatch-like public games and electoral bribery, imposed exigent demands on leading men. (Leading women poisoned leading men.) The upshot is misunderstood by Finley and others blinded by Keynes's (1936) *éclat*. Finley conflates the 'land' fallacy of Chapter 17 of the *General Theory* with mercantilist ideas, favoured by Keynes (1936), that money supply is negatively correlated with the real cost of capital.

> Complicating this ravenous hunger for acquisition in the upper strata was the fact that their basic wealth was land, and that they therefore faced chronic shortages of cash [read gold and silver coin] whenever they needed larger sums [for personal or political purposes].
>
> Finley (1985, p. 56)

This cannot be true. Finley explains elsewhere that non-monetary precious metal holdings were immense. Any threat of a chronic shortage of cash would have been countered by a flow from non-monetary to monetary precious metal holdings.

Interpolation

We have it on the uncertain authority of Robert Graves's *Claudius the God* (1934/1954, p. 84) that Claudius, on his accession, obtained 1 million gold pieces by melting down the huge gold statue Caligula had had placed in his temple. The easy transition, back and forth, between monetary and non-monetary gold and silver, is crucial for a correct theory of commodity money. Again see Barsky and Summers (1988) and Chapter 8 of (1989a).

* * *

As for *public (imperial) policy*, Finley complains that not even during credit crises (when creditors may try to reduce their assets to specie) did the state do more than make futile gestures urging hoarders to disgorge stocks. This is unfair. Emperors sometimes became gods, but never alchemists. If they played out the state treasure too freely, panic could become complete once people saw that no mass of manoeuvre was left. True, in a more supple system, rulers might call for temporary moratoria (as in nineteenth-century America). But, in ancient times, formal moratoria would have impelled people to cease to pay out coin and to refuse further grants of credit. Effects would have been ghastly.

10.7.1 Money and Credit Redux: Money Supply and Growth

Finley's interesting *further thoughts* (1985, pp. 177–207) centre on money supply and growth. Alas, he confuses effects of poor mobilization of savings (so that saving may be discouraged by inadequacy of mediation) with insufficiency of the supply of money.[1] And he confuses mediation of credit with its creation. The first fault is visible in the following passage, strikingly akin to improper analyses of British North American monetary conditions in the eighteenth century – which I discuss in (1966/1988) as well as in 'Alexander Hamilton'.

> It remains beyond dispute that even Rome suffered an occasional crisis attributable to a shortage of coin . . . It is also beyond dispute that, Rome and other imperial states apart, ancient states were faced with chronic shortages except when they had windfalls through conquest or a lucky strike in mining.
>
> Finley (1985, p. 196)

Finley's conclusion looks vulnerable to this criticism. At a low enough price level (a high enough real value for a unit of money), real monetary balances are large enough to meet any demand. *But it is not!* The value of monetary silver or gold was substantially less than that. This implies that money supply was perfectly elastic at a critical value of money (or non-monetary precious metal stocks); indeed nobody denies that the *total* supply of gold and silver was sufficient. *Finley is wrong.*

As for the *second fault*,

> However, my concern is with credit rather than with coin, and specifically with the machinery for credit beyond the lending of coins. In the original edition, I stressed the absence of devices, familar from the late Middle Ages . . . which permit the *creation* of credit, i.e. the extension of the society's resources by techniques permitting lenders . . . to deal with tokens . . . as if they were cash. I noted in particular the lack of negotiable paper, the corresponding absence of bourses or exchanges and the absence of a public debt in the form of official bank notes or similar fiduciary money.
>
> Finley (1985, pp. 196–7)

Finley, like so many others, confuses money with credit while confusing qualitative properties of financial mediation with volumes of credit taken. But he properly says that the primitiveness of the Roman financial markets precluded financial provocation of real fluctuations along lines taken by Thornton (1802), and many modern writers too . . . Agreed, Roman finance was heavily flawed. Credit markets were too primitive for savings to be efficiently directed into optimal uses. The utility of markets in debt *was* insufficiently appreciated.

10.7.2 Liquidity Crises

It remains to discover a plausible mechanism that may have generated liquidity crises in the Roman economy.

Potentials for instability nest in the following factors.

1. *Elastic expectations* encourage *more* hoarding when precious metals are in excess demand, so that prices are falling.
2. Enhanced precious metal preference induces *calls* (i.e., pressing demands for debt payment), forcing debtors to offer non-monetary assets in markets that may collapse under the weight of such offers. Resulting bankruptcies feed back to liquidity preference so that it heats up still more. But the stabilizing immensity of ancient reserves seems to have disarmed feedback channels in ways Finley, and so many others, misperceive.

Finley sees the reserve principle from a slant common in his salad days. Emperors were financial cripples; Finley finds the resulting lack of a central banking principle a grievous fault. But a central bank, inevitably attuned to politics, may impose a powerful forcing vibration on an economy whose intrinsic vibration is mild: the resulting compound vibration may be severe. More importantly, when reserves are as huge as they were anciently, 'mass of manoeuvre' is unimportant.

Decentralization seems to have worked quite well. Liquidity crises were localized. Think of an electricity transmission grid on which local failures are frequent but widespread *pannes* are avoided. The conservative ancient laissez-faire reserve management principle achieved its limited objectives: crises did not spread. Put differently, a huge reserve army prevented global crises by virtue of its size – but the army was not subtly deployed. (Cf the British appraisal of General Eisenhower's strategy in 1944–5.) Centralized systems are more likely to override circuit breakers – as happened in America *circa* 1931–3.

10.8 DEPRECIATION OF THE VALUE OF MONEY IN ROMAN TIMES

The edict of maximum prices of Diocletian (AD 245–316; emperor, 284–305) is widely cited as a supreme example of the futility of price control; and as an example of endemic confusion of improper qualitative explanations of price behaviour with proper quantitative ones. It is said that sense-of-number was so feeble that qualitative rationales cropped up again and again: 'something is wrong with the money'; 'merchants are ganging up and gouging'. But a lot was wrong with the money. Ancient coinages were chronically degraded in order to obtain pseudo-seigneurage profit. The root cause was fiscal shortfall, as Finley and his copious references explain. Of course, since then, inflation taxes have been extracted at levels undreamt of by Caesar.

10.8.1 Reconciliation of the Quantity Theory of Money with Qualitative Approaches to Ancient Inflation

(See Chapter 2.)

If ancient prices are measured so that a well-defined quantum of gold or silver, or of an amalgam, is numéraire,[2] necessarily crude time series of prices look stable enough; to that extent there was little inflation in antiquity. But the value of monetary objects chronically depreciated against gold or silver or goods in general. Diocletian *et al.*, seeking to arrest such depreciation, tried to impose lacking on the economy in favour of Crown expenditure. The market resisted him by crying down the bullion price of the coinage and contriving metrics for which official coin is not numéraire. These conclusions are buttressed by some remarks on the theory of monetary standards, on implications of high elasticities of demand for precious metals in Roman times and on specifics of Roman coinage debasement.

Remarks

(a) *Some Theory of Monetary Standards*

As time passed, coins were lightened (sweated, clipped, abraded, etc.)

> sometimes retaining their original names, sometimes acquiring new ones. Measures of value became disjoint from measures of weight. Coins came to be accepted by *tale* rather than by weight. A one-mark coin ceased to weigh one mark.
>
> Burstein (1986, p. 5)

Silver weighing one mark might retain its purchasing power; but a silver coin that weighed but a fraction of a mark would command much less than a full-weighted one-mark coin.

(b) *High Elasticity of Demand for Silver and Gold*

Substantial infusions of gold and silver into the empire would not have much affected prices; the purchasing power of gold and silver would not have fallen much. Very elastic demand for non-monetary precious metals would cause such infusions to be absorbed into stocks without leaving much of a trace on prices.[3]

(c) *Coinage Debasement*

Consider the *Aureus* – important in Chapter 2 and in (1989a, especially Chapter 6). Its history is one of debasement. This full-bodied coin of the Roman Republic was retained by Augustus[4] at 42 to the Roman pound, but debased by Nero and again by Caracalla, etc. (For an admirable quick reference see the article on 'Coinage, Roman' in the *Oxford Classical Dictionary*.)

Notes and References

1. Finley (1985, p. 182) fully documents references to models of Keith Hopkins and Thomas Pekáry. Pekáry insists that an insufficient stock of coinage throttled growth; Hopkins says that there was significant growth and plays down 'money shortage'. The British North American analogy

favours Hopkins. But Finley, supporting Pekáry, claims that Hopkins insufficiently considers exploitation of the provinces; that Hopkins misinterprets trade balance data, confusing exploitation by Rome with 'mother country' growth. Also see Whittaker (1980).

2. Finley's discussion of symmetallism must grip the reader of Chapter 2.

> Only the gold-silver alloy, white gold or electrum, was beyond control [i.e., money changers could not evaluate electrum objects]. Whether minted from a natural alloy or alloyed artificially, the popular electrum staters of Cyzicus in Asia Minor could not be assayed before Archimedes's discovery of specific gravity, and they therefore circulated at a conventional value.
>
> Finley (1985, p. 167)

(Finley cites Bogaert, 1963 and Eddy, 1970 in this connection.)
'Circulation at a conventional value' is a short step from reckoning in imaginary money, a procedure that has long incensed governments: it blocks collection of inflation taxes.
The Romans were sophisticated enough to take this 'short step'. Discussing the Roman law of obligations, in particular contracts, Nicholas writes

> (ii) *The Price*. There must be a money price. This requirement meant that the *permutatic* (exchange or barter) was not sale . . . The Proculians prevailed. Their argument was that if the price were not in money, it would be impossible to distinguish buyer from seller, the implication being that since their duties, and the actions by which they were enforced, were different, the law would then be unworkable.
>
> Nicholas (1962/1969, p. 174)

Even today tabular standards, together with sophisticated giro-clearing concepts, are often rejected because their upshot looks like barter. Roman resistance to the Proculians is impressive. It is possible that Roman law would have closed the intellectual gap separating money of account from money *propre* sooner than modern law will have done if the Romans had had a still longer run.

3. Gibbon interestingly comments on the 'adequacy' of the supply of precious metals in the Roman world; nor does he (mistakenly) centre on supplies of monetized precious metals instead of those of precious metals *propre*.

> It was a complaint worthy of the gravity of the senate, that, in the purchase of female ornaments, the wealth of the state was irrecoverably given away to foreign and hostile nations [citing Tacitus, Annal., iii, 53 while indicating that the matter was taken up by Tiberius before the senate; Professor Bury's annotation is considered below]. The annual loss is computed . . . at upwards of eight hundred thousand pounds sterling. Such was the style of discontent brooding over the dark prospect of approaching poverty. And yet, if we compare the propor-

> tion between gold and silver, as it stood in the time of Pliny, and as it was fixed in the reign of Constantine, we shall discover . . . a very considerable increase. There is not the least reason to suppose that gold was become more scarce; it is therefore evident that silver was grown more common; that whatever might be the amount of the Indian and Arabian exports, they were far from exhausting the wealth of the Roman world; and that the produce of the mines abundantly supplied the demands of commerce.
>
> Gibbon, *Decline and Fall* (Bury edn, 1909/1974, vol. I (of 7 vols) pp. 60–1)

See *Gibbon (1909/1974 edn)* note 114, p. 60 Professor Bury, referring to copious sources, asserts that 'there was certainly [*sic*?] a gradual diminution in the amount of gold and silver *in circulation* in the second century [emphasis supplied]. Yet . . . Gibbon has grasped [the] facts; the spirit of his observation is right'.

The amount of gold and silver *in circulation* was endogenous, responding to demand; while aggregate supplies of precious metals were immense, dwarfing monetary circulation.

4. I think Augustus possessed *measure* to a supreme degree. *Measure* is easily defined: Napoleon I lacked it. My short list includes the emperor Hadrian, General Washington, the Duke of Wellington and Otto von Bismarck.

11 Conclusion

Scanning more than two thousand years of economic history, it is hard to discern spontaneous monetary impetus to real economic fluctuations. But systematic vibration in the action of monetary authorities (MAs) may induce systematic 'real' vibration. Of course, an MA might impart a regular vibration to an economy it makes less volatile.

11.1 PRELIMINARIES (CHAPTER 6)

Economic cycles are apt to be illusory. Much random behaviour looks cyclical. And properly-defined wave action is dominated by *diffraction*. Study of diffraction (or of interference) turns up a striking property of the algebra of wave action – cancellation; or coincidence, leading to intensification that may induce resonance.

11.1.1 Monetary Background

Flexible interest on money erodes distinctions between financial assets the way Wallace's (1983) legal restrictions theory does: in the limit financial assets become an amorphous mass.

Flexible interest on money also disarms the *inflation tax*, a variant of *forced saving*, so central to most monetary approaches to business cycles. Much forced saving theory flows from Wicksellian economics, which need not be the economics of Wicksell. Wicksellian theory is based on an improperly specified, or unspecified, notion of 'money market' equilibrium; and it 'forgets' that the business of the financial intermediary sector is to swap paper claims against itself for less liquid claims. A cumulative process entails real effects only if supine, if not stupid, agents trade away claims to real product for paper whose yield has fallen while, according to Wicksellian theory, the yield of real assets has increased.

A principal conclusion of the study, exhaustively illustrated, is that potential for business cycles is especially feeble in innovated open economies. Then the relation between *money* and cycles is hopelessly weak.

Spontaneous crises, or acute episodes flowing from excess demand for liquidity, are indeed *possible*, but they do not induce *regular* vibrations; and historically have tended to nest in flaws of regulatory systems.

MA action may vibrate quite strongly. Such vibration, sometimes associated with MA over-reaction to or misperception of impulses received on a feedback channel, may induce real fluctuation. (Rational expectations require that truly systematic MA vibration be anticipated so that its impact on real action is muffled.)

Many strands of thought are woven together to form the hypothesis that monetary motivation for cyclical behaviour is supplied by MA action. Examples include Keynes's (1930) bismuth/castor oil model, Friedman's (1951/1953) 'formal analysis', extensions of Friedman's set-up to wave mechanical paradigms, Poole's (1970) model, Wicksell's *cumulative process*, driven by a neurasthenic MA and purgative Bank rate policy (see Chapter 3).

11.2 IMPLICATIONS OF EMPIRICAL PROPERTIES OF A HYPOTHETICAL OPEN ECONOMY (CHAPTER 7)

Chapter 7 concerns empirical orders of magnitude. In view of its simplicity, it is surprisingly revealing. Orders of magnitude of *changes* in variables directly affected by MA action, or of changes resulting from spontaneous action of the banking system, are swamped out by the intrinsic vibration of the global system. Well-known theories of trade fluctuations concern tiny tempests in huge teapots, even in closed economies. *A fortiori*, in open economies, impulses generated by MAs or the banking system fade away still more rapidly. Then almost all monetary or financial variables are endogenous.

Remark

Barsky and Summers (1988) are studied in Chapter 10, and in Chapter 8 of (1989a). It is shown that money supply is endogenous in closed, as well as open, commodity money systems. But monetary theories of trade cycles were proposed for economies on commodity standards. Theorists groped in darkness from the beginning.

* * *

Quite massive changes in data for hypothetical, mostly open, economies are considered. In no case is there substantial interference with the economy's autonomous action; and autonomous action looks cyclical only in the way continuous variegated random shocks generate pseudo-cycles. There is not much for theories based on monetary action to explain.

Simulated shifts in savings rates of 25 per cent require trade balance changes of less than ¼ of 1 per cent of GDP for equilibrium to be restored. Even 50 per cent declines in planned capital formation lead to GDP shortfalls from full employment (cf aggregate demand gaps) of less than 1.2 per cent – in a starkly Keynesian analysis ignoring equilibrating effects of myriad relative price adjustments.

There are more plausible, if non-monetary, sources of fairly regular real fluctuation. If sectoral demands and supplies shift frequently and erratically, differentials in price inertia lead transiently to distortion of relative prices abetting unsustainable expansions of the industrial sector that run into bottlenecks, leading to cumulative contraction. Non-linear dynamic models of the sort developed by Hicks and Goodwin imitate this upshot at a very high level of aggregation. And fluctuations of terms of trade explain much of the fluctuation in nineteenth-century American growth rates – and are always important for small open economies.

* * *

Turning to *finance*, scenarios are developed in which investment surges in Economy *E* are readily financed by domestic savings and capital inflow. Austrian scripts describe the sequel: the structure of production is distorted so that the period of production is unsustainably long, impelling a spontaneous reversal, etc.

But this study centres on *banks*.

Since banks do not generate flows of real resources, they typically contribute little to real expansionary impulses. But acute contraction of financial intermediary credit can provoke crises of liquidity inducing real contraction. The upshot is asymmetrical. Acute contraction of credit may disrupt the matrix of claims. Expansion of the nominal credit of the financial intermediary sector is *not* disruptive: temporary excess supply of liquid claims does not make for a crisis!

Admittedly-sketchy empirical work supports these conclusions. The banking industry's contribution to real credit taken is quite slight, especially in open economies. Monetary theories of real economic fluctuations are not supported empirically.

11.3 SOME THEORY OF INNOVATED FINANCIAL NETWORKS (CHAPTER 8)

(See Chapter 4.)

Wallace's (1983) *legal restrictions* theory, flowing from the Modigliani–Miller corporate finance theorem, is crucial. Spontaneous free market processes swamp out, or offset, official sector monetary actions and freely cross national borders, often in ways that cannot be picked up statistically. And ongoing innovations sap the ability of central banks to control credit flows and money supplies within their jurisdictions.

What if local base money growth changes? Spontaneous counteraction is induced. If there is a spurt in the E-dollar monetary base, options entitling holders to E-dollar payments, or their equivalents, will run off without replaced or will be closed out prematurely. Or consider a security market analogy. Supplies of virtual shares are not determined by boards of company directors: cf forward and futures transactions, together with options writing. Quasi-issue may be negatively correlated with supplies of underlying stocks – although real potential earnings streams constrain possibilities in ways not common in monetary-theoretic counterparts. The open-economy equivalent to the quasi-share issue case concerns the way $\bar{E}$ banks may generate E-dollar issue, perhaps frustrating E's monetary authorities. ($\bar{E}$ = not-E.)

The illustrations lead up to *financial denationalization*. In an innovated open economy, a representative agent contracts for liabilities (obtains resources) in various measures and arranges for cover like agents with short commodity positions. In the upshot, monetary authorities are unable to exercise control over the volumes of locally-denominated liquid assets in their jurisdictions. And what is worse for such MAs, local agents will sometimes contract out of measures sensitive to MA action, doubtless to its distress: Danish traders may formulate internal transactions in DM, arranging for credit in Germany and laying off any resulting DM exposure in global foreign-exchange options markets.

The analysis is sucked into the field of the theory of *currency competition* – or, better, competition between metrics. In the upshot, liquid holdings of Economy E are not assigned an exclusive E-dollar designation; and options dealings transform apparent E-dollar holdings into virtual $\bar{E}$-dollar ones (i.e. not-E-dollar ones) in ways that cannot be tracked.

There is more! Monetary theories of fluctuations of real economic action are surely sapped if the evolution of virtual local money stocks lies outside the sphere of influence of local banking systems and MAs. And *more* is happening: the ideas of money as such and of intermediation are crumbling. Development of extended tabular systems and full giro transfer modalities, studied in Chapter 4, pushes the idea of monetary properties (let alone money) back to a new defensive line – *viz*. liquidity properties of larger subsets of financial substances. But the *securitization* idea, going *beyond the banking principle* (see 1988) overruns the new trenches. Securitization makes a wide range of assets monetarily indistinguishable: compound claims to *many* mortgages are as intrinsically liquid as even a claim against a fully reserved intermediary. (On 2 May 1989 the press reported that Citicorp is planning to securitize part of its consumer credit portfolio.)

Chapter 8 essays considerable 'thought experimentation'. In one instance, the Banque de France, instructed by the Ministre des Finances, seeks to damp down credit flows. Citicorp barges in, massively increasing its French lending. It may raise capital in France, Frenchmen may effectively sell French stock to Citicorp for Citicorp stock: Citicorp invests the proceeds of share sales in French franc securities markets, thus evening up its book subsequent to expanding its French franc lending. French shares purchased by Citicorp may be traded in deep, thick markets and so be virtually as reserve competent as formal reserves.

A generalization of other illustrations shows how banks anywhere can 'issue' monetary liabilities in *E*-dollars, obtaining cover by selling long securities, including their shares, in *E*'s securities markets (or in Euro-markets), thus evening up *E*-dollar exposure on their books. In the upshot, residents of Economy *E* simply alter the texture of their collective equity portfolio. In an innovated global economy, central banks cannot exercise much control.

Chapter 8 also explores an interface with the *free banking* literature, extensively explored by L. White and interestingly reviewed by Schuler (1988). Thus Selgin (1988) argues that, under free banking, banks modify their portfolios so that they respond sympathetically to public demand for their liabilities and are barred by competitive pressures from forcing their liabilities on the public, as may happen under central banking. However, Chapter 9 shows that 'forcing' attempts are apt to fail for reasons Ricardo gave in 1817.

Selgin makes another point. Along the lines of Hayek's information theory (cf socialist economic calculation) central planners are prone to big mistakes instead of the small ones of competitive entrepreneurs. This helps explain why, in Wicksell's model, MA action is the main monetary source of real economic perturbation.

Remark

If the small mistakes of competitive entrepreneurs are statistically independent, the variance of the aggregate perturbation may be very small – and will be large if such mistakes are strongly positively covariant, as is often true in securities markets. Alternatively, if wave properties are ascribed to individual action (including forecasts), frequences and amplitudes of 'aggregate' waves depend on the extent of cancellation – as against superimposition.

11.4 BANKING POLICY AND ECONOMIC FLUCTUATIONS (CHAPTER 9)

Dennis Robertson's *Banking Policy and the Price Level*, bottomed on a *real* theory of economic fluctuations, is important for Chapter 9. Robertson argues that optimal real fluctuations require more substantial and more fluid fluctuations in *Lacking* than occur spontaneously. Committed to closed-loop financial control (cf fine tuning), Robertson proposes that the banking system intervene to correct this fault by appropriate adjustments in the volume of bank lending, acknowledging that there is a trade-off with price stability. I argue that Robertson's still influential major premiss is flawed: banks are *not* well placed to monitor flows of real resources into investment; they are lucky to know what is happening!

What, then, do banks really do? They offer their paper for higher-yielding, less-liquid, paper, living off their *spread*. An episode in which banks substantially increase their issue on their own initiative (as they do in Robertson's schema) should find bank spreads narrowed and bank paper relatively higher yielding; but in Wicksellian scenarios massive increases in issue are accompanied by *lower* yields on bank paper. Something is wrong. The standard scenario for MA induced disjunction of market rate from natural rate should be reassessed.

Milton Friedman gets to the heart of the matter in the following passage.

> It seems entirely satisfactory to take the anticipated real interest rate . . . as fixed for the demand for money. There the real rate of

> interest is at best a supporting actor . . . The situation is altogether different for saving and investment.
>
> Friedman (1974, p. 40)

I am inclined to push Friedman's point further, stopping just short of Knight's Crusonia plant, whose growth rate is exogenous; Knight's is an ultimate extension of the core proposition of classical macroeconomic theory. The banking system cannot regulate the hire price of a product (real capital) it does not produce – as Ricardo showed so ably in 1817.

11.4.1 Robertson (1926/1932)

The MA (Robertson's banking system) acts pro-cyclically. Robertson saw that his programme for supplementary expansion and contraction of bank credit amplifies real fluctuations and imparts a secondary vibration to the system, a vibration that is a product of official action.

Robertson's programme is a variant of the *forced saving* idea. If the banking system rapidly expands its credit, offers of newly-issued claims on banks for goods disequilibrate goods markets; in the ensuing scramble, the new borrowers crowd out others' demands. Agents fail to fulfill purchase plans; and the real value of their holdings of money-fixed claims erodes – leading to induced lacking. Keynes (1923) explains how attempts to rebuild cash balances lead to curtailment of planned expenditures: ergo Induced Lacking and, indeed, the *inflation tax*: new cash will be voluntarily absorbed in order to keep real cash balances intact.

11.4.2 Secondary Vibrations

If the supply of reserves to the banking system is elastic, acceleration of prices by bank lending activates a feedback channel. Since banks 'create' currency *and* procure short lacking (*sic*?), 'any cause aggravating the rise in prices directly tends to aggravate it also indirectly by tempting businesses to scale up the money values of their outstanding obligations to the banks' (Robertson, 1926/1932, p. 76).

How is secondary vibration to be coped with? One device may be manipulation of Bank rate – subsumed by Robertson under 'money rates of interest' (p. 76). Another concerns open-market operations in government securities. Reflection produces two strands of analysis. (1) On Robertson's premiss, efforts to subdue secondary vibration can easily overcompensate, so that the potentially salutary primary thrust is more than offset. (2) Robertson's premiss is flawed: the banking system is incapable of exerting such power.

Elaborating on (1), endemic insufficiency of information available to MAs makes overcompensation quite plausible; MA intervention programmes may increase intrinsic variances or boost amplitudes of intrinsic waves. Ironically, the fatal flaw in Robertson's stabilization programme, premissed on the ability of the banking system to monitor flows of real resources, is implicit in his prescient *ex ante/ ex post* formulation of inventory movements, along lines developed by the Stockholm School.

Elaborating on the flaw in Robertson's major premiss, when the underlying paradigm is corrected, the banking system cannot rechannel real resources. The controlling logic clusters around two core concepts. Under an extended tabular standard (like the Aureus standard of Chapter 2), expansion and contraction of the volume of bank paper merely affects its price. Under monetary standards *en vigeur*, the upshot is like that of a Keynesian elastic liquidity preference paradigm. In innovated economies in which money flexibly yields interest, additional bank paper is readily pumped into portfolios – offset by contractions in other financial asset holdings induced by small changes in relative yields, in turn implying that velocities of any but very broadly-defined monetary aggregates (financial stocks) are volatile. The reciprocal proposition is that little else is affected.

11.4.3 Real Foundations of Robertson's Theory

Robertson's is a theory of *humped investment*, rooted in technological characteristics of modern industry. Surges in investment may be followed by quite lengthy intervals on which industrial investment expenditures are depressed for wholly technical reasons. Dual to humped investment is humped lacking – its equivalent being easily accomplished in open economies where capital inflow supplements domestic saving and capital outflow dissipates excess lacking. In Robertson's empirically unsupported closed economy, there are solid theoretical foundations for weak correlation between fluctuations in investment impulses and spontaneous lacking: persistence of the propensity to consume is central to the modern theory of consumption, anticipated by Robertson.

And there is another characteristic dissonance. All may know that demand has increased for the product(s) of a competitive industry.

But there may be an expectations failure: each firm may regard itself as 'the special protégé of providence' and prepare to provide too large a portion of augmented production – leading to disappointment and retrenchment.

Interpolation

The secondary cycles of Robertson's theory are substantially psychological. And the closed-loop structure linking up MA action with that of the private economy is susceptible to psychological impulses: private agents guess what the MA plan is, and how it might be eluded, leading to revision; the MA ponders on how private agents plan to react to what they think the MA plans to do. See Frydman and Phelps (1983). Channels of influence may overheat. And sequences can be forecast no more accurately than chess games, as I explained (in 1986, Chapter 6).

(a) *Rational Expectations*

Rational expectations curtail the range of scenarios based on expectations failures: rational expectations bar systematic over-optimism, followed by recoil. Sources of real economic fluctuations become confined to purely technical factors like lumpiness and indivisibility, mandating humped investment.

(b) *Another Cause of Divergence of Actual From Appropriate Output*

This 'second cause' divines innovations in theory that took root about fifty years after publication of *Banking Policy*. Thus increases in prices received by producers may be misperceived as increases in relative prices instead of reflections of a higher general price level. When the signals are finally correctly read, output plans are reversed. Successive expansionary and contractive pulses, distributed among many agents and products and subject to the bizarre calculus of wave mechanics, are easily envisaged.

(c) *Consumer Durables/Some Subtleties in the Theory of Saving*

Moving towards a reconstructed, updated theory, admittedly unaccommodating to systemic macro-economic vibration, Chapter 9 takes up consumer durables in the context of a quite subtle savings theory.

Why is consumer durable accumulation so neglected, even by Robertson and Keynes? Such accumulation accounts for a substantial portion of investment. And there is much more. Expenditures on consumer durables are easily postponed or accelerated. The ease with which they can be switched on or off makes it much easier for increases in industrial investment to be supported or decreases to be offset – going far to solve Robertson's problem. When humped investment in chemical or power plants is called for, finance is generated by making it slightly more attractive to postpone plans for landscaping, piscine enlargement, etc. in favour of participation in industrial investment. And consumption (but not necessarily consumer expenditure) is fairly impervious to transitory events: forward-looking theories of consumption imply that savings rates tend to increase during booms and fall during downturns – relative to disposable income.

Less transparently, durable goods are a more plausible social contrivance than money to accomplish intergenerational transfers. *Inter alia*, claims to durable sources of consumption services are transferred by the old to the young as the old sustain expenditure levels exceeding the sum of their 'unearned' and shrivelling earned income.

11.4.4 Properties of a Proposed Theory of Banking Policy and Economic Fluctuations

The first job is to cut the banking industry down to proper size. Indeed as more assets become competent to discharge debt and as securities markets gain in sophistication (see securitization taking us beyond the banking principle, for example) traders will be substantially indifferent between alternative asset holdings from a monetary point of view. Tiny changes in relative yields will induce large changes in volumes of mediation; the aggregate balance sheet of financial intermediaries will fluctuate substantially. It becomes more plausible still that the evolution of the real cost of capital is autonomous for monetary analysis.

In the proposed theory, changes in the volume of financial mediation do not *per se* affect supplies of net real credit to the market. Nor do sellers of goods elect a temporary (paper) abode of purchasing power and then discover that they have been too slow to react; indeed sellers of goods for paper are guaranteed against loss – and are as fast on thc uptake as borrower-spenders. So induced lacking, as well as the inflation tax, are barred; and systematic automatic lacking is transformed into fairly uniformly distributed shortfalls of realized from planned purchases of goods.

Indexation blocks induced lacking and, less evidently, impedes automatic lacking in several ways. It creates property rights in favour of 'depositors', indemnifying them for depreciation of their claims. Financial intermediaries will require indemnification in turn: primary borrowers will know that surcharges, quasi-inflation taxes, will be imposed on them. And indexation blocks automatic lacking in another way. Agents not now taking credit will speed up planned spending upon realizing that they risk being forced into undesired lacking; they will correctly anticipate revenues from inflation premia components of yields of their assets. And they will seek lines of credit so that they are not crowded out. Robertson's process is transformed into one of pure inflation (depreciation of paper claims) with little or no real impact.

Under a *tabular standard*, an expansion of financial intermediary issue obviously has no impact. Market makers mark down Aureus prices of paper pouring onto the market. Aureus prices of goods and services barely twitch.

11.4.5 Spontaneous and Induced Crises of Liquidity

Real secular data seem to evolve fairly indifferently to neurasthenic episodes in financial markets, although Professor Kindleberger ably describes conspicuous exceptions. Still some remarks are in order.

A contraction of credit in Economy *E*, perhaps engineered by its MA, may disrupt the equilibrium of its matrix of claims, inducing attempts to build up liquid balances that undermine others' liquidity. (An ancillary effect is a fall in monetary velocity.) More often than not, such contractions are contrived by MAs, sometimes obeying 'belt tightening' ukases of the IMF. And spasms of monetary expansion are sometimes engineered by MAs responding to gnomic advice to become locomotives of global growth.

Finally, liquidity preference vibration is ordinarily easily accommodated by open economies; world markets easily cope with such vibration save for strong positive covariance.

11.4.6 On Finance: An Instructive Episode in *Dogmengeschichte*

Finance is properly a *real* concept. Thus in a crude, closed multiplier model a permanent unit increase in investment generates its own finance, once GDP has increased by lambda units. But investment expenditure is initially underfinanced, so far as we have gone; and the dynamics of the traverse are quite intricate.

If resources are elasticaily available, banks can finance investment on the traverse so long as the public are prepared to increase their holdings of bank paper *pari passu* – as they are when liquidity preference is highly, let alone absolutely, elastic. Monetary velocity slightly decreases while the proportion borne by investment expenditures to total income increases (on the traverse) . . . In a fully employed economy, there is a transient trade deficit and small changes in relative yields induce postponement of consumer durable purchases.

But non-banking agents can supply finance as readily as banks by exchanging claims on banks for the paper of deficit spending units, so that monetary velocity slightly increases.

Keynes (1937a) concludes that the upshot buttresses the liquidity theory of interest in which the rate of interest is 'determined by the interplay of the terms on which the public desires to become more or less liquid and those on which the banking system is ready to become more or less unliquid'. And Robertson, after supplying a scintillating real analysis, concludes that banks are pivotally important. They are not. A correct analysis may elide banks altogether.

Does spontaneous, unregulated action induce lower real interest rates during slumps, and higher ones during booms? As I explained in (1976), the answer is surprisingly opaque.

If firms produce 'too much', so that realized proceeds fall short of expected ones, they must *finance* the gap. But, especially in open economies, it is plausible that real pure rates evolve autonomously against local monetary action so that improvement in the trade balance fills in a dual aggregate demand gap, just as does a reduction in aggregate output in a simple closed case.

11.4.7 Concluding Observation: What Does the MA Really Do?

It is more fruitful to study the behaviour of liquidity premia obtained on money market assets than chimerical MA influence on pure real rates of interest. The MA *does* influence liquidity premia. The MA *can* supply legal tender or virtual legal tender, just as it *cannot* supply real resources. Will liquidity premia fluctuate perversely under open-loop control? Will liquidity premia behave better under closed-loop control?

11.5 MONETARY FEATURES OF TRADE FLUCTUATIONS IN ANCIENT ROME (CHAPTER 10)

Caesar paid hard cash in advance. But the feeble, irregular pulse of the ancient economy's vibration does not seem to have been led by monetary pulsation. A number of high elasticities permitted human and non-human resources to shift smoothly between sectors; and precious metals moved agilely between monetary and non-monetary stocks.

The slave system and *panem et circenses* (the welfare system) are shown to explain high elasticity of supply of labour to industry, especially the building industry.

Non-monetary precious metal stocks much exceeded monetary ones. It seems that the quantity of monetary gold and silver was governed by the convenience yield of non-monetary stocks; and this convenience yield may have been exogenous for the money market. Two conclusions follow. (1) Sources of finance included stocks of non-monetary gold and silver. Humps in investment expenditure could be financed from non-monetary stocks. Temporary increases in the monetary circulation (as elastically supplied labour and materials were purchased) were in time refluxed back into non-monetary stocks. (2) There was no inflation problem in ancient Rome; the purchasing power of precious metals was steady. There was a *depreciation* problem: the chronically debased monetary circulation depreciated in real value.

The *primitive financial structure* of the Roman economy seems to promote lively potential for liquidity crises which could lead to economic *implosion*. There was a vast amount of personal lending on call, and no systemic back-up of the sort provided by modern economic authorities. And indeed there were occasional localized panics. Why did the upshot fall so far short of chronic crisis? The answer is bottomed on huge stocks of non-monetary precious metals in ancient and modern times.

The ancient significance of *cash in advance* is questionable the way conventional definitions of M-1 are undermined by 'sweeping'. Anciently the easy transition, back and forth, between monetary and non-monetary precious metals greatly eroded the force of 'cash in advance'. The upshot is intrinsic to commodity standards: see Barsky and Summers (1988) and Chapter 8 of (1989a).

Ancient experience illuminates *liquidity preference*. Finley conflates the fallacy that preference for land clogged capital accumulation (*General Theory*, Chapter 17) with mercantilist fallacies, also favoured by Keynes: ancient hunger for land and cash clogged ancient development (*sic?*). This cannot be true. Any looming shortage of cash induced a flow from non-monetary to monetary precious metal holdings, save for possibilities of panic not relevant for Finley's secular proposition. And the price of land fully reflects 'land hunger'. Non-monetary precious metal holdings are of paramount importance.

11.5.1 Money Supply and Real Growth

Arguments that growth is impeded by insufficiency of the money supply also look vulnerable on the following point – *but are not!* At a low enough price level, real monetary balances are large enough to satisfy any demand. *But* the value of golden or silver money could not rise substantially above that of a unit of non-monetary precious metal. Indeed this point illuminates the principal characteristic of the ancient monetary economy: money supply was perfectly elastic at a critical value of money (i.e., at a critical general price level).

11.5.2 Ancient Inflation

I explained in (1988) (cf 'Alexander Hamilton') that, until the fairly recent predominance of fiat paper standards, the counterpart to chronic inflation (still not properly defined in dictionaries) was depreciation of money-stuff against pure gold or silver. And the upshot illuminates the quantity theory of money (or, better, prices).

It is said that for many centuries people mistakenly perceived price behaviour qualitatively instead of quantitatively: 'something is wrong with the money'. A *lot* was wrong with the money! Debasement was endemic. The 'qualitative' approach is quite consistent with quantity-theory logic (said to begin with Jean Bodin). Ancient inflation *was* a matter of deterioration of the coinage; and *is* controlled by the logic controlling the Bullionist controversy following the Restriction of 1797 – spawning a literature still central for monetary theory.

The motor force behind ancient inflation was greed for *seigneurage*. Emperors cried up the price of specie – measured by *tale*, not weight. They lightened the coinage. As coin flowed into the imperial treasury, it was clipped, sweated and abraded – so that the coins flowing *out* of the treasury, including light coins fashioned from the sweat of received coins, comprised a larger *nominal* stream than the inflowing one. (Frightful punishments were inflicted on private persons caught playing this game.)

11.5.3 Concluding Remarks

The ancient economy behaved like an innovated one in important respects; the economy of the day before yesterday importantly resembles that of the day after tomorrow. Thus substantial infusions of gold and silver into the empire did not much affect either relative prices or the general price level. Recall how high was the elasticity of demand for non-monetary precious metal stocks. So the ancient economy exhibited a pseudo-Keynesian feature as well: cf perfectly elastic liquidity preference.

Real economic fluctuations in the Roman empire seem to have evolved invariantly against spontaneous monetary events. Business cycles or trade fluctuations may never have had robust monetary foundations.

Bibliography

ALLEN, R. G. D. (1958) *Mathematical Economics* (London: Macmillan).

ALLEN, R. G. D. (1967) *Macro-Economic Theory: A Mathematical Treatment* (London: Macmillan).

ALLINGHAM, M. and M. BURSTEIN, (eds) (1976) *Resource Allocation and Economic Policy* (London: Macmillan).

ANDREAU, J. (1977) 'La banque antique et l'économie moderne', *Annali . . .* Pisa, 3rd series, 7, pp. 1125–52.

ASIMAKOPOULOS, A. (1983) 'Kalecki and Keynes on Finance, Investment and Saving', *Cambridge Journal of Economics*, 7, pp. 221–33.

BAGEHOT, W. (1873/1927) *Lombard Street* (London: John Murray) 14th edn, posthumous.

BARRO, R. J. (1974) 'Are Government Bonds Net Wealth?', *Journal of Political Economy*, 82.

BARRO, R. J. (1984) *Macroeconomics* (New York: John Wiley).

BARSKY, R. and L. SUMMERS (1988) 'Gibson's Paradox and the Gold Standard', *Journal of Political Economy*, 96, p. 528.

BECKER, G. S. (1971) *The Economics of Discrimination* (Chicago: University of Chicago Press) 2nd edn.

BIRMAN, I. (1983) 'Will Andropov Purge the Passbooks', *Wall Street Journal* (21 March).

BLACK, F. (1970) 'Banking and Interest Rates in a World Without Money: The Effects of Uncontrolled Banking', *Journal of Bank Research*, 1, p. 9.

BOGAERT, R. (1963) 'Le cours du statère de Cyzique au Ve et IVe siècles avant J.-C.', *L'Antiquité classique*, 32, pp. 85–119, further discussed in 34 (1965, pp. 199–213) and by S. K. Eddy (1970).

BRANSON, W. H. (1979/1989) *Macroeconomic Theory and Policy* (New York: Harper & Row) 2nd and 3rd edns.

BRITTAN, S. (1989) 'Roots of Britain's Inflation Problem', *Financial Times* (London) (22 June) p. 19.

BUCHANAN, J. (1958) *Public Principles of Public Debt* (Homewood, Il.: Irwin).

BURSTEIN, M. L. (1963) *Money* (Cambridge, Ma.: Schenkeman).

BURSTEIN, M. L. (1968) *Economic Theory Equilibrium and Change* (London: Wiley).

BURSTEIN, M. L. (1978) *New Directions in Economic Policy* (London: Macmillan).

BURSTEIN, M. L. (1986) *Modern Monetary Theory* (London and New York: Macmillan and St Martin's Press).

BURSTEIN, M. L. (1988) *Studies in Banking Theory, Financial History and Vertical Control* (London and New York: Macmillan and St Martin's Press).

see in particular: 'Knut Wicksell and the Closure of his System: Critique and Reconstruction of the Cumulative Process', Chapter 5, p. 48; 'Beyond the Banking Principle', Chapter 6, p. 63; 'Colonial Currency and Contemporary Monetary Theory', Chapter 7, p. 87; 'Homer on the History of Interest Rates', Chapter 8, p. 99; 'The Political Economy of Alexander Hamilton', Chapter 9, p. 110.

BURSTEIN, M. L. (1989a) *Open-Economy Monetary Economics* (London and New York: Macmillan and New York University Press).

BURSTEIN, M. L. (1989b) 'The Classical Theory of Money and Interest Vindicated', Roskilde, Denmark (May).

BURSTEIN, M. L. (1989c) 'Monetary Authorities and Monetary Induction of Business Cycles', Rungsted, Denmark, IEA Conference (June).

CAGAN, P. (1972) *The Channels of Monetary Effects on Interest Rates* (New York: Columbia University Press).

CAGAN, P. (1980) 'Comment on Shiller, 1980', in Fischer (ed.) (1980, p. 156).

CARANZA, C. and A. FAZIO (1983) 'Methods of Monetary Control in Italy, 1974–1983', in *The Political Economy of Monetary Policy: National and International Aspects*, Proceedings of a Conference at Perugia, pp. 65–92.

CASSEL, G. (1927/1951) 'The Rate of Interest, the Bank Rate and the Stabilization of Prices', *Quarterly Journal of Economics*, 42, reprinted in F. Lutz and L. Mints (eds). *Reading in Monetary Theory* (Philadelphia: Blakiston) pp. 319–33.

CASSEL, G. (1932) *The Theory of Social Economy* (New York) (new rev. edn, trans. S. L. Barron – see Cassel, K. G. (1918) *Theoretische Sozialökonomie* (Leipzig: C. F. Winter)).

CLOWER, R. W. and M. L. BURSTEIN (1960/1988) 'On the Invariance of Demand for Cash and Other Assets', Review of Economic Studies', 28, reprinted in Burstein (1988, Chapter 1).

COTTARELLI, C., G. GALLI, P. REEDTZ and G. PITTALUGA (1986) 'Monetary Policy through Ceilings on Bank Lending', *Economic Policy: A European Forum*, 1 (3) (October) published by Cambridge University Press for the Centre for Economic Policy Research and Maison des sciences de l'homme.

CRAWFORD, M. H. (1970) 'Money and Exchange in the Roman World', *Journal of Roman Studies*, 60, pp. 40–8.

DACEY, W. M. (1951) *The British Banking Mechanism* (London: Hutchinson).

DACEY, W. M. (1956) 'The Floating Debt Problem', *Lloyds Bank Review* (April).

DAVIDSON, D. (1916) 'Comment on Thornton and Wicksell', *Ekonomisk Tidskrift*, Stockholm, p. 391.

DYKES, S. and M. WHITEHOUSE (1989) 'The Establishment and Evolution of the Federal Reserve Board: 1913–23', Federal Reserve *Bulletin*, 75 (4) (April) pp. 227–43.

EDDY, S. K. (1970) 'Discussion of Bogaert, 1963', *Museum Notes*, 16, pp. 13–22.

EINAUDI, L. (1936/1952) 'Teoria della moneta imaginaria nel tempo da Carlomagno alla revoluzione Franchese', *Rivista di Storia-Economia*, 1,

trans. as 'The Theory of Imaginary Money', for *Enterprise anc Social Change* (Homewood, Il.: Irwin for the AEA, 1952).
EINAUDI, L. (1937) 'The Medieval Practice of Managed Currency', in A. D. Gayer, (ed.), *The Lessons of Monetary Experience*, (New York:) pp. 259–68.
ELTIS, W. (1984) *The Classical Theory of Economic Growth* (London: Macmillan).
FABRA, P. (1988) 'British Monetary Affairs', *Le Monde* (8 November, p. 44).
FAMA, E. F. (1980) 'Banking in the Theory of Finance', *Journal of Monetary Economics*, 6, p. 39.
FELDSTEIN, M. (1980) 'Fiscal Policies, Inflation and Capital Formation', *American Economic Review*, 70, p. 636.
FEYNMAN, R., R. LEIGHTON and M. SANDS (1963) *The Feynman Lectures on Physics* (Reading, Ma.: Addison-Wesley vol. 1.
FEYNMAN, R., R. LEIGHTON and M. SANDS (1963) *The Feynman Lectures on Physics* (Reading, Ma.: Addison-Wesley) vol. 1.
FINLEY, M. I. (1985) *The Ancient Economy* (London: Hogarth Press), 2nd edn.
FISCHER, S. (ed.) (1980) *Rational Expectations and Monetary Policy* (Chicago: University of Chicago Press).
FRIEDMAN, M. (1948/1953) 'A Monetary and Fiscal Framework for Economic Stability', *American Economic Review*, 38, pp. 245–64, reprinted in Friedman (1953a, pp. 133–56).
FRIEDMAN, M. (1951a/1953) 'Commodity Reserve Currency', *Journal of Political Economy*, 59, p. 203, reprinted in Friedman (1953a).
FRIEDMAN, M. (1951b/1953) 'The Effects of a Full Employment Policy on Economic Stability: A Formal Analysis', in Friedman (1953a, pp. 117–32), originally published as 'Les effets d'une politique de plein emploi sur la stabilité économique: analyse formelle', *Economie Appliquée*, 4 (1951), pp. 441–56.
FRIEDMAN, M. (1953a) *Essays in Positive Economics* (Chicago: University of Chicago Press).
FRIEDMAN, M. (1953b) 'The Case for Flexible Exchange Rates', in Friedman (1953a, pp. 157–203).
FRIEDMAN, M. (1968) 'The Rôle of Monetary Policy', *American Economic Review*, 58, p. 1.
FRIEDMAN, M. (1969) *The Optimal Quantity of Money and Other Essays* (Chicago: University of Chicago Press).
FRIEDMAN, M. (1974) 'A Theoretical Framework for Monetary Analysis', together with replies to critics, including Patinkin (1974), in R. Gordon (ed.) (1974).
FRIEDMAN, M. (1977) 'Nobel Lecture: Inflation and Employment', *Journal of Political Economy*, 85, p. 451.
FRIEDMAN, M. (1984a) 'Financial Futures Markets and Tabular Standards', *Journal of Political Economy*, 92, p. 165.
FRIEDMAN, M. (1984b) 'The Taxes Called Deficits', *Wall Street Journal* (26 April).

FRIEDMAN, M. (1986) 'The Resource Cost of Irredeemable Paper Money', *Journal of Political Economy*, 94.
FRIEDMAN, M. (1987) 'Monetary Policy: Tactics versus Strategy', in Dorn, J. and A. J. Schwartz (eds), *The Search for Stable Money* (Chicago: University of Chicago Press).
FRIEDMAN, M. and A. J. SCHWARTZ (1963) *A Monetary History of the United States* (Chicago: University of Chicago Press).
FRIEDMAN, M. and A. J. SCHWARTZ (1982) *Monetary Trends in the United States and the United Kingdom* (Chicago: University of Chicago Press).
FRIEDMAN, M. and A. J. SCHWARTZ (1986) 'Has Government Any Rôle in Money?', *Journal of Monetary Economics*, 14 (January).
FRYDMAN, R. and E. S. PHELPS (1983) *Individual Forecasting and Aggregate Outcomes: Rational Expectations Examined* (Cambridge: Cambridge University Press).
GALIANI, F. (1750) *Della Moneta*.
GALLI, G. and R. MASERA (1988) 'Government Deficits and Debts: Their Necessity and Cost of Adjustment; the case of Italy', in Eltis, W. and P. Sinclair (eds), *Keynes and Economic Policy: The Relevance of the General Theory after Fifty Years* (London: Macmillan).
GIBBON, EDWARD (1776–1787) *The Decline and Fall of the Roman Empire* (London) see the J. B. Bury edn, 7 vols (London: Methuen; 1909) reprinted by AMS Press New York (1974).
GOODHART, C. A. E. (1985) *The Evolution of Central Banks* (London: London School of Economics) rev. and reissued by the MIT Press, Cambridge, Ma. (1989).
GOODHART, C. A. E. (1987) 'Why do Banks need a Central Bank?', *Oxford Economic Papers*, 39, pp. 75–89.
GOODWIN, R. (1951) 'The Nonlinear Accelerator and the Persistence of Business Cycles', *Econometrica* (January) pp. 11–17.
GORDON, R. J. (ed.) (1974) *Milton Friedman's Monetary Framework: A Debate with his Critics* (Chicago: University of Chicago Press).
GOWLAND, D. (1984) *Controlling the Money Supply* (London: Croom Helm) 2nd edn.
GRAVES, R. (1934/1953) *I Claudius* (London: Penguin).
GRAVES, R. (1934/1954) *Claudius the God* (London: Penguin).
GREENFIELD, R. L. and L. B. Yaeger (1986) 'Competitive Payments Systems: A Comment', *American Economic Review*, 76, p. 848.
HABERLER, G. A. (1937/1964) *Prosperity and Depression* (London: Allen & Unwin) 5th edn.
HAMILTON, ALEXANDER (1790/1962) *Report on Public Credit*, reprinted in Syrett, H. and J. Cooke (eds), *The Papers of Alexander Hamilton* (New York: Columbia University Press) vol. 6.
HAMILTON, ALEXANDER (1791/1963) *Report on a National Bank*, in Syrett, H. and J. Cooke (eds), *Papers of Alexander Hamilton* (New York: Columbia University Press) vol. 7.
HAWTREY, R. G. (1932) *The Art of Central Banking* (London: Longmans, Green).

HAWTREY, R. G. (1938) *A Century of Bank Rate* (London: Longmans, Green).
HAWTREY, R. G. (1947) *The Gold Standard in Theory and Practice* (London: Longmans, Green) 5th edn.
HAWTREY, R. G. (1950) *Currency and Credit* (London: Longmans, Green).
HAYEK, F. A. (1932) 'A Note on the Development of the Doctrine of "Forced Saving"', *Quarterly Journal of Economics*, 47.
HAYEK, F. A. (1935) *Prices and Production* (London: Routledge & Kegan Paul).
HAYEK, F. A. (1933/1966) *Monetary Theory and the Trade Cycle* (New York: Augustus M. Kelley) a reprint of the 1933 edn, trans. from the German by N. Kaldor and H. M. Croome.
HAYEK, F. A. (1939) *Introduction* to Thornton (1802/1939/1962).
HAYEK, F. A. (1960) *The Constitution of Liberty* (Chicago: University of Chicago Press).
HAYEK, F. A. (1976) *Denationalization of Money* (London: Institute of Economic Affairs).
HICKS, J. R. (1946) *Value and Capital* (Oxford: Clarendon Press) 2nd edn.
HICKS, J. R. (1950) *A Contribution to the Theory of the Trade Cycle* (Oxford: Clarendon Press).
HICKS, J. R. (1967) *Critical Essays in Monetary Theory* (Oxford: Clarendon Press).
HOOVER, K. (1988) 'Money, Prices and Finance in the New Monetary Economics', *Oxford Economic Papers*, 40, pp. 150–67.
HOPKINS, K. (1980) 'Taxes in the Roman Empire, 200 B.C.–400 A.D.' , *Journal of Roman Studies*, 70, pp. 101–25.
HORACE (Quintus Horatius Flaccus, 65–8 BC) (1978) *Satires, Epistles and Ars Poetica* (Cambridge, Ma. and London: Harvard University Press and Heinemann, Loeb Classical Library).
JEFFERSON, THOMAS (1984) *Writings, etc.* (New York: Library of America).
KALDOR, N. (1960) *Essays on Economic Stability and Growth* (London: Duckworth).
KALDOR, N. (1970) 'The New Monetarism', *Lloyds Bank Review*, 97.
KAMIEN, M. and N. SCHWARTZ (1981) *Dynamic Optimization* (New York: North-Holland).
KELSEY, D. (1988) 'The Economics of Chaos', *Oxford Economic Papers*, 40, pp. 1–31.
KEYNES, J. M. (1923) *A Tract on Monetary Reform* (London: Macmillan) reprinted, with some corrections, supplements, etc. as vol. IV of Keynes's *Collected Writings*.
KEYNES, J. M. (1931) *Essays in Persuasion* (London: Macmillan): see especially 'The Economic Consequences of Mr Churchill'.
KEYNES, J. M. (1933) *Essays in Biography* (London: Macmillan).
KEYNES, J. M. (1930/1971) *A Treatise on Money* (London: Macmillan) 2 vols, reprinted, with corrections, etc. as vols. V and VI of Keynes's *Collected Writings*.

KEYNES, J. M. (1936) *The General Theory of Employment, Interest and Money* (London: Macmillan).

KEYNES, J. M. (1937a) 'Alternative Theories of the Rate of Interest', *Economic Journal*, 47, reprinted in vol. XIV of Keynes's *Collected Writings*, p. 201.

KEYNES, J. M. (1937b) 'The "Ex Ante" Theory of the Rate of Interest', *Economic Journal*, 47, reprinted in vol. XIV of Keynes's *Collected Writings*, p. 215.

KEYNES, J. M. (1937c) 'The General Theory of Employment', *Quarterly Journal of Economics*, 51, pp. 209–23.

KEYNES, J. M. (1938) 'Mr Keynes and Finance', *Economic Journal*, 48, reprinted in vol. XIV of Keynes's *Collected Writings*, p. 229 – a rejoinder to Robertson, 1937.

See a set of three books, *The General Theory and After*, D. Moggridge (ed.), (Macmillan, for the RES) brought out in a set, with some revision of Parts I and II (Macmillan, 1987):

vol. XIII (1973/1987) *Preparation*.
vol. XIV (1973/1987) *Defence and Development*.
vol. XXIX (1979/1987) *A Supplement*.

KINDLEBERGER, C. (1978) *Manias, Panics and Crashes: A History of Financial Crises* (New York and London: Basic Books and Macmillan).

KINDLEBERGER, C. (1984) *A Financial History of Western Europe* (London: George Allen & Unwin).

KINDLEBERGER, C. (1989) 'Business Cycles, Manias and Panics in Industrial Societies', Rungsted, Denmark, IEA Conference (June).

KING, W. T. C. (1936/1972) *History of the London Discount Market* (London: Frank Cass).

KLEIN, B. (1975) 'Our New Monetary Standard: The Measurement and Effect of Price Uncertainty, 1880–1973', *Economic Inquiry*, 13, pp. 461–84.

KOOPMANS, J. G. (1933) 'Zum Problem des "Neutralen" Geldes', in Hayek, F. A. (ed.), *Beiträge zur Geldtheorie* (Wien: Julius Springer) pp. 211–359.

LAIDLER, D. (1988) 'British Monetary Orthodoxy in the 1870s', *Oxford Economic Papers*, 40, pp. 74–109.

LAIDLER, D. and P. HOWITT (1980) *Recent Canadian Monetary Policy: A Critique* (London, Ontario: University of Western Ontario).

LANDO, H. (1989) 'Economic Consequences of Debt Deflation', Roskilde, Denmark (May).

LAVINGTON, F. (1921) *The English Capital Market* (London: Methuen).

LEIJONHUFVUD, A. (1968) *On Keynesian Economics and the Economics of Keynes* (New York: Oxford University Press).

LEIJONHUFVUD, A. (1981) *Information and Coordination* (New York: Oxford University Press).

LERNER, A. P. (1952/1953) 'The Essential Properties of Interest and Money', *Quarterly Journal of Economics*, 66, reprinted in his *Essays in Economic Analysis* (London: Macmillan).

LINDAHL, E. (1939) *Studies in the Theory of Money and Capital* (London: Allen & Unwin).

LORENZ, H.-W. (1989) 'Strange Altractors and Endogenous Business Cycle Theory', Rungsted, Denmark, IEA Conference (June).

LUCAS, R. E. (1976) 'Econometric Policy Evaluation: A Critique', in Brunner, K. and A. Meltzer (eds), *The Phillips Curve and Labour Markets*, supp. to the *Journal of Monetary Economics*, 4, pp. 19–46.

LUCAS, R. E. (1981) *Studies in Business Cycle Theory* (Cambridge, Ma.: MIT Press).

MAJNONI, G. and E. ZAUTZIG (1980) 'Techniques of Monetary Control in Italy: Developments and Problems', MAJNONI, G. and E. ZAUTZIG, pp. 74–93.

MAKINEN, G. (1977) *Money, the Price Level and Interest Rates: An Introduction to Monetary Theory* (Englewood Cliffs, NJ: Prentice-Hall).

MARSHALL, A. (1887/1925) 'Remedies for Fluctuations of General Prices', reprinted in Pigou, A. C. (ed.), *Memorials of Alfred Marshall* (London: Macmillan) pp. 188–211.

MARSHALL, A. (1923) *Money, Credit and Prices* (London: Macmillan).

MARSHALL, A. (1926, op. post.) *Official Papers by Alfred Marshall, J. M. Keynes* (ed.) (London: Macmillan for the RES)

MASERA, R. S. (1987) 'European Currency: An Italian View', Strasbourg (IEC/EP), (28 October) reprinted in Giavazzi, F., S. Micossi and M. Miller (eds), *The European Monetary System* (Cambridge: Cambridge University Press, 1989).

MASERA, R. S. (1989) 'The European Monetary System Ten Years on: Problems and Perspectives', Bergamo, University of Bergamo (May).

MEIGS, J. (1962) *Free Reserves and the Money Supply* (Chicago: University of Chicago Press).

METZLER, L. A. (1948) 'Three Lags in the Circular Flow of Income', in L. A. Metzler *et al.*, *Essays in Honour of Alvin H. Hansen* (New York: Norton).

MILL, J. S. (1940, reprint) *Principles of Political Economy* (London: Longmans, Green) – the 1st edn was published in 1848.

MINTS, L. A. (1945) *A History of Banking Theory* (Chicago: University of Chicago Press).

MODIGLIANI, F. (1986) *The Debate over Stabilization Policy* (Cambridge: Cambridge University Press).

MODIGLIANI, F. and T. JAPPELLI (1988) 'The Determinants of Interest Rates in the Italian Economy', Banco di Roma *Review of Economic Conditions in Italy*, 1 (January–April) pp. 9–34 – the Italian version is 'L'effetto della politica fiscale sul tasso di interesse', *Economia Italiana* (Banco di Roma), 1, (gennaio–aprile) pp. 9–38.

MODIGLIANI, F. and M. MILLER (1958) 'The Cost of Capital, Corporation Finance and the Theory of Investment', *American Economic Review*, 48, pp. 261–97.

MODIGLIANI, F. and L. PAPADEMOS (1980) 'The Structure of Financial Markets and the Financial Mechanism', in *Controlling Monetary Aggregates*, vol. III, Conference Series 23, Federal Reserve Bank of Boston, p. 111.

NICHOLAS, B. (1962/1969) *An Introduction to Roman Law* (Oxford: Oxford University Press) 3rd edn.
NICOLET, C. (1971) 'Les variations des prix et al "théorie quantitative de la monnaie" à Rome, de Cicéron à Pline l'ancien', *Annales: Economies, Sociétés, Civilisations*, 26, pp. 1203–27.
OHLIN, B. (1937) 'Some Notes on the Stockholm Theory of Savings and Investment', *Economic Journal*, 47 (March and June, pp. 53, 221).
Oxford Classical Dictionary (1970), N. G. L. HAMMOND and H. H. SCULLARD (eds) (Oxford: Oxford University Press) 2nd edn.
PATINKIN, D. (1956/1965) *Money, Interest and Prices* (New York: Harper & Row) 1st and 2nd edns.
PATINKIN, D. (1961/1972) 'Financial Intermediaries and the Logical Structure of Monetary Theory', reprinted with some rev. in Patinkin (1972) p. 31. See *American Economic Review*, 1961, 51, pp. 95–116.
PATINKIN, D. (1972) *Studies in Monetary Economics* (New York: Harper & Row).
PATINKIN, D. (1974) *Comment* on Milton Friedman's 'A Monetary and Fiscal Framework', followed by Friedman's rebuttal and his surrebuttal, in Gordon (ed.) (1970).
PATINKIN, D. (1981) *Essays on and in the Chicago Tradition* (Durham, N. C.: Duke University Press).
PATINKIN, D. and O. STEIGER (1989) 'In Search of the "Veil of Money" and the "Neutrality of Money": A Note on the Origin of Terms', *Scandanavian Journal of Economics*, 91 (1).
PEKÁRY, T. (1980) *Les 'dévaluations' à Rome*, no. 2 of a series published by l'Ecole française de Rome, pp. 103–20.
PEKÁRY, T. (1981) 'Zur Bedeutung des Handels in der Antike', in *Aspekte der historischen Forschung in Frankreich und Deutschland*, G. A. Ritter and R. Vierhaus (eds) (Göttingen) pp. 30–9.
PHILLIPS, W. (1954) 'Stabilization Policy in a Closed Economy', *Economic Journal*, 64 (June).
PHILLIPS, A. W. (1957) 'Stabilization and the Time Form of Lagged Responses', *Economic Journal*, 67.
PIERCE, J. (1980) 'Comment on Shiller', in Fischer (ed.) (1980).
PIGOU, A. C. (1929) *Industrial Fluctuations* (London: Macmillan) 2nd edn.
PIGOU, A. C. (1932) *The Economics of Welfare* (London: Macmillan) 4th edn. (Robertson, 1926/1932, cites the 1st edn).
PIGOU, A. C. (1949) *The Veil of Money* (London: Macmillan).
PONTRYAGIN, L. S. *et al.* (1962) *The Mathematical Theory of Optimal Processes* (New York: Wiley).
POOLE, W. (1970) 'Optimal Choice of Monetary Policy Instruments in a Simple Stochastic Macro Model', *Quarterly Journal of Economics*, 84, p. 197.
POOLE, W. (1978) 'The Theory of Monetary Policy under Uncertainty', in R. Teigen, (ed.) (1978, pp. 327–33).
RICARDO, D. (1817/1951) *The Principles of Political Economy and Taxation*, in Sraffa, P. and M. Dobb (eds), *The Works and Correspondence of David Ricardo* (Cambridge: Cambridge University Press; 1951–5) 10 vols.
ROBERTSON, D. H. (1915) *A Study of Industrial Fluctuations: An Enquiry*

into the Character and Causes of the so-called Movements of Trade (London: P. S. King), reprinted by the London School of Economics and Political Science, University of London (1948).
ROBERTSON, D. H. (1922/1948) *Money* (London: Pitman).
ROBERTSON, D. H. (1926/1932/1969) *Banking Policy and the Price Level* (London: P. S. King), reprinted with a new introduction in 1932 and republished by Augustus Kelley (New York: 1969).
ROBERTSON, D. H. (1936) 'Some Notes on Mr Keynes's "General Theory of Employment"', *Quarterly Journal of Economics*, 51, p. 168.
ROBERTSON, D. H. (1937a) 'Mr Keynes and "Finance"', *Economic Journal*, 47 (June and September).
ROBERTSON, D. H. (1937b) 'Alternative Theories of the Rate of Interest: Three Rejoinders', *Economic Journal*, 47 September) (The rejoinders are by R. G. Hawtrey, B. Ohlin and D. H. Robertson).
ROBERTSON, D. H. (1937c) 'Note on J. M. K.'s "The 'Ex Ante' Theory of the Rate of Interest"', *Economic Journal*, 47 (December).
ROBERTSON, D. H. (1948) *Money* (London: Pitman) (The 1st edn was published in 1921).
ROBERTSON, D. H. (1966, op. post.) *Essays on Money and Interests*, J. R. Hicks (ed.) (London: Collins).
RODEWALD, C. (1976) *Money in the Age of Tiberius* (Manchester).
RUSSO, M. and G. TULLIO (1988) 'Monetary Policy Coordination within the EMS: is there a Rule?', CEC, Bruxelles, Internal Paper, 63 (April).
SAMUELSON, P. A. (1947/1983) *Foundations of Economic Analysis* (Cambridge, Ma.: Harvard University Press).
SAMUELSON, P. A. (1958) 'An Exact Consumption Loan Model of Interest With or Without the Social Contrivance of Money', *Journal of Political Economy*, 66.
SARGENT, T. (1979) *Macroeconomic Theory* (New York: Academic Press).
SARGENT, T. (1987) *Dynamic Macroeconomic Theory* (Cambridge, Ma.: Harvard University Press).
SARGENT, T. and B. SMITH (1987) 'The Irrelevance of Open Market Operations in Some Economies with Government Currency being denominated in Rate of Return', *American Economic Review*, 77, pp. 78–92.
SARGENT, T. and N. WALLACE (1981) 'Some Unpleasant Monetarist Arithmetic', Federal Reserve Bank of Minneapolis *Quarterly Review*, 5, p. 1.
SAYERS, R. S. (1957) *Central Banking after Bagehot* (Oxford: Clarendon Press).
SCHULER, K. (1988) 'Free Banking', *Humane Studies Review*, George Mason University, 61 p. 1.
SCHUMPETER, J. A. (1954) *History of Economic Analysis* (New York: Oxford University Press).
SELGIN, G. A. (1988) *The Theory of Free Banking: Money Supply under Competitive Note Issue* (Totowa, N. J.: Rowman Littlefield).
SHAW, E. S. (1938) 'False Issues in the Interest-Theory Controversy', *Journal of Political Economy*, 46 (December).
SHAW, E. S. (1938/1979) 'Letter to J. M. Keynes' (dated 29 March 1938) printed in vol. XXIX of Keynes's *Collected Writings* pp. 176–9.

SHEFFRIN, S. (1983) *Rational Expectations* (Cambridge: Cambridge University Press).

SHILLER, R. (1980) 'Can the Fed Control Real Interest Rates?', in Fischer (ed.) (1980) p. 117.

SIEVEKING, H. (1933) 'Loans, Personal', *Encyclopaedia of the Social Sciences*, 9, p. 561.

SMITH, ADAM (1776) *An Inquiry into the Nature and Causes of the Wealth of Nations* (London).

SMITH, B. (1988) 'The Relationship between Money and Prices: Some Historical Evidence Reconsidered', Federal Reserve Bank of Minneapolis *Quarterly Review*, 12, p. 18.

STEIGER, O. (1987) 'Monetary Equilibrium', in Eatwell J., M. Milgate and P. Newman (eds), *The New Palgrave: Money* (London: Macmillan) pp. 223–8.

STIGLITZ, J. (1969) 'A Re-Examination of the Modigliani–Miller Theorem', *American Economic Review*, 59, pp. 784–93.

SVENSSON, L. (1988) 'Trade in Risky Assets', *American Economic Review*, 78, p. 375.

TEIGEN, R. (ed) (1978) *Readings in Money, National Income and Stabilization Policy* (Homewood, Il.: Irwin) 4th edn.

TEMIN, P. (1969) *The Jacksonian Economy* (New York: Norton).

THOMPSON, W. E. (1979) 'A view of Athenian Banking', *Museum Helveticum*, 36, pp. 224–41.

THOMPSON, W. E. (1982) 'The Athenian Entrepreneur', *L'Antiquité classique*, 51, pp. 53–85.

THORNTON, H. (1802/1939/1962) *An Enquiry into the Nature and the Effects of the Paper Credit of Great Britain* (London: Allen & Unwin; 1939) (the 1962 (London: Frank Cass) edn reprints the 1939 edn, including a famous introduction by F. A. Hayek; the 1802 edn was published in London by Hatchard).

TOBIN, J. (1974) 'Friedman's Theoretical Framework', in R. J. Gordon (ed.) (1974).

TOBIN, J. (1978) 'Monetary Policies and the Economy: The Transmission Mechanism', *Southern Economic Journal*, 44, p. 421.

TOBIN, J. (1980) *Asset Accumulation and Economic Activity* (Chicago and Oxford: University of Chicago Press and Basil Blackwell).

TOBIN, J. (1985) 'Financial Innovation and Deregulation in Perspective', Second International Conference of the Institute for Monetary and Economic Studies, *Financial Innovation and Monetary Policy: Asia and the West*, Bank of Japan, Tokyo (29–31 May).

TOOKE, R. (1838–1839) *History of Prices* (London).

TULLIO, G. and F. CONTESSO (1987) 'Causes of the Development of the Private ECU and the Behaviour of its Interest Rate, Oct. 1982–Sept. 1985', Commission of the European Communities, Brussels, Internal Paper, 56 (July).

VINER, J. (1927) *Studies in the Theory of International Trade* (New York: Harper).

VIRGIL (Vergil: Publius Vergilius Maro, 70–19 B.C.) *The Aeneid*, etc. – see especially the Loeb Classical Library edn.

WALLACE, N. (1981) 'A Modigliani–Miller Theorem for Open-Market

Operations', *American Economic Review*, 71, pp. 267–74.
WALLACE, N. (1983) 'A Legal Restrictions Theory of the Demand for Money and the Rôle of Monetary Policy', Federal Reserve Bank of Minneapolis *Quarterly Review*, 7, pp. 1–7.
WHITE, L. H. (1984a) 'Competitive Payments Systems and the Unit of Account', *American Economic Review*, 74, p. 699.
WHITE, L. H. (1984b) *Free Banking in Britain: Theory, Experience and Debate* (Cambridge: Cambridge University Press).
WHITTAKER, C. R. (1980) 'Inflation and the Economy in the Fourth Century A.D.', in *Imperial Revenue, Expenditure and Monetary Policy in the Fourth Century*, C. E. King (ed.), *British Archeological Reports*, Intl. Series, 76, pp. 1–22.
WICKSELL, K. (1898/1936) *Geldzins und Güterpreise* (Jena: Gustav Fischer). R. F. Kahn (trans., published as *Interest and Prices* (London: Macmillan, 1936).
WICKSELL, K. (1907) 'The Influence of the Rate of Interest on Prices', *Economic Journal*, 17
WICKSELL, K. (1935, op. post.) *Lectures on Political Economy: Money*, vol. 2 (London: George Routledge) English trans. ed. and introduced by Lionel Robbins.
WOOD, G. E. (1989) 'Banking and Monetary Control after 1992: A Central Bank for Europe?', City University Business School, Barbican Centre, London EC2Y 8HB, Discussion Paper, 67 (April).
YAVORSKY , B and A. PINSKY (1975) *Fundamentals of Physics* (Moscow: Mir Publishing Co.) 2 vols, N. Weinstein (trans.).

Index of Names

Index of Subjects